A
Suitable Job
for a
Woman

A *Place of Execution*

The Kate Brannigan Novels
Dead Beat
Kick Back
Crack Down
Clean Break
Blue Genes
Star Struck

The Dr. Tony Hill Novels
The Mermaids Singing
The Wire in the Blood

The Lindsay Gordon Novels
Report for Murder
Common Murder
Final Edition
Union Jack
Booked for Murder

A
Suitable Job
for a
Woman

Inside the World of Women Private Eyes

by Val McDermid

Poisoned Pen Press

First U.S. Edition 1999

10 9 8 7 6 5 4 3 2 1

Library of Congress Catalog Card Number: 99-60514

ISBN: 1-890208-15-9

Front Cover Design by: Alexander J. Perovich
                          www.alexander-jp.com

Poisoned Pen Press
6962 E. First Ave. Ste 103
Scottsdale, AZ 85251
www.poisonedpenpress.com
sales@poisonedpenpress.com

Printed in the United States of America

For Diana Muir;
*for friendship, for support, and for being
a constant reminder of the true journalistic values
of integrity, accuracy and alcohol.*

Val McDermid grew up in a Scottish mining community then read English at Oxford. She was a journalist for sixteen years, spending the last three as Northern Bureau Chief of a national Sunday tabloid. She is the author of fourteen crime novels, including six featuring the female PI Kate Brannigan. *Crack Down* was short-listed for the Crime Writers' Association Gold Dagger award, and *The Mermaids Singing* won the Gold Dagger in 1995 (Best Crime Novel of the Year). Her 1998 Kate Brannigan novel, *Star Struck*, received France's Grand Prix des Romans d'Aventure.

Acknowledgements

The idea for this book surfaced at a party in London one night. Unlike most similar drunken ideas, this one looked just as interesting sober. Between conception and delivery, a lot of people gave generously and patiently of their help, support, time and knowledge to make it happen. It's a long list, and I've probably missed off some crucial people, to whom I tender abject apology. First, I have to thank all the women private investigators who let me into their lives and were so generous with their time and their expertise, in particular Zena Scott-Archer who invited me into the inner sanctum of the Association of British Investigators and opened her contacts book to me. Without her help, the book would never have become a reality. Others whose assistance was invaluable include: Janet Rudolph, Diana Muir, Kate Mattes, Carol Andrus, Priscilla Ridgeway, Edna Buchanan, Janet Dawson, Lorraine Petty and Chris Humphries. Thanks also to Michell Doek who performed the drudgery of transcribing my tapes without complaint.

I owe particular thanks to Mary Wings, Sue Grafton, Minette Walters and Sara Paretsky, true comrades who rescued me from the motels from hell and made me feel at home when I was a long way from my security blanket.

My eternal gratitude goes to the friends who held my hand during the panic attacks, especially my editor, Val Hudson, and BB, whose tolerance goes way above and beyond the call of duty.

Foreword

I was in law enforcement with the National Park Service for eight years, serving in Isle Royale, Guadalupe Mountains, Mesa Verde, and the Natchez Trace Parkway. For another eight years I've written about a woman in law enforcement. I've known scores of women in the profession and yet the world of the female private eye remained largely fictional for me, from the bobbling bosoms of television depictions to the "spunky" women of novels.

Though the law enforcement professions have come forward leaps and bounds in the realm of equality for women, we are still not entirely accepted, not welcomed. The mystique of macho is prevalent and to have a woman come onto the scene shakes that illusion, contaminates the boy's club with a nasty dose of reality.

Val McDermid's A *Suitable Job For a Woman* is vivid with that reality. In an impressive body of work, she has interviewed women P.I.s from both sides of the "pond." Val has a remarkable talent for capturing the essence of these women's experiences and, most delightfully, the absurdity of life on the mean streeets. Law enforcement provides drama and heroics off and on but mostly, delving into the seamier side of human nature provokes pathos and laughter—much of it cynical, but laughter none the less. Val captures this undercurrent of sadness and hilarity with remarkable clarity. She has recreated the vocal patterns and the attitutdes of women from Los Angeles to Liverpool and deftly painted the myriad situations they are called upon to deal with in their day to day work. From the sublime, a woman who delights in her work because she's "had a few defendants who were actually innocent," to the ridiculous, murder by house dog.

I don't know if there are other books that focus on women in private investigation. If there are, I've not run across them. A *Suitable Job For a Woman* is a wonderful read, a concise and eye-opening trek through the competence, humor and humanity of women.

Nevada Barr
Mississippi, 1999

Contents

Acknowledgements vii

Foreword by Nevada Barr ix

Prologue xiii

Short and Curlies 1
1   Getting Started 2

The American Nightmare 20
2   Separated by a Common Language 23

Career Case 37
3   In the Beginning 42

In the Nick of Time 56
4   Wonder Women 59

While the Balance of his Mind... 81
5   Playing with the Big Boys 83

Short and Sweet 91
6   On the Job 92

Memories are Made of This 122
7   Target Practice 124

Once is Unfortunate... 139
8   Criminal Elements 142

Charles and I... 159

9   I Spy... 162

...And Never Called Me Mother 177

10   Human Elements 181

That'll Do Nicely... 198

11   Going Underground 201

Truth, Justice and the American Way 210

12   Legal Liaisons 216

Everybody Loves Good Neighbours 230

13   Techno, Techno, Techno,.. 234

Where There's a Will... 245

14   Women Against Violence Against Women 248

René and Anna's Excellent Adventure 258

15   Point of Impact 263

The Slave Trade 276

16   Truth is Stranger than Fiction 278

An Interview with Val McDermid by Adrian Muller ... 286

Prologue

By the time I read my first woman private eye novel, I was an investigative reporter on a national newspaper. We had a lot in common, it seemed to me. We were both driven by the urge for truth and some kind of justice that wasn't supplied by the official system. We both used unorthodox means to reach our goals. We were each to some extent only as good as our contacts and our abilities to persuade people to confide in and trust us. We both had to be tenacious and prepared to take risks to get the results we craved. And we sometimes had to accept that the outcome we wanted wasn't the one we were going to get.

But as I read that book—Sara Paretsky's *Indemnity Only*—I realised there was another strand that bound me as a journalist to the women who really pounded the mean streets searching for answers. I was familiar, from fiction and film, from *All The President's Men* to *The Front Page*, with the distortions that happen when reality is translated into fiction. The first thing that gets lost is the boredom factor. The hours spent on fruitless stakeouts, the finger-drumming, chain-smoking days sitting waiting for the one call that you need to move the investigation forward, the frustration of time wasted on false trails and empty leads. None of that ever translates on to the page or the screen, and for good reason. It's humdrum enough doing it; it would be mind-numbingly boring to have to go through it at second hand. So fiction is forced to give a picture that's highly selective.

When I first created my own private eye, the Manchester-based fast-talking, kick-boxing computer whizz Kate Brannigan, I knew I was almost certainly as guilty of perverting reality as all those novels and films that had left me protesting to my friends that honestly, journalism was nothing like as glamorous as it looked. But then, I told myself and anybody else who would listen, I was aiming to write fast-paced, intricate crime fiction, not produce a documentary.

That didn't stop me wondering just how big the gap was between the creatures of my imagination and the real-life women private eyes who take on the cases that make real differences in people's lives. The more time I spent writing about Kate Brannigan, the more curious I became about the other side of the coin.

Four years ago, I gave up journalism to become a full-time writer of crime fiction. But I couldn't resist picking up my old trade in a bid to discover if the real Kinsey Millhone or Kate Brannigan exists. This is the story of that quest.

Short and Curlies

People do tend to go up in the air a bit when you serve them with legal papers. We had to serve this chap in South Ockenden with an injunction. I banged and banged on the door and eventually it opened to reveal this man who must have been nearly seven feet tall and about as wide. He was a big man. He was wearing nothing but a towel round his middle because he'd been in the bath.

When I served him with the papers, he blew his top. He was literally jumping with rage, and his towel fell off. By this time all the neighbours had come out to see what all the shouting was about and I'm standing there trying to keep a straight face. He followed me down the path and he was literally dancing with rage on the lawn. Everything flapping up and down! If he hadn't been such a big man it wouldn't have been quite so funny but he was fat with it as well, and everything was wobbling around.

I couldn't contain myself and just burst out laughing. The whole neighbourhood was holding each other up laughing. I had to go back and serve subsequent papers and he did apologise to me for his outburst but every time I go to South Ockenden I think of that man dancing on the front lawn starkers and it brings a smile to the grimmest day.

DIANA MIDDLETON
Hornchurch, Essex

1

Getting Started

Does anybody grow up thinking they're going to be a PI?
I think we always come from somewhere else.

BLAIR
Berkeley, California

I never had a burning desire to become a detective.
I suspect that's one of the prerequisites. You mustn't have stars
in your eyes. If you go into it thinking it's glamorous and
wonderful you are going to be disillusioned.

ZENA SCOT-ARCHER
Liverpool

'Have you considered becoming a private detective?' are seven words that have never passed the lips of a careers teacher. I'd bet money on that. Maybe that's because of the image of private eyes as seedy middle-aged male emotional cripples with drink problems and an unreliable bank balance. Maybe it's because being a good private eye, like being a good novelist, generally requires a chunk of life experience that the practitioner can draw on. Or maybe it's something as simple as the fact that there's no career structure. It's not like you can take a college course, start on the bottom rung and claw your way up the corporate ladder until you become VI Warshawski.

There's not a lot of careers guidance from the fictional women PIs either. They're mostly mavericks who started off in some area of law enforcement then fell into the job because they couldn't work within the system either from conviction or temperament. Sara Paretsky's VI Warshawski was a lawyer who realised that she and her colleagues were simply papering over the cracks while society crumbled around them, the weak falling prey to the legal system as much as to the powerful forces that exploited them outside it. Linda Barnes' Carlotta Carlyle was a cop who wasn't prepared to brown-nose her bosses. Sue Grafton's Kinsey Millhone was an insurance investigator with far too much attitude to make it in the corporate world. And Sandra Scoppettone's Lauren Laurano quit the FBI after she accidentally killed her lover in a shoot-out.

The mavericks who do the job for real have arrived from a much wider range of jobs and motives. Of the thirty-four women I spoke to, exactly half of them became private eyes by accident. The reasons vary from falling in love to financial necessity, from political conviction to frustration at the system. Of the remaining half, a third came to it from the police, a third from the secretarial side and another third because of family connections.

Only one of them was a career gumshoe. Like my fictional detective Kate Brannigan, René Olsson needed money to help fund her student courses. Kate went to work part-time for a private investigation agency, while René chose a security firm. They both decided this was the most fun they'd ever had without laughing or exchanging body fluids, so they became PIs. René, slightly more cautious than Kate, finished her degree in sociology first.

That out of the way she sent her CV out to private investigation companies, but while they were all impressed with what they saw, each thought that she was too young for the job. One company, however, was willing to give her a chance.

'They didn't hire me right then, but the boss said they really liked me and they wanted me to stay in touch. So I said, "Tell me what I can learn about, just tell me something to go study that will make me a better prospect for you." He told me to go and research old sixteen-millimetre wind-up Bolex cameras! God knows why. I went to the library and looked up everything I could then wrote up a report. Everything there is to know in the whole world about Bolex cameras! He was pretty impressed, and I asked for another assignment. I did this every week for about four months, all sorts of weird stuff, and finally Windsor, the boss, said, "I'm going to hire you to do a real job."

'It was a background check on this guy who was trying to get someone to invest a whole bunch of money in some scheme. I uncovered some seams he'd pulled in the past, mainly because I talked to everyone and went every place I could think of. I researched every single possible thing that was a matter of public record about this guy. I ended up giving Windsor a twenty-seven-page report and he about fell over! I didn't know what I was doing, I could have cut it down, but we were able to give the client very good reason not to invest his money. Boy, was I thorough!' The hard work paid off; Windsor hired René.

The most conventional route into the job is from the police. The vast majority of male PIs have previously been in one branch of law enforcement or another, but for all but a handful of women, a career as an officer of the law has only become a serious option in recent years, so in sheer numerical terms, there haven't been that many of them leaving the police to start with. Brenda Balmer and Diana Middleton both joined the police in Britain in the fifties when there were hardly any women in the Force and left in the sixties, for very different reasons.

Diana works just outside London in Hornchurch, Essex. She was a police officer for fourteen years, climbing to the rank of sergeant. She left in 1965 when this part of Essex amalgamated with the Metropolitan Police in London. 'I didn't want anything to do with the Met,' she explains. 'The ethos was totally different, and I knew I wouldn't feel comfortable there. A former police colleague had started an agency and he was looking for a partner, so I joined forces with him.'

Brenda Balmer didn't have any choice in the matter. Back in the early sixties when she was a policewoman in Sunderland, there was no such thing as maternity leave. 'I'd been a policewoman for ten years, and I was good at my job, bwt in those days, when you fell pregnant, you were on your bike,' she says. For Brenda, now a fifty-nine-year-old grandmother, the move into private investigation was a more circuitous one. She started work as a store detective at Sunderland's premier department store the week after she quit the force and stayed for twenty years, collaring 13,500 shoplifters in the process.

'I was the scourge of the shoplifters. If they saw me walking across the floor, they went over the other side of the road to Woolworths. Once or twice I got hurt in the course of work, and the bosses would ring me up and say, "We dinna care how many bumps and bruises you've got, we need you to come in and be seen!"'

So successful was she, that in 1970 she was offered the chance to set up her own security company. Only her husband's objections stopped her taking up the opportunity. Eight years later, Brenda found herself in need of a private detective to investigate her philandering husband. Since the only PIs in town were ex-policemen whom she knew from her days on the Force, she felt she could not approach them. It was this painful experience that gradually led her into investigation work.

'I couldn't turn to anybody so when I had to go through my divorce I had no evidence at all. I felt bitter about that. Then some of the staff at the store started coming to me and saying, "You know, Bren, my husband's off with another woman. Can you do something about it?" So I started to do observations for members of the staff, because I knew how they felt. I thought, at least I can help people in the same state I was in. I would write out what I had discovered and send a copy to the solicitor and then those solicitors started ringing me and asking me to do jobs for them. That's basically how I started. I was still working in the store for maybe five years after that. I was working for them from nine to five and working for myself between five and nine!' Eventually, Brenda decided she preferred being her own boss. Fifteen years later, she still runs Castle Investigations, but now she has the full-time help of her daughter Susan and son-in-law Mark.

Other PIs who came from the police left for domestic reasons—the need to spend more time with their family than their busy, high-pressured job allowed. But for Jean Mignolet, an outspoken, strong-minded woman who more than holds her own in the macho world of South Florida, it was the frustrations of the job, especially for an ambitious woman.

'I reached the point in law enforcement where I'd had enough of the bureaucracy, the inefficiency, the sexism. I was one of the few women in the unit, but I was making more money on merit than all the men in my office and they hated that. I had a lifestyle that wasn't ghettoised into law enforcement. I was married at the time to a European tennis pro, I was travelling, I didn't socialise with them, I didn't fit. Then I got beat up and shot at in Miami on a case and I thought, what am I doing? For $19,000 a year? Becoming a private investigator felt like a natural transition.'

It is a move that has certainly paid off. After four years as a partner in an extremely successful agency, Jean decided to go it alone and now runs her own agency, and even charges other PIs and attorneys for consultancy work on their cases.

Policing and private eye work may be similar in many ways but moving from one to the other is far from straightforward. All the ex-police officers spoke of the difficulties they had adjusting to not having the power of the warrant card, or the security of back-up. Christine Usher, who worked as a detective in Gloucestershire before becoming a PI, explained.

'I did find it difficult to make the transition from the police service. In the service I had my warrant card, I was someone, and when you come out you've really got nothing. Who are you? We don't have any powers, we have nothing, so you have to learn to communicate better than you did in the police service. Also, I think you feel conspicuous as a police officer, even though you might be in plain clothes. That's certainly how I felt, and for a little while I had to make the effort to blend in, although in reality I probably was blending in.'

Yet despite these problems not one of the women eyes expressed regrets at their decision to make the change. They share a love of independence that makes private investigation their perfect occupation.

Another route into private investigation is through legal work—from jobs as legal secretaries, paralegals and probation officers. For many of the women eyes who came into the job this way it was the kind of frustration with the system that Jean Mignolet felt as a cop that finally drove them to become PIs.

When she dropped out of a PhD course at Berkeley, Nancy Barber found work as a legal secretary and quickly worked her way up to the position of paralegal. Two things finally drove her into becoming a licensed PI. 'I had one colleague that I worked with very closely on asbestos [litigation] cases, and he was a wonderful, wonderful man. He had a really creative approach to the work. The more we worked on it, the more fascinating it became.

'Then he died suddenly. I thought, I could stay in this very comfy little position and make a lot of money but it doesn't mean anything. His death made me realise that you have to be willing to take risks and chances. He loved murder mysteries too. We had this fantasy about what our life would be like if we went into the investigation business together, and after he died, I thought, well, why not? I could do it by myself.

'The other thing that drove me to it was that I hired an investigator way ahead of time to work on a trial. We paid him a lot of money and he did nothing, absolutely nothing. Shortly before the trial, I realised if we were going to get anything at all, I was going to have to get it myself. And I did. Late in the day, I did what he was supposed to and he still sent us an outrageous bill. I was so angry. I said, "How dare you charge so much?"

'He said, "This is a big name law firm, they can afford it." Like, "Oh, this is asbestos litigation, everybody can make a lot of money out of it." I was furious! He thought people's pain could be turned into a cash cow. It felt like everybody had lost sight of what was going on here. I thought, enough is enough. And that's when I started up on my own, six years ago now.'

It's the stuff of all the best feminist fantasies. The secretary watches what the boss does, figures she can do it herself, and takes over the operation. That's how four British women started their careers, and each of them has made a good living out of the job for more than a decade.

Pat Storey's experience is typical. In spite of being married to a police officer, Pat had no ambitions to be a detective herself until she became the secretary to a private investigator. 'I was like most of the general public who think that you run around in fast cars getting shot at. Of course, it was nothing like that at all. After about two or three years, my boss decided to retire, so I said, "Right, I'm interested enough, I'll buy the business.

Pat hadn't actually been out on the road at that stage, but had learnt the trade from inside the office. This wasn't enough to convince her bank manager so she had to mortgage her home to raise the capital. But she was willing to take the risk. 'I never doubted that I'd make a go of it.'

Yvonne Twiby, Jackie Griffiths and Pam Quinney also learned the job from the inside, watching the detectives, learning from their mistakes, and getting a feel for how the job is done. Yvonne branched out on her own after making the move from secretary to investigator; Pam Quinney was handed the business by her boss who had lost interest and let the agency run itself into the ground.

And Jackie Griffiths set up in business for herself. We met at her home, a trim bungalow that doubles as her office. As we talk, it becomes clear she's not had an easy life; widowed young, with two small daughters to bring up, one afflicted with chronic illness, scarred emotionally and physically by a car crash that left her mother dead. But there is no trace of self-pity, just a stoic determination to get on with life without complaint.

'I started off doing secretarial work for a private investigation agency and the chap I was working for had a minor stroke so he asked me if I fancied doing some of the enquiries,' she says in her soft voice with its slight Welsh lilt. 'I thought I knew enough about it from doing the office work, so I agreed.' When the investigator retired, Jackie went back to secretarial work, until her new employer suggested she start up on her own as a private eye. Within three weeks, Jackie's husband had bought her a desk and had a phone line connected, and she was in business.

While most women eyes come to the job late in life after having tried other things, some, at the other extreme, have been involved in private investigation since childhood. Susan Balmer is one of these. 'Susan's been a store detective since she was about nine days old,' her mother Brenda admits proudly. 'She was bred to the job! I worked until I was seven months and three weeks pregnant. I was back at work nine days later, with Susan in the pushchair. I used to dump her with whichever sales assistant was nearest when I had to make a collar.'

'The canteen was on the top floor, and customers would see me struggling up the stairs,' Susan chips in. 'They would say, "Eh, hinny, are you lost? Have you lost your mam?" And I would say, "No, I work here!" I used to have problems opening the staff door to the staircase to the canteen because it was so heavy. It got to the point where if the staff saw me heading for the doors, they'd just desert the customers to open the doors for me! I suppose I never really had any choice in what I was going to do for a living; the job chose me.'

Zena Scott-Archer, the longest serving woman investigator in Britain, also grew up in an investigative environment. In a career that has spanned five decades, she climbed from humble filing clerk and report typist to sole proprietor of one of the country's most successful and respected confidential investigation agencies.

No small part of the reason for her success is that she couldn't look less like most people's idea of a gumshoe. No one would ever guess, sitting next to her on a train or in a restaurant, that this elegant, immaculately groomed senior citizen is more familiar with the seedy side of life than the average convicted criminal. I first met Zena when we were both taking part in a local radio chat show. I arrived in the reception area, and announced my presence to the receptionist. I didn't pay a lot of attention to the elderly woman sitting there, except to notice that she looked smart enough to be the captain of the local championship bridge team. I hope I hid my confusion when the presenter's assistant finally emerged and gathered us together to do the programme. By the end of the interview, I had discovered her genteel facade also disguised a quick brain and a wicked sense of humour. If she hadn't been a PI, she'd have made a great actress; whenever she tells a story, she slips into the intonations and body language of the characters, till you can see the whole tale unfold before your eyes.

Now a semi-retired consultant, Zena followed in her father's footsteps. A retired Scotland Yard detective, he opened his agency in Liverpool in 1937. When she joined the busy firm, she had no intention of being a detective. 'I only joined him as a secretary/dogsbody. I did the filing and I used to type the reports of his agents and I realised that they were very poor accounts. They never described the houses they'd been to, they never managed anything but the sketchiest and most superficial descriptions of people they'd seen. They may have been detectives, but they had no skills in report writing and I got so exasperated that I said to my father one day that I could do better myself! So he said, "Well, go ahead and do it," and that's how it started! I never had a burning desire to become a detective. I suspect that's one of the prerequisites. You mustn't have stars in your eyes. If you go into it thinking it's glamorous and wonderful you are going to be disillusioned.'

Zena became a partner in 1950, and when her father died in 1953, she took over the business. 'My father was an empire builder; he had a lot of employees. But when I took over the business I decided to be small and good. And it worked out extremely well for me. I've had a wonderful life in the business.'

Being a private eye seems to be in the blood for Susan Neary. Her parents started their agency forty-five years ago. Now semi-retired, they still take on assignments from their retirement homes in the Isle of Wight and Spain. Their agency is now run by Susan's brother and her uncle. 'My sister's the only one who got away,' she laughs. 'When I was at school, you daren't tell anybody what your mum and dad did for a living, because back in those days, they still did a lot of the old-style divorces where you had to prove all the naughty goings on, and private investigators had a really sleazy image. I didn't care; I knew that what they did was legal, and that's all that bothered me.

'I really enjoy what I do, but I don't think this would have crossed my mind as a career if it hadn't been for the example of my parents.'

Jennifer Paul and Maureen Jacques-Turner both found the world of private investigation opening up to them because their husbands were in the business. Glasgow-based Jennifer is a mother of two in her late thirties. She looks more like the teacher she used to be than the investigator she now is. 'I always say it was the male menopause that got me into this. My husband, Brian, was fed up with his job in the garage trade. His brother is a solicitor and he said "You can come and work for me taking statements, it's easy. You don't need any qualifications."

'I'd quit teaching to have the kids, and I used to type up Brian's reports and statements. One night he said, "I've got to go to Motherwell Police station to take a statement later on, and I fancy a drink, but I can't have one." So I said I'd go and do it. It's a very Scottish way to get into it—going to do a job so my man can have a drink!'

It may have been chance that got her into the job but it was the job itself that made her stay. 'I'd felt I was slowing down mentally being at home all day with the kids so I was quite glad to start doing this sort of work. It gave me a challenge which I'd missed. It got so that I was out doing the work more and more, and Brian stayed home looking after the kids. Once they both started school, he came back to work full-time and now we've got a secretary so I don't have to do the typing any more!'

Jennifer's chance entry into the profession is typical of many of the women eyes who fell into the job— having friends in agencies who had vacancies when they needed a job, meeting a PI and deciding it was the job for them, even reading about it in a magazine and setting out to do it. They have come from careers as different as theatre administration, journalism and computing and their stories are as varied and interesting as the women themselves.

For some the path has been a struggle against convention and institutionalised sexism. Sarah Di Venere is a woman who seems more than ready to take on the world and come up winning. An irrepressible blonde in her late forties, she's stylish and bursting with energy. A former commodities broker and realtor, she always nursed a secret desire to become a private eye, following in the footsteps of her fictional heroines Nancy Drew and VI Warshawski. Within five minutes of starting our interview, she was showing me her snub-nosed Smith & Wesson with all the eagerness of a child at Christmas.

Packing the pistol back in its shoulder holster, she reveals, 'I'd always had this fantasy about being an investigator. Then about fifteen years ago, I was in Florida on holiday and I read an article in the local paper about this female PI and she was sixty years old! I thought, this older woman is doing everything I want to do in my life! So I came home and told my boss I was quitting to become an investigator. He said, "How can you do that? You make good money here, and you're going to be dealing with sleazy people!" I'd been selling real estate in an affluent area of Chicago, dealing with three-piece suit people that don't have any assets half the time and always tried to welsh on their contracts. I told him, "At least the people I'm going to be dealing with now, I know they are crooks and they know they're crooks."'

Sarah went through the state Police Academy, then served her three years' apprenticeship in one of the city's biggest agencies. 'When I started in the business, there were very few female investigators. My boss was an ex-Deputy Superintendent of Police. He thought he was the best investigator in the state of Illinois, and I was the first female investigator he'd ever taken on. He really did not like women. I worked for this guy for four years and if there was a horrible case, I got it. If there was a case on at Christmas, I got it. On Super Bowl day, I got it. A lot of the hours I wasn't even paid because I was riding shotgun to one of the other investigators and the client was only paying for one person. But I very badly wanted to learn the business and so I did it. They want you to say you won't do it. They want to throw in your face that you're a girl. I can honestly say in twelve years in this business I have had to fight that all the time. I still do, but now I don't take any shit. I'm my own boss.'

For Byrna Aronson it wasn't just sexism that had to be contended with. She's a blue-collar radical lesbian feminist living and working in Boston, one of the most conservative and class-ridden cities in America.

'The banks run Boston,' Byrna explains. 'They run it in more ways than you usually think of. There's something called the Vault which is an unofficial group of executives from all the banks and big corporations who meet. Every mayor, every executive of the city has to deal with them and if they don't like your policies then you have a problem. These are not elected people, this is a self-perpetuating oligarchy.'

Growing up in a city so driven by politics, it's scarcely surprising that they have played a large part in Byrna's choice of career. 'My political background is the major reason why I'm a private investigator,' she admits, lighting another of the long slim cigarettes that punctuate her conversation. When she first graduated, Byrna wanted to become a lawyer but research showed that since the Bar Association, which ultimately decides who becomes an attorney, had a morals clause, she would have little chance if she were an open lesbian. 'If I was going to be open about being a lesbian the best I could hope for was being a test case with no guarantee about the outcome.'

Unwilling to go through four years of under-grad school, and three years of law school to be a test case, she dropped out of her law degree and went to business school in Philadelphia to learn secretarial skills.

One evening Byrna was arrested in a police raid on a lesbian club. 'That night was the start of my real political education. We got moved around from precinct to precinct all night, they were bouncing us around, treating us like shit, screaming at us, sexually handling

15

us, making fun of us, not letting us sit down, not letting us stand up, not letting us go to the bathroom. I'd had a matron attempt to shove my head down a toilet when she finally let me go to the toilet after three hours of asking. It was a really remarkable and charming night!

'We got into the courtroom next morning, tired and dirty, and to my amazement there was a lawyer there waiting for us, and there was this handful of women sitting there from one of the gay organisations. They had stayed up the whole night, following us from precinct to precinct. Then the cops read out their story, which was full of lies. So we were charged with sodomy and some other things. But the judge just dismissed all charges. I heard tell later that he had been bought off, but I don't know if that's true. Unfortunately, we all now had an arrest record with fingerprints which also goes to the FBI, standard operating procedure.

'But I am eternally grateful for that hideous night because of the way it affected me for the rest of my life. I started to understand that a lot of what I believed about this country wasn't true. And that who ran things wasn't who we were told ran things. That the privileges and rights we thought we had we really didn't. That the police were corrupt. And that a lot of people liked it that way.

'That night was also probably the first in a series of events that brought me into investigating for a living. I started wanting to know what was really going on and who really ran things. I started doing investigations from a political perspective. I wanted to know who really owns things. I wanted to know what the laws really said. I wanted to know who made those laws. I wanted to know the names of the people behind the corporations. I wanted to know who was paying the money to the corrupt cops.'

Byrna started researching legal and corporate records, doing surveillance, taking photographs, many of the jobs that make up a private investigator's work.

It took a very public event to turn Byrna from political activist to private eye. She was walking down a street in Philadelphia hand in hand with her girlfriend, Val, when a police patrol car pulled up across the street and the patrolman hailed them. Thinking it was just the usual hassle lesbians and gay men had been fighting for so long, Byrna got stroppy with him. The patrolman said he wasn't interested in hassling them, but that Val looked just like Susan Sachs, a woman on the FBI's Most Wanted list. Within minutes, the street was choked with police cars, state police cars, FBI—a hundred cops, all with their guns cocked and pointing at Byrna and Val.

The officer had been right, 'Val' admitted to Byrna that she hadn't told her the truth about her identity, and that she was indeed Susan Sachs, one of the two Most Wanted women in America. The reason Susan was on the Most Wanted list was because of her participation in a bank robbery where a cop had died. Susan was involved with the radical Anti-War Movement, protesting against the Vietnam War, and to raise funds, they'd taken to robbing banks. In this instance, Susan had been one of the three robbers. The lookout man left behind got into a shoot-out with the cops and one cop died.

Byrna stood by Susan and began working as an investigator for the lawyers on her case. The trial ended with a hung jury and Susan opted for a plea bargain that gave her seven years in prison because she didn't want to exploit the resources of the community any further with a second trial, and she already had an eightv-year sentence on other charges. Byrna may have hoped for a better outcome, but working on the trial gave her new inspiration.

'I decided that I could do this for the rest of my life. I moved back to Boston, and started working for a law firm here. The more I did it, the more I liked it. I watched the difference it made when we got involved in a case from day one and the legal resources of our firm were applied to that person's case. How between the good lawyering and the good investigating and the good research, we could make a huge difference in people's lives, not least because police investigations were so shitty.

'The gay community, the women's community, the left community had nobody they could trust. If they got charged with crimes, not necessarily politically associated ones, they needed someone who had some credibility within the community to work on their behalf. Now, I knew that people would talk to me who wouldn't talk to anybody else. I felt that my community, however broadly you want to define that, could use the resources of somebody with my skills. So I eventually decided that I wanted to become a licensed investigator and open my own business.'

She had to fight against prejudice to get her licence. Women detectives were rare at the time, let alone open lesbians with FBI records. The political beliefs that made her determined to fight such prejudice now inform the work she does.

'Some of my clients pay me off at $25 a month. It's very important to me to spend not only my private time but also my work time working for change and even though it's a Band Aid approach, not only do I not have any trouble looking at myself in the mirror every morning, but I know I make a difference and I know I can be counted on for the people that I end up doing work for and they tend to be people that wouldn't have access ordinarily.'

As Byrna and Sarah's experiences show, getting into a masculine profession isn't always easy but each woman who does it paves the way for others. Most of the women eyes I spoke to actively support others in the field, employing women in their agency and helping each other out on cases. When Joan Beach first got her licence she had to struggle to get work, and most of it came from female attorneys who were also struggling against sexism in their chosen profession. These women gradually developed a solid and supportive community of friends.

'Now some of them are judges, some are heading up firms and they've become a great source of referrals. And now guys think it's great for their image hiring women.' With positive support like this, it seems likely that there will be more women finding their way into private investigation in the future.

Already, some women eyes, like Sandra Sutherland, have built up their businesses into international concerns and become leaders in their fields. Others prefer to keep their businesses small and local but they all pride themselves in the job they do. Whatever their choice, and whatever way they came into the work, these women have found independence and satisfaction in being a PI. Despite any difficulties their gender may cause them, they firmly believe it is a job perfectly fitting to their sex.

The American Nightmare

One of the things Miami-based Jean Mignolet reckons keeps her sane is doing pro bono work. She can pick and choose the cases she takes on, allowing her to do work that interests and fulfils her when the paying cases are not as inspiring as she would like. One of her charity cases has turned into the complex investigation she now calls her career case. 'This guy has been completely stiffed,' she says as she drops me off at my hotel. 'You need to meet him, to hear his story. I'll fix up for us to have lunch with him tomorrow.' With a wave that jangles her collection of silver bracelets, she's off.

Up until five years ago, Joe Seriani was the American Dream made flesh. A working-class boy from a northern steel town, Joe was cursed with bottle-bottom glasses and eye problems so severe he needed half a dozen operations. 'I grew up idolizing my eye doctors,' he says. .'So I worked hard, won scholarships and after eight years of studying, I got to be an optometrist.'

The dark, handsome eye doctor started working for a company pioneering the concept of spectacle stores in shopping malls. 'I worked my butt off for six months, and saved up enough to open my own business, providing a service from a shop front, $99 glasses. I did really well, and the business expanded fast. I started a service where my customers could get replacement contact lenses for only $10 each by mail order. No one had ever done this before. I was a pioneer.'

Then the law changed, forcing optometrists to release prescriptions to their patients so they could get them filled wherever they chose. Seeing the perfect opportunity, Joe sold his shopping mall stores and launched a mail order firm where customers could send their prescription and obtain contact lenses for a mere $19.95 a pair. 'It took off,' Joe reveals, pride still obvious. 'Twenty-six years old and I was living the American Dream. The boy from nowhere had a business turning over $2 million a year.'

Joe decided to float the company to raise the capital to expand. But before he could complete the formalities, he was approached by a wealthy Jewish father and son. 'They said, "Hey, Joe, you don't have to go public. We've been customers of yours for a long time now, we'll invest in your business." If I'd known then what I know now, I'd have called Jean and got her to check them out. But I was a trusting guy, and they seemed to be on the level.'

What Joe didn't know was that his new partners had made their money in drug running. Their efforts at laundering their money through Joe's company were so successful that they decided they wanted a bigger piece of the action. That meant ditching Joe. So they set him up.

'We had 125,000 satisfied customers. But we'd had five complaints from people saying they hadn't had their lenses. Every one of those complaints was dealt with, but my partners realised that by "losing" orders and by claiming I'd told them to fill prescriptions with the incorrect lenses if the right ones weren't in stock, they could frame me for mail fraud. And mail fraud is a major felony.'

The fit-up worked. Joe, bewildered at finding himself in the dock, and badly served by an attorney who didn't bother to hire an investigator to build a defence case, was found guilty. He served three years behind bars and lost his right to practise as a doctor. While he was in prison, his rabbi persuaded Jean to talk to Joe. One meeting convinced her. She went to work. 'I did a lot of digging,' she says. 'Subsequently, the guys who did this to Joe got arrested for money laundering, but they did a deal with the cops and informed on everybody and his dog. They ended up out of prison before Joe did because of the deal they cut. The fact that they've been convicted of drug-related money laundering still doesn't mean that the courts are automatically going to take Joe's word against theirs. After all,' she adds sarcastically, 'he's a convicted felon now too!'

The first big break came when one of Joe's former employees, a woman whose evidence had been crucial against him at trial, discovered she was dying from AIDS. 'When she was looking death in the face, she repented,' Jean reveals. 'She recanted her testimony on her deathbed, before two ministers of the church, telling how she'd helped to set him up.'

Two years after his release, Jean has amassed enough evidence, including twenty witnesses who were never called at the original trial, to win Joe Seriani a retrial. He says, if it wasn't for Jean, I'd have no chance of having my conviction overturned and regaining the right to practise as a doctor. She's amazing. She deserves to be on the front cover of Newsweek for the stuff she does. She took me on knowing I had no money, and that's never stopped her from going the extra mile for me.'

Jean shrugs off Joe's appreciation. 'There are more ways to repay someone than money. I've been welcomed into Joe's family like they were my own. And now he's running a massage training school, I get all the free massages a woman could want. A case like this, the best reward is seeing the client get their life back.'

2

Separated By a Common Language

I think I'd rather be walking the streets of the East End of London than be in some neighbourhoods in Southern California.

NANCY POSS-HATCHL
Santa Ana, Calilornia

From garbage to guns, the Atlantic Ocean symbolises the cultural divide that differentiates the work of the women eyes. There's a lot of overlap between the work that the American and the British women do, but the way they do it is dictated as much by their different cultures as their different rules and regulations. Comparisons are as odious as generalisations, but who cares? We all make them all the time. McDonalds looks the same, but the burgers taste different. For me, what tells you all you need to know is the contrasting attitudes to access to information. In America, they have a Freedom of Information Act; the public has a right to know and everything is deemed to be in the public domain unless there are specific prohibitions against it. In the UK, the opposite holds true; we're like mushrooms, kept in the dark except for the rare occasions when someone opens the door and shovels manure over us. Nothing is in the public domain unless some government at some point has decided that it wouldn't cause any harm if we the people were permitted to have access to some information relevant to our lives.

In the UK, anyone has legal access to registrations of births, marriages or deaths, the electoral register and the phone book. We have access to information about companies—who owns them, what their balance sheet shows. We can find out who rents Post Office box numbers by applying to the Post Office. We can now get Land Registry details, records of divorces. But we have no legitimate access to ex-directory numbers, no right to information from the Department of Social Security. Medical records are almost impossible to get hold of. Adoptions are a closed book, as are criminal records and motor vehicle details.

Most of this and more is available in almost any state in the USA. One prominent American crime writer told me how she'd received a letter in the mail from one of her fans who had checked her out in the state property database. He now knew her address, when she'd bought her house, how big it was, what she'd paid for it, how much was outstanding on her mortgage, that she was up to date with her property taxes and that she owned the property jointly with her husband. This guy had no legitimate reason for his database search; he'd just paid his fee and accessed the information. He told her that he wasn't a crazy, that he had no intention of using the data he'd acquired, but he thought she might be interested in how easy it was to come by the details. It might, he thought, come in handy for researching how her private eye character gets background. The downside of freedom of information, of course, is that the hurters can get their hands on it too.

It's a difference in attitude that seems to me to say a lot about the open, relaxed Americans versus the buttoned-up Brits. That cultural difference revealed itself in so many ways as I researched this book. More often than not, I was a stranger ringing up out of the blue asking women to give me a chunk of their valuable time and to reveal something of their lives and themselves. Almost without exception, the Americans were delighted to meet me, relaxed and open whether or not I came armed with a reference from someone they knew. The British women, on the other hand, were far more wary, often checking out my credentials with third parties. Some refused point blank to have anything to do with me, a few to the point of rudeness. The only woman I interviewed who demanded anonymity was British.

The Americans showed no surprise that I wanted to talk to them. They expected people to be interested in what they did, they were delighted to have the chance to dispel the myths about their professional lives, and they had no doubts that what they had to say was interesting not just to me but to the world out there. The British were far more diffident. More times than I can count, my blood pressure rose as I heard variations on, 'I can't think why you want to interview me, I'm so dull and ordinary. There's nothing glamorous or interesting about me or my work. I feel I've got you here under false pretences.' And then they proceeded to tell me tales every bit as gripping as those I'd heard in America. In America, my interviewees were aware of the bad publicity some private eyes have generated, and were eager to show the other face of the .job. In Britain, the women I spoke to were often slightly nervous that they were going to find themselves contributing to that bad publicity.

The most refreshing thing was the strong sense of ethics that these women bring to the work they do, on both sides of the Atlantic. They are committed to their principles as much as to their clients, they run themselves ragged to get results, but they don't resort to illegal, underhand, sleazy tricks to do it. It's not for nothing that the PIs who cut corners, break the law and place the end above the means are called cowboys.

In practical terms, one of the key differences between the USA and the UK is licensing. In America, you have to have a licence to be a private investigator. In Britain, anyone can be a PI. No experience necessary. You can quit your job as a check-out operative in a supermarket one day and set yourself up as a PI the next. You can walk out of jail and run a small ad in the local paper offering your services as an inquiry agent. There are no rules, no examinations, no fees, no need for insurance.

There is a degree of voluntary regulation, in the form of the Association of British Investigators. To become a full member, applicants must have worked exclusively as private detectives for two years and they must have no criminal record or civil debt judgements against them. They have to pass examinations in process serving, matrimonial inquiries, court procedures and general inquiries, and they have to acquit themselves in an interview with members of the Association's selection committee.

Zena Scott-Archer, who started in the business in Liverpool in 1946 and is a past president of the ABI, is an ardent advocate for the licensing of British private investigators. 'It would legitimise professional standards, there's no doubt about that. And with luck, licensing might give us access to records that are not currently in the public domain. For example, when you join the Association of British Investigators, we want to know whether you have a criminal record. Now, criminal records are available only to the police. But what we can do is tell applicants to write to the police themselves asking for confirmation that they have no criminal record. The police will write back and say yes or no. There are usually ways around everything.'

Pat Storey is one of four partners in a Birmingham agency and has fourteen years' experience. She's also a past president of the ABI and another supporter of licensing detectives. Pat, in her fifties but looking younger, is a powerhouse of energy. She's a passionate defender of the integrity of her profession. She believes it's important to campaign for professional ethics backed with formal licensing arrangements. 'People come to us when they're vulnerable,' she says. 'They deserve not to be ripped off. It pains me to admit it, but there are a lot of unscrupulous operators about. The sooner we have licensing in this country, the better.'

Pat describes a recent case in which a young man had approached the ABI after a private investigator had conned him out of £13,500. The PI was not a member of the ABI but they did everything they could to resolve the situation. After investigating the investigator they were able to present the Crown Prosecution Service with evidence which gave them a solid case of fraud and he was found guilty. It turned out that the man had done the same scam seven times before, had a criminal record and had even served time in prison.

Every woman I spoke to in Britain agreed that licensing would help the profession, if only on the practical level of making sure people are trained. Because of current unemployment levels, all sorts of people are setting themselves up as private detectives, offering cheap rates that undercut the reputable agencies. But not knowing what they're doing leads to all sorts of cock-ups, which invariably end up on the desk of the more experienced operators. It wastes time and costs the clients money.

Jackie Griffiths, a one-woman agency in Wrexham, explains, 'People think process serving is dead easy. They're wrong. There are lots of different kinds of paper to be served and they all have to be served in different ways. There are different court rules to abide by. You can't just set up in business as a process server. You really need to know what you're doing.

'If we had licensing, I would hope it would have provisions where you would have to work in the business for a couple of years getting hands-on experience under someone else so you get a working knowledge of what you're doing. It shouldn't be a matter of walking out of the police force and automatically becoming a licensed PI. Most policemen round here will tell you their job is so different it wouldn't qualify them to do my kind of work, It's all right going somewhere with a warrant for someone's arrest with all their back-up. It's not the same thing as serving injunctions and bankruptcies. The system is totally different and the attitude has to be too.'

In spite of pressure from the ABI, the British government, wedded to the political dogma of deregulation, remains opposed to setting up a training and licensing system. Now the ABI have taken their fight to Europe, hoping that the EC will adopt community-wide licensing regulations that will clean up the business by the back door.

In America, the picture is very different. Even though the requirements vary from state to state, a licence is compulsory if someone wants to advertise herself as a private eye. What all the states demand as a minimum is relevant experience. Paradoxically, that often effectively discriminates against women. Having been a police officer, an FBI or CIA agent, an investigator with the Drug Enforcement Agency or some similar federal body is usually an automatic experience qualification. But until relatively recently, those were virtually exclusively male preserves, and even now, women are still very much in the minority. So for women who want to become licensed investigators, the route they generally have to take is to work in an agency under someone else's licence until they have enough experience to go for their own licence. You have to really want to do this job if you're prepared to work every anti-social hour in the book for three years, often for as little as $7.50 (£5) an hour, before you can even think about qualifying on your own bat. Especially when you know your boss is charging clients anything up to $75 an hour for your services.

Then, in most states, you have to take an examination. Helen Kliner, a former police sergeant in Chicago, outlines the process she went through to become a PI. 'To be a private investigator in the state of Illinois, you have to meet certain requirements before you can take the exam. When I took the test in 1992, you had to have three years' experience as a law enforcement officer or working for a private investigator, and you had to have some education in criminal justice. Even as a law enforcement officer I had to prove I had investigative experience, that I wasn't just a patrol cop. I had to get letters from my supervisors to explain what my duties had been.

'I had worked undercover in Narcotics and done investigative work in the Youth Division which included trying to locate missing persons and investigating child neglect and child sexual abuse. That qualified me. Then I had to do a lot of reading and studying. It was a struggle to keep my eyes open; most of the reading material is pretty boring. Then I took the test, which is a multiple choice written examination. It's not easy. I failed it the first time, because I ran out of time. I passed on my second attempt.

'Most people have to take the test more than once and I have heard of a man who took the test ten times. When I took it, it cost $125, so you can imagine how much he must have wanted his licence!'

Then you have to pay your licence fee, which varies from $50 to $1000. As if that's not enough, the aspiring PI has to post a bond. Byrna Aronson explains.

'Massachusetts statutes require you to be bonded for various licences. If you're sued by somebody in the course of your work, the bonding company puts up however many thousands of dollars the law requires to make sure that if you lose, the plaintiff gets their money. For that availability you pay a fee every year. If you're sued and you lose, you have to pay the bonding company back. Consequently, bonding agencies don't want to bond you if you don't own a house or have some form of material asset that they can attach as collateral in order to get their money back if they have to put up the bond. That also helps make sure that the people that get licences are heterosexual, mainstream, male. A man who is an ex-cop or ex-FBI agent is unlikely not to have a house at least, and maybe some investments. There are not a lot of single, twenty-five-year-old women who own property. When I went for my licence, the only property I owned was my car. It took me a long time before I found an agent who was prepared to take the risk!'

Once you've jumped through all those hoops, you're finally ready to roll. But only in the state you're licensed for. One of the many controversies that has raged as a result of the OJ Simpson case centres round this very issue. The private investigators that were hired by the defence were from out of state and weren't licensed in California, where the crime and the trial took place. Local investigators argued that their work product should therefore be inadmissible as evidence. There are two key issues here. One is that an investigator who is called to give evidence in a state in which they are not licensed has no official standing; they are not an expert witness, they are merely members of the public. The other is that an operative who isn't licensed in the state isn't subject to any sanction if they break the rules; they can't be stripped of their licence because they haven't got one to be stripped of.

Jurisdictional problems like this mean that most scrupulous investigators only work within their own state or else they make sure they're licensed in all the states they work in. René Olsson is a financial investigation specialist based in Seattle whose work involves spending time in various parts of the country. She's licensed in six separate states. It means paying six lots of dues, but for her it's worth it because of the particular work she does.

But licensing doesn't scrub the business clean of all the sleaze merchants, however much the ABI hopes it will. Nancy Barber, a San Francisco environmental investigation specialist, says, 'It's not my perception that this industry is well regulated. The biggest problems are the issue of scruples and right to privacy. It's not the availability of the information that bothers me so much, it's how it's used. That bothers me a lot. When people call me and ask me to do something I perceive to be unethical, I say, "Would you like this done to you?" There is a theory that if you file a lawsuit then you've made yourself vulnerable; if you say to someone, "You owe me money because you injured me," then the other party has the right to discover how much money you make, how long you've worked, to calculate your economic status. But where is the line drawn? Who draws the line? Often, it seems to me that plaintiffs' lives are turned inside out in the attempt to find anything, however small, that might discredit them. Using licensed operatives somehow legitimises that.'

And no matter how much information exists in the public domain, there will always be private eyes willing to bribe, cheat and steal their way to the stuff they're not supposed to have. It happens on both sides of the Atlantic. For example, California has closed down public access to their Department of Motor Vehicle information following the murder of Hollywood actress Rebecca Shaeffer who was killed by an obsessive stalker after he found her home address in the public records of the DMV. Already, private eyes have been prosecuted for attempting to buy DMV information.

Friday night. Five unrelated homicides in the city tonight. Everybody says, 'So what?' It's just another night in New York city, where they've turned paranoia into one of the fine arts. It's hardly surprising the city is so manic; the street noise is constant, waking me staring-eyed and panic-stricken every night in the small hours. No one here has had a proper night's sleep since about 1943. The whole city is jittery with sleeplessness, as wired as if they're constantly on speed. It couldn't be more different from the tranquil atmosphere of the English countryside. Come to that, it's a long way from inner-city Manchester, where the midnight whoop of sirens is still unusual enough to draw people to their windows.

Inevitably, the job is shaped by the environment. Some things are broadly similar—tracing missing persons, investigating internal theft and fraud for companies, serving process. But in general, a private eye in rural Gloucestershire has a very different case load and lifestyle to one in New York. Not least because America's street culture is so heavily defined by drugs and guns. In Britain, neither has reached the epidemic proportions of the USA, though the drugs are heading in that direction, with the guns following, thankfully still a long way behind. With so many illegal guns on the street, I was surprised by how few of the American women eyes choose to exercise their First Amendment right to bear arms. They rely on other techniques to defuse difficult situations. Oakland's Francie Koehler speaks for most of them when she says, 'I don't believe in carrying a gun. You talk to the guys and most of them carry weapons and believe in it. They would never go in a bad neighbourhood without one. I think it's crazy. Just what you need. One more gun in the neighbourhoods.'

But then, the reason most of the American women PIs are in the neighbourhoods in the first place is that they're doing criminal defence work. They are perceived as being on the side of the inhabitants, unlike their British counterparts, who are probably in the inner city no-go areas to serve injunctions for domestic violence or papers relating to debt. In America, the state is more inclined to shell out for a private eye to work for the defence in serious criminal cases, partly because of the awful finality of the death penalty. It's a symbol of a commitment to the principle of a fair trial, a principle that too often goes by the board in a country addicted to the plea bargain as the basic machinery for making sure the legal system doesn't collapse under the weight of its caseload.

In England, the Legal Aid Board is reluctant to fund an investigator's fees to assist the defence. In Scotland, with its entirely separate legal system based on a different set of first principles, there is a closer parallel to what happens in America. But even that is under threat now. Jennifer Paul, who is a criminal defence specialist in Glasgow, explains. 'There's talk about changing the system here in Scotland. At the moment, defence solicitors hire someone like me to go out and take statements from the prosecution witnesses. I don't think it would be in the interests of justice to stop that.

'The police do not get the same statement as I do. The police are out there looking for a case and they're only interested in what substantiates that case. When I go out, that case is already in position so I'm not looking for a case, I'm looking for all the facts plus any angles. I take all the good and all the bad. I want all the information. Some of the witnesses don't want to tell you everything because they know that what they're going to say may be detrimental to the accused. Perhaps they're friends of the accused but they're being called as a prosecution witness, so I explain that the defence solicitor doesn't want any surprises. The solicitor doesn't want to know the facts of the case on the day of the trial, he wants to know them beforehand. It's in the interests of justice that we have that sort of fair play.'

Differences in the law make for differences in the work at every level. Even the details are different. A British investigator was recently fined by magistrates for stealing the contents of somebody's rubbish bin. The arguments raged in court over whose property the rubbish was—did it belong to the person who threw it out or did it belong to the council? Eventually, it was decided the crucial issue wasn't ownership, but the fact that the detective had broken the law by 'intending permanently to deprive' whoever the lawful owner was. The PI would have been OK if he'd brought the rubbish back after he'd probed it!

In America, it's acceptable to take someone's garbage; it's assumed that if they've thrown it away, they have no further claim on it. Often, investigators who steal the garbage will replace it with their own bin bags so that the victim doesn't realise they've been the victim of what one PI calls 'garbological investigation'. René Olsson again, on the unexpected side of financial investigation: 'I jumped into a huge construction dumpster one time. I was looking for bank statements, payroll slips, company accounts, anything that would give me a lead on this guy's finances. There was broken glass in there, decomposing unidentifiable stuff and things I don't like to think about even now. I hadn't thought it through before I did it, but these giant containers, they have the ladder on the outside but once you jump in there there's no ladder on the inside. There was a slight moment of panic! I just had to pile stuff up on the inside and climb up till I could jump clear. Don't let anybody tell you financial investigations are dull.'

Another area the Americans have to worry more about than the Brits is the civil courts. America, as every citizen will tell you, is lawsuit heaven. One woman PI I interviewed is currently fighting the threat of a lawsuit from a company she was hired to investigate. Her secretary sold them the incriminating evidence she had uncovered against them, and they are now suing her for invasion of privacy as a result of her initial undercover investigation.

Sarah Di Venere, the proprietor of an agency in Chicago, tells a similar story. 'I was at a fund-raising dinner one time and I was talking to a bunch of cops from the 18th District vice unit. They'd had an apartment in an expensive downtown building for a month because they suspected the doorman of providing cocaine to residents and their friends. The cops were complaining because they only had one day left on the operation and they still didn't have anything solid on this guy.

'I said, "Let me try." They had nothing left to lose, so they agreed. I went up to this doorman and gave him a song and dance about how I had some girlfriends coming to town and I had to get some stuff for a party. And he told me he would sell me some stuff.

'Meanwhile the guys in the vice unit were all stationed outside the glass lobby of the complex, waiting for me to give them the signal to move in. I'm bullshitting this doorman, saying I could use more than he had, so he called his dealer! This dealer came over the apartment building and I talked to him. All this is happening in the lobby and these vice guys are wondering what the hell is going down!

'The dealer and I are gossiping about different people in town and eventually, I say I could really use a lot more than he'd brought me. So he called up a runner who came over on a motorcycle. Meanwhile the cops outside are getting real twitchy, wondering what in the world I am doing, this is taking forever. Eventually, the runner arrives and I finally give thc signal and all these cops came running in and made the arrests. Because I was just an informant, I never had to give evidence at trial. But I did have to go and give evidence in front of the Union arbitrators because the doorman had been fired while he was on bail awaiting trial and he was filing for unfair dismissal! Can you believe that?'

Only in America.

Career Case

When you ask most investigators about a career case, they tell you about the case that's made their career. When I say career case, I mean the one that has spanned the whole of my career. I've been tangling with this family for nearly forty years. The story begins around 1957 when a woman committed suicide by jumping off a railway bridge in front of a train. I was still in the police force and I remember going to deal with the body. Her head was chopped off and it wasn't a pretty sight. She had a daughter called Lizzie Crichton. I did Lizzie regularly for shoplifting, starting in the early sixties. And among her many kids, nearly all of whom I've done for shoplifting at one time or another, Lizzie Crichton had a daughter called Sandra. Sandra must have been about thirteen when I ended up taking her off Lizzie Crichton for being in need of care and protection. This was back in the days when you could take children off their parents! Sandra was put into care for about three years and then she had several children and then she eventually got married to a fella called George Botham.

She probably had about three kids to him. Sandra Botham is about five foot three, long straw hair, shaped like a Michelin man, she'd be about forty-five now. She used to drive me round the bloody bend with her shoplifting when I was a store detective. I remember one Christmas shoplifting spree her and George went on. The ground floor in the store was shiny marble, and there were two doors between the shop floor and the street. If the inner door was open then you had a shiny surface all the way to the front door. I was hiding in the stationery department, watching them. They were already loaded down with stuff, and I saw them pinch a wig and a pair of gloves. So I ran out of my hiding place and down the stairs. I dove from the stairs on to George's back and he fell to the ground and with my weight on top of his, we slid right to the front door and he hit his head on it! It took our nursing sister about two hours to bring him round and I'm going 'Oh, God, I could be done for manslaughter here!' But he did come round, so we did him for shoplifting.

Then Sandra left him and started going with women. She took up with this lass called Christine, and the pair of them started writing letters to the Kray Twins in prison. They were making up to them on the pretext that they were in love with them and they'd end up marrying the twins when they came out of jail. What they were really up to was getting these love letters from Reggie and Ronnie Kray so they could sell them to the newspapers for vast sums of money.

Next thing I know is I'm being asked to act for the Krays! I ended up serving papers on these two for the Kray Twins. The brothers got their injunction order to stop Sandra and Christine writing letters to them and to prevent them getting the brothers' letters published. We were doing observations on the block where Sandra was living, waiting for her to show up so we could serve the injunction. And we noticed a car at each entrance to the street full of enormous fellas, and we're thinking, 'Who are they looking for? They're not coppers, that's for sure.' It turned out that these guys were the Kray Brothers' heavy mob, looking for Sandra and Christine to explain the error of their ways to them!

For all that this is my patch and I know it like the back of my hand, I could not find Sandra anywhere. Finally, I got a tip that she was doing belly dancing in this dive in Sunderland. My daughter Susan must have been about eight months pregnant at the time, but she was like me, worked right up to the last, and so she served Sandra with the Kray Twins' injunction in this pub while she was doing her belly dance and that was the end of that chapter.

Next thing is that Sandra is up at Durham Crown Court for shoplifting. This time, she broke her bail and she was nowhere to be found. The five kids she'd had before George were in care, but George's sister had taken out wardship proceedings for the other three because Sandra had a habit of turning up and pinching the kids and running off with them. Also, George was wanting a divorce. So I had the wardship papers and the divorce papers to serve on Sandra, and we didn't have a bloody clue where she was.

So I had to go round and speak to George and when I got there, he had these two great big Rottweilers in the garden so of course I couldn't get up the path. George came to the front door and the language that he came out with! He didn't want no fucking police at his door, he was going to set the fucking dogs on me, I could just fuck off. I just stood there with a smile on my face and I said, 'But I'm working for you, George. Your solicitor's hired me to serve the papers on Sandra.'

'Oh,' he said. 'You'd better come in, then.' Not long before this, he'd had his nose bitten off. Not by the Rottweilers, by a human being. They're like that, the people we work with. George had had his nose repaired by a skin graft from his bottom. Well, he had a dark, tanned rugged face, and there's this stupid little pink nose in the middle. I couldn't take my eyes off his nose and he's getting more and more wound up. It was a terrible struggle to keep a straight face. I ask him if he knows where Sandra is and he tells me she's buggered off to Amsterdam to work as a go-go dancer in some sex club. Of course, the solicitor says there's no money for me to go to Amsterdam looking for her, so the whole thing went on hold.

I'm watching the telly one night and suddenly I'm looking at George's front door and there's a reporter saying that George has been shot dead on the doorstep. I couldn't believe it! I rang the police and said, 'If Sandra's not already involved with the murder, she will be in Sunderland in twenty-four hours. I've got some papers to serve on her, and there's a warrant for her arrest for jumping bail from the Crown Court.'

'Oh,' says this copper. 'What do you think we should do?' It's worrying, isn't it?

'Well,' says I, 'I think you start by arresting her.' I asked them to ring me as soon as they'd got her so I could serve the wardship papers on her. They promised but the police never ever keep any of their promises. I sometimes wonder why I bother helping them. Next morning I found out they'd picked her up off the Amsterdam flight, taken her passport off her and let her go. I could have smacked them!

I thought she might go looking for her bairns so I went up to George's sister's house and the place was full of women. I said 'Is Sandra in?' and they told me I'd just missed her, that she'd created merry hell and they'd had to call the police to cart her off. I said, 'Oh God, no! Get the bloody kettle on.' I'd had enough.

Then this weedy old woman in her eighties came in from outside and she's staring at me because obviously I was the only stranger there and she says, 'And who the fucking hell are you?' Charming people we get in this job, but you get used to it.

I said, 'I'm naebody, I'm just the fucking Bailiff around here!' I don't normally swear, but I couldn't help myself; I was so bloody mad that I hadn't caught up with Sandra.

She said, 'Are you looking for San Botham? I know where she is.'

I'm exasperated by now, so I say, 'Don't talk daft, man, she's just been arrested.'

She said, 'I know. They put her in the car and they drove her out the street and when they got round the corner, they chucked her out the car. I followed her and she's in that house over there.' I could have kissed the old woman!

I knew I couldn't go out the front door because that was visible from the house where Sandra was holed up. That left the back door. There was a bloody six foot wall round the yard. I didn't care, I had Sandra in my sights. I had a skirt on, so I hitched it up and climbed over the back wall, went up the back alley, crossed over the road and crawled back down the street on my hands and knees below window level. The front door was on the latch so I just walked right in and there was Sandra on the other side of the room with a baby in her arms. I walked over, gave her a kiss and a cuddle and the wardship papers and said, 'Eh, Sandra, you're the best lass in the world.' Well, you can imagine the language!

The last chapter of the story—well, it's the last chapter so far—came in 1992. It turns out that George got murdered over a drugs deal. He'd got a supply of drugs from a Pakistani bloke in London, and he hadn't paid for them. So this bloke came up from London and got himself a local sidekick, and they'd done for George. And I got hired by the defence to make inquiries on their behalf for their so-called alibi evidence! I couldn't believe this bloody family were still haunting me!

It's been a long family saga. I wish I could believe I'd heard the last of Sandra Botham and her clan, but I doubt it.

BRENDA BALMER
Sunderland

3

In the Beginning

*One phone call sent me in a direction I'd never
have considered before. And I love it!*

JANET WILSON
Dover

Because of the accidental way so many women come
into the job, they often don't have a clear idea of what
kind of cases they want to specialise in. Like any job,
it's hard to appreciate what's involved until you're
doing it. When I was a journalist, the one thing I ever
wanted to do was investigative reporting. That was until
I tried it and realised I was far too impatient for the
painstaking research, the endless hours of waiting for
that crucial phone call and the mindless tedium of
stake-outs. After a short spell of that kind of work, the
relief of returning to the private lives of soap stars was
indescribable. I still went back to investigations at
regular intervals, but I knew I couldn't hack it full time.
In the same way, often the first cases the woman eyes
are involved in sharpen their focus and point them in a
direction they hadn't imagined they would take.

Bouncing down the pavement in sneakers, Francie
Koehler doesn't look like the president of a sizeable
corporation. Around five two in blue jeans, pearl-

studded denim overshirt and white teeshirt, she isn't dressed for the part. Closer up, I see the signs of the well-groomed professional woman; the thick hair, more salt than pepper, is immaculately cut, there's not a single chip on the dusky red nail varnish, the subtle make-up emphasises lively blue eyes, and the pearl earrings match the detail on the shirt.

The offices of Rand Investigations Inc. is an impressive set-up. Past the wide reception desk, offices line the perimeter of a central rectangle lined with waist-high shelves containing the phone book archive—yards and yards of it. Going round anti-clockwise, there's a conference room cum library with an oak table and chairs. The shelves contain city directories going back to the fifties, textbooks on everything from forensics to construction regulations to interview techniques, plus video and audio tapes about thieves and about how to avoid losses in business. There's also a comfortable looking three-seater sofa with a thick comforter; obviously this is a place where people work late, maybe even camp out in the office. Next door is her husband Randy's office, complete with his polygraph machine.

There are offices for other investigators, including a specialist document examiner, an administration area, a kitchen, and offices for their subsidiary companies, one of which tracks down copyright infringements for film and TV merchandise. Currently, they're working on rip-offs of The Simpsons—everything from clothing to soft toys.

It's all housed in a pleasant modern building just off the main street in downtown Oakland. Oakland is a split city; it's white and upper middle-class in the hills, blue-collar and ethnically mixed down in the city itself. In the past, Oakland has been supported by the military, with army and navy bases there. But both are winding down prior to closing, unemployment is rising and in tandem with that goes street crime, drugs and murder. All of which means that Francie Koehler is never short of work.

Francie got her first case the very evening that she resigned her job in retail management to join her husband's agency as a marketing specialist and administrator. 'Randy got paged as we were having our celebration dinner! It was a missing person case involving a Palestinian girl, a senior in high school, she's seventeen and she's about to be forced into an arranged marriage with a man she had met only once. The father barely spoke English, he was a very strict, traditional Middle Eastern patriarch.'

The girl's car had been left by the Golden Gate Bridge, with her purse and a suicide note inside. But after talking to the parents, Francie felt the idea that she had killed herself didn't seem to fit.

'What was also strange was that her two best friends really were not helping find her. The next day we'd organised posters, and we took a look at the area where these friends had been assigned to fly-post. Their posters were not up. By now, we were pretty sure something was going on, and so we just kept putting pressure on these two kids and finally the girl surfaced and went to an attorney. She had faked her suicide because she didn't want the marriage. The important thing was that the family was reconciled.

'So much for managing the office and marketing investigative services! I really got thrown in at the deep end. But once I got a taste of that...I figured out what I wanted to do when I grew up! I said, "Randy, gimme some cases!"' She spreads her hands in a gesture of gathering things to her. Francie is one of those people who'd be struck dumb if their hands were cut off.

Her husband specialises in loss prevention and employment theft and wished to train her in the same field, but when she got her first taste of criminal investigation she knew that that was where her heart lay. Francie firmly believes that finding the thing you like doing most is the key to success. 'When your heart is in it, you go the extra mile. You tell yourself that little piece of key evidence is somewhere. I've been really fortunate in that I've had a few defendants who were actually innocent and because of my evidence they're not in jail. I have always said that if I had one of those it would make a whole lifetime worthwhile. Just one, But I have been fortunate enough to have had several and that's really rewarding.'

Sometimes, that first taste makes it just as clear what kind of work a woman does not want to do. That's what happened to Nancy Poss-Hatchl, anthropologist, chemist, former columnist for a Spanish magazine, co-author of a children's book about Chemar the armadillo, painter, and collector of photographs of benches. A fifty-nine-year-old grandmother, she's the last person you'd mark down as International Investigator of the Year.

Her trim white bungalow on a quiet suburban street in Santa Ana, California, continues the deception. Take a walk down the back yard, through an orchard of fruit trees with rubber snakes hanging from the branches to scare the birds, and what looks like a big shed at the end of the garden is revealed as the high-tech offices of Helios Investigations, base for Nancy and her half-dozen employees. She's been her own boss since 1979, when she decided it was time to stop working for other people.

'I got into the investigating business as a result of a divorce. I had three teenagers, and I had to earn a living. There aren't many jobs open for middle-aged women anthropologists. And even if you get a job as an anthropologist the pay is probably less than you would get as a dishwasher.' Nancy had a girlfriend that worked for a PI, and they needed an undercover worker in a factory where there had been a number of narcotic deaths. This seemed an opportunity to try something exciting and earn some money. 'I've always loved adventure, even as a little kid. I used to be into things like Agatha Christie, Sherlock Holmes and Dashiell Hammett. So I said I'd give it a go. I was willing to try anything that paid reasonably well.'

The management of the factory suspected there was a drugs ring operating and needed to find out who was involved so Nancy had to learn to solder so she could work undercover on the factory floor. This didn't prove as easy as it might seem, as Nancy relates. 'I kept my eyes peeled and every Friday I'd rendezvous in a bar with the agency boss, Maxwell Smart, who actually wore a trench coat! He was a retired military CIA type, so he was really into the undercover stuff. The only problem was, I soldered so well I kept getting promoted out of the department, and they kept saying, "Get back in there and make more mistakes." That department was the key, so I had to get myself demoted again!'

Work problems aside, it didn't take long for Nancy to find out what was going on in the factory. 'Every Friday, the pay cheque would come. Every Friday the drug dealers would have these little bags and counters, and they would say, "What do you want? The store is open." I would just watch it happen and that's how I found out who was participating in the ring. I don't think they ever suspected me while I was there. I would read their tarot cards and that would make them like me. Also, they didn't know I'm bilingual. They would talk to me in broken English but they didn't know I could understand what they were saying when they talked among themselves in Spanish.

'One morning, Maxwell Smart called me up at about quarter to five and said, "Don't go to work, you'll be killed." The whole thing was wound up then and there.'

Being an undercover agent wasn't exactly what Nancy had expected. As she points out, standing doing soldering all day can get very boring. Nevertheless, she had caught the investigation bug, although it would lead her into a very different area of the field. 'I knew then and there that I wanted to be a private investigator. But that early morning phone call made me realise that as a mother, I couldn't do something that dangerous, so I began working as an insurance investigator.'

Seattle is a small, civilised city curling round Puget Sound and Lake Washington. The streets of Seattle are generally safer than most major American cities, but there's still more than enough dishonesty to keep the private eyes busy. Not to mention the crime writers. There are probably more mystery novelists per head of population than anywhere in the United States; and more bookstores.

Most of all, Seattle feels like a young city, a place with more future than past. Appropriately enough, René Olsson was the youngest investigator I met. Though she's only thirty-one, she's already got ten years' experience under her belt. While she was still a student, she took a part-time job as an emergency despatcher for a security company to help pay her way through college. 'It was a horrible job. I sat in a little room that was four foot by four foot, answering alarms and doing my homework,' she recalls. It was there that she fell into her first case, which set her on the path to a career in private investigation.

'This company had probably the majority of all the accounts in Seattle. Everything from franchise stores, stereo stores, drugstores to private residences. We held the codes for all their alarm systems and we had security guards who patrolled our subscribers' properties. A couple of the security guards who worked there were also despatchers and one of them was coming on to me, trying to impress and he asked if I wanted a new stereo. I was curious, so I let him talk.

'He started telling me how he can get anything he wants all over town because him and his buddy are ripping off all the accounts and there's no record of it. This was supposedly impossible, because every time you enter or leave a building when it's closed, there's a password that has to be used and there's always a record printed out on indestructible tape back at the despatch centre. He told me they would just slip another piece of paper over the alarm tape so that when the print head came down, it didn't print on the tape, it printed on the scrap paper that you just threw away. They had furnished their apartments and traded goods for drugs and everything! The only reason it ever came to light was this guy was a little too cocky.'

René didn't want to get involved, and informed her employers of what was going on. The police were brought in and they asked René to work with them on a sting operation. She was to tell the guard she wanted a stereo but to insist that she go with him when he picked it up. That way the police would know when and where they were going and could have the place staked out and catch the guy red-handed. It sounds a simple plan but, as René describes, it didn't quite work out that way.

'The police handled it really badly. We were going to hit this hi-fi warehouse in the middle of the night. It took two people minimum, because one person had to enter the building and take the stuff and the other person had to be in the despatch centre to slip the paper over the tape, so there was no record, and also to check no one else went in or out of the building. So we'd told the despatcher that we were going to go out and get stuff that night and we'd call him on the radio when we were ready to go in so he could slip the paper in.

'We got down there and we found ourselves in a radio hole. We kept calling the despatcher, but the guy couldn't hear us. So he said, "We'll drive up the hill and call him from there." And I'm thinking, shit, all these cops are out there hiding, when they see us driving off they're going to think we've changed our minds, and they're going to leave, and then we're going to come back and really burgle the store!

'So as we're driving out, I'm desperately trying to get the guy on the radio, and finally he said, "I can't hear you, I don't know what you're saying, but I'm putting the paper in now." Huge sigh of relief!

'The guard runs in the building and I'm left in the car with this huge mean guard dog in a cage in the back. Before the guard comes back, a policeman sneaks around the side of the car, and whispers, "Put your hands up and let me cuff you now," because I told them, if I help you, I don't want these guys to know it was me. So I put my hands up, and the dog all of a sudden went wild. The cop dives in front of the car, the guy comes running out of the building, saying, "What's going on, what's the matter with the dog?" And I'm sitting there with handcuffs on, going "I don't know, he just freaked out, I didn't see anything."

'He goes back in and when he comes out with the speakers, I just hear click, click, click, hammers going back on guns, and the cops are all leaping out of hiding, the place is surrounded. They tell him to freeze, because of course he's armed, and at that moment I also realise, this is kind of dumb. I'm the only unarmed person here and I'm in handcuffs and I'm between the cops and the robber and I really don't like the way they're handling this at all!

'The guard won't freeze. He thinks the whole thing is a mistake, and he's flailing around, saying, "This is crazy, I'm the security guard!" And the police are screaming, the tension is getting really high. Finally, the police close in, still screaming and he gets so scared he puts his hands up and they pull the gun away and they throw us both in the cop car.

'When we get to the police station, they do this totally stupid thing. They put me in a holding cell adjacent to the guard, then they go off to arrest the despatcher. Meanwhile, the custody officer, who does not know what is going on, is talking about getting transport to take us to the jail, and I can't say anything because the guy in the cell next to me would hear every word, and I don't want these guys to know I'm the informer! The custody officer can't find any paperwork on me, because of course I haven't been arrested, but when he asks me what I'm in for, all I can do is grin and say, "Second degree burglary."

'Finally it all got straightened out, but the next morning, all over the front page of the Seattle Post Intelligencer is, "René Olsson, informant, busted up a big burglary ring." So much for confidentiality.'

After such an experience, most people would vow never to do anything similar again, but not René. She was interviewed by an investigator prior to the guards' trial and what he told her about the job of PI convinced her it was the career for her.

Those first jobs stick in the mind long after other assignments are deleted from the brain's memory banks. After a while, even the most exciting job in the world develops its routine side, where every case looks much like something that has gone before. But in the early days, it's all fresh and new. Every client brings an original story, every interview is unfamiliar and demanding territory. Every day is a challenge, another notch higher up the learning curve. So even the most mundane tasks that wouldn't merit a footnote in the diary in years to come are stories that never fade.

In 1946, Liverpool was still one of the world's busiest ports. The huge docks stretched for miles along the Mersey estuary, haven for cargo ships and passenger liners alike. The city first got rich through its trade across the Atlantic in the nineteenth century, and the sea was still the source of its prosperity. It was also the source of Zena Scott-Archer's first case.

'It was just after the war and there was a lot of divorce work, because soldiers were coming home and finding that there was an extra baby in the family,' she recalled with a chuckle. 'My first case was very simple, really. It was the serving of a divorce petition on a woman who was a stewardess on a ship that came into Liverpool. Several of the men in the agency had tried already, but none of them could get hold of this wretched woman who was really playing ducks and drakes with them. She was a stewardess on a passenger ship and whenever anybody asked for her by her official title, it sent warning signals out and she did a disappearing act.

'I had her description and I went on board the ship. You can wander on to any ship but as usual, I was wearing high heels and a skirt and they are not the best things for going up gangways! Anyway, I walked around until I saw the woman I thought might be her. So I called out her first name, Elsie. She turned round and realised the game was up. Once people have been rumbled they usually will admit it.'

For Yvonne Twiby, it was a similar story; a routine process service drew her into the business that has been her career for the last twenty years. She was working as a secretary for a PI and when her boss could find no one free to serve a bankruptcy notice, he turned to her. The job didn't prove quite as simple as she'd expected.

'The problem with serving him was that he didn't live on the mainland and by the time the client found out he was on the mainland, he was back off again,' Yvonne explains. 'So I spoke to the booking department at the BBC to find out who his agent was, then phoned his agent to find out where he was working next, acting like I was the secretary of somebody who wanted to see his act with a view to booking him. To me that was just common sense. My boss was over the moon. And from there, he started giving me jobs.'

Not all first cases are so mundane. For Lynn McLaren in Santa Barbara, it was literally a matter of life and death. Her first big case came in 1989. It was a murder, the killing of Phillip Bogdanoff, a high-profile case that became the subject of a book, Death in Santa Barbara. Bogdanoff was sunbathing with his wife on a nude beach when he was shot by two gunmen. At first the police thought it was just a random killing, but when they started to dig deeper, they discovered it was a hit. Diane, Bogdanoff's wife, was charged with conspiring with her daughter and the daughter's boyfriend to kill the husband. Lynn was hired by the defence to try to get the death penalty excluded, which meant finding serious mitigation.

'My job in essence was to write this woman's life story. I spent a lot of time talking to Diane, getting to know her, then back-tracking right through her past, and I discovered all sorts of terrible stuff. This had been a really abusive marriage. She had been repeatedly battered, and it was not as straightforward a crime as it looked on the surface. The work I did helped to establish enough mitigation for the death penalty to be dispensed with, and we got a hung jury at the first trial.

'The second trial was less of a knife-edge thing as a result, because the DA had decided not to ask for the death penalty. Of course, our strategy at the second trial had to be a bit different because we didn't just want to repeat the defence that the DA already knew about, so I had a different task this time. I had to find witnesses and organise them, make sure they were properly prepared to give testimony and that they knew what to expect in the witness box. The whole process was fascinating.' At that second trial, Diane Bogdanoff was found guilty of first degree murder and sentenced to life without parole. But it's thanks to Lynn McLaren's work that she isn't sitting on Death Row waiting for her execution date.

That sense of gratification can often be the key factor that makes a woman certain she's on the right path. So it was for BJ Seebol. BJ trained as a lawyer and found herself working as a legal investigator almost by accident when the job she'd started part-time to pay her way through college became her bread and butter after she failed the bar exam. At first, she felt like a failure because she hadn't succeeded at the one thing she'd ever wanted. Investigation was not so much a choice as a necessity to pay the bills. Then, within weeks of her reluctant decision, a case came along that gave her confidence the boost she needed and made her realise that she had found her forte almost by accident.

The case involved a feud between the landlord and tenant of a restaurant. When the landlord had negotiated the lease he had made it clear to the tenant that he planned to build on the two empty parcels of land on either side. However when work began, the tenant tried to sue the landlord because of the noise and dirt produced.

'I had to go out and video-tape the actual construction. I had to monitor our own guys just to make sure they weren't doing anything that was extraordinary for a construction site. Without that tape, it's just our word against his. Well, the case went to trial and we won.'

In the lease there was an attorney's fees clause, which meant that the parties had agreed that in the event of any litigation between them, the loser had to pay the winner's legal fees. A separate hearing was arranged to agree costs but the tenant claimed that BJ's were too high.

'I couldn't believe this, but the judge gets up and he starts lambasting this guy and saying, "You've just got sour grapes because you don't have somebody like BJ Seebol on your team. It's so obvious that she did so much of the work." And I was just so astonished. I was walking on air after that. I asked my client, "Do you think it would be obnoxious if I requested a copy of the record and plastered it all over my wall?" That was accolade city!'

Sadly, accolades and encouragement are rare for PIs, especially when they are just starting out. Being a private eye can be a fearful business, whether it's worrying about where the next job is going to come from or working on a case which is a race against time. For Nancy Barber, striking out on her own was an adventure in terror.

'I absolutely remember my first case,' she says vehemently. 'Partly because of the fear of not having business. You've hung out your shingle and you're thinking, now what? My very first case came to me from my previous employer, which I was glad about because it showed that somebody had faith in me!'

The case involved a man who had been exposed to asbestos during construction and later working on an oil refinery out in Iran. He had developed mesothelioma as a result and was bringing a case against the Iranian oil company. The investigation was a difficult one. Getting information direct from Iran proved almost impossible, while Iranians resident in the States—many of them illegal immigrants—were hard to track down and often frightened to talk.

Through a combination of smart thinking and hard work, Nancy eventually established who was responsible in law. Unfortunately the plaintiff died before the case was settled. It's a painful outcome which comes with the territory for Nancy. 'When I get a case and someone is very, very sick, I'm working against the clock. It's not like the usual run of things when you know you have a comfortable time to do the discovery and investigation. But if somebody's dying, you have to move it right along. I had less than two months to settle the case, and sometimes that just ain't enough time to get everything. But it's one hell of an incentive to get the job done.'

In the Nick of Time

A gas station attendant was shot in the course of a robbery. Three men were arrested: Alexander, Johnny B and Willy. Alexander was convicted and was serving twenty-five to life. Johnny B turned state's evidence and got probation even though he had a record a mile long. The charges against Willy were dropped and he moved to another state. He wasn't involved in the murder, he was just living with the mother of one of the killers and he got caught up in the investigation.

He'd started afresh, met a woman, got married, had kids, bought a house and became a minister of religion. Unknown to him, the charges against him had been refiled. He never knew that there was a murder warrant out for him. Now it's ten years later and he gets picked up for a traffic violation. They run him through the computer and up pops this ten-year-old murder warrant in California. So they extradite him back here.

When you first get a case, you never believe they're innocent. Everybody says they're innocent, but you get cynical about it after a while. But there was something about this guy that rang true and so I drove down to San Luis Obispo to interview Alexander in jail. His story was wobbling all over the place and it gradually emerged that the DA's investigator had been down to see him a few days before. Alexander's parole hearing was coming up, and the investigator pretty much told him that if he could help them out at Willy's trial then they would speak favourably on his behalf in front of the parole board. But Alexander knew that he would have to lie to do that because he knew that Willy wasn't involved with this crime. I could see he was really struggling between self-interest and the right thing to do.

I knew that somehow I had to make sure that Alexander told the truth. I found out that Alexander's father was a Pentecostal pastor of some kind in Las Vegas and I ended up calling him. I explained the prosecution were bringing Alexander up for the hearing, convinced that he would testify in their behalf. And that would nail Willy. Alexander's dad drove through the night—I still can't believe this—all the way from Las Vegas to get to this hearing. He had two motives; he wanted to see his son but he was also committed to helping us get Alexander to tell the truth. He was going to sit in the front row of that courtroom and he would just look his son in the eye.

Reverend Jefferson wanted to be able to talk to his son before the hearing. We had a battle with the judge to allow it, and eventually it was agreed he could talk to Alexander provided neither I nor the DA's investigator were present. So the Reverend went off to the holding area to see his son. I'm sitting in the courtroom when they bring Alexander in and swear him in! They haven't let him see his father! I raced down to the holding area, and the Reverend is still waiting. I said, "Sir, the court has started, Alexander's on the stand!" He looked at me and his mouth dropped open. The Deputy had this really weird look on his face. I said, "He's supposed to be either talking with his son or upstairs in court."

The Deputy said, "They told me to hold him here."

I took the Reverend Jefferson back upstairs and told our attorney what happened and he went ballistic. He stopped the proceedings right there and he marched up to the judge and confronted him. The judge was just sitting opening and closing his mouth like a goldfish. If I hadn't been so angry it would have been comical. Finally, the judge pretty much admitted that the Reverend was being held up deliberately.

After all of this, Alexander testified, and he told the truth.

And Willy walked free. But by this time he had been in jail six months and he lost his house. His wife is questioning whether she really knew the man she married. In spite of that, Willy finally got out a very, very happy man.

FRANCIE KOEHLER
Oakland, California

4

Wonder Women

Ask the public what they expect a private eye to be and they'll probably say, 'a bloke in a dirty raincoat.'

DIANA MIDDLETON,
Hornchurch, Essex

I approach every job with the idea that I might have to stand up in court and back up my work. I'm doing what the client requires, but at the same time, I have my own mental standard of proof that I know will stand up in court. Some investigators just want to do the job and get their money.
Not me. I want the job done to the highest standard.

CHRISTINE USHER
Hampshire

Women detectives think women make better detectives. To paraphrase Mandy Rice Davies, they would, wouldn't they? But do they? And if so, why? To answer that, the first question probably should be, what makes a good private eye? Integrity, tenacity, curiosity, empathy, courage, discretion, resourcefulness, a built-in bullshit detector and a sense of humour seem to be the basic prerequisites if the idealised fictional blueprint is anything to go by. On all of those counts, the women I interviewed seem to score higher than the average population.

At present there are relatively few women in the field; women might hold up half the sky, as the feminist catch-phrase has it, but down on the mean streets, the ratio is a lot lower than that. Statistics are hard to come by, but in the UK women seem to account for between five and ten per cent of PIs. It's more in America, but it varies enormously from state to state. In the Hispanic-dominated South Florida area, there are only a handful of women operatives. But in California, the figure seems to be nearer the twenty-five to thirty percent mark.

The women themselves have clear ideas about what qualities are important. And those ideas are what convinces them that women are better at the job than the men. Zena Scott-Archer expressed the opinions of most of the women eyes I spoke to when she explained why she tended to employ women in her agency. 'They are extremely good, so attentive to detail, so observant. When I sold my business, I sold it to a woman who had worked for me. I knew that I could rely on her. She never misunderstood me, she was always on the ball and would get on with the job. Men need a lot of bolstering up, I'm afraid!

'I think you need a knowledge of human nature and body language. The majority of men who came to me looking for a job had the idea that it was very exciting and they would tell me that they thought it was all about shooting people and they'd be perfect because they knew all about guns! I wasn't really interested in that sort of thing! I was more interested in whether they could do an eight-hour stint on surveillance without wandering off. With the men, I would say, "Does your wife know you've applied for this job?" And they'd say yes. How does she feel about it? "Oh, fine!" Then I'd take them on and three weeks later they'd come in saying their wives don't like them going out every night!

Women are better at the sheer plod and the routine stuff; they don't expect excitement and glamour.

'To be successful in this business, you need to combine tenacity and expertise. Often, if I found someone who had the gumption to stay there for eight hours without going away, they didn't know what to do when the surveillance subjects did come out; and those who knew what to do when they came out wouldn't have stayed there for eight hours. Marrying the two together was very difficult. It seems to me that women have a greater sense of personal responsibility. They don't just shrug their shoulders and walk away if a job isn't working out the way they hoped. They look at the problem and try to find another way round the situation. With most men, if they can't tackle it head on, it can't be done.'

Yvonne Twiby recognised a similar arrogance in the men she has employed in the past; an arrogance with which she has little patience. 'The fact that I've been doing this successfully for twenty years and they've just started means nothing to the men I've taken on. They always want to do it their way. Say I send them on a straightforward job to collect a credit card. I tell them they have to do this, this and this. If they do it wrong the first time, I say, "OK, you didn't get it quite right." If they do it wrong the second time, then that's it. Out the door. Because I'm the one who's speaking to the client, I'm the one getting the load of aggravation because they've screwed up. There's enough aggravation in the job without having to generate more because I've employed a pillock.'

So what do women have that makes them different? For a start, because most of them don't come from a formal law enforcement background, they have a different perspective. They have never had the power of a warrant card or the knowledge that back-up is only a radio call away. They have had to be self-reliant and use their wits from day one on the job. They haven't spent their lives in the disillusioning pursuit of low-lifes and inadequates, facing the dispiriting knowledge that no matter how many they put away today, their places will be taken by others tomorrow. They don't arrive in the business with the expectation that the world is entirely populated by scumbags who hate them and what they stand for. What cynicism they possess comes from a quite different set of experiences, that of being second-class citizens in a man's world.

Pat Storey explains. 'Most male PIs are ex-bobbies, and that's a big problem for the way the job is perceived by the public. These blokes have great difficulty getting away from the fact that they are not still police officers. They tend to forget they haven't got the uniform, they haven't got the badge, they have no right to demand information or cooperation. I've seen them get people up against the wall and say, "Look, tell me what I want to know, I know your sort." They forget they're no different from the rest of us. They don't realise they're committing a common assault. Most women have never been in that position of authority, so they realise right from the word go they're only going to get anywhere if they behave in a civilised manner.'

Not everyone does realise that. Some women inevitably think the way to success is to imitate the boys. Jean Mignolet reckons that some women forget the importance of the differences they bring to the private eye's world. 'The only way to survive in this business is to work out what you like to do, who you really are, and stick to that. I've seen some women thinking they have to play it as tough as the guys. They act like they wish they could grow a penis too. It's like they lose sight of all the advantages there are to doing the job in a way that's true to themselves. Women have got it made in this business if we only recognise the qualities in ourselves that make us so good at it.'

There's more to the difference between men and women than the fact that they've come to the job of private investigators from different perspectives. Society assigns us roles based on gender that are deeply ingrained. Even the most liberal, non-sexist parent knows that moment of despair when their little daughter encounters peer group pressure for the first time and comes home demanding her dungarees be replaced with a frilly frock and her building bricks with a Barbie doll. From childhood, women are schooled to defer to men. We are socially conditioned to listen and observe, to take a passive rather than an active role. There have been changes in this area in recent years, some of them profound, but anyone who thinks there has been a revolution only has to walk into a classroom where there are fewer computer terminals than pupils to see which group is not only disenfranchised but is accepting of the position.

Sandra Sutherland, with twenty years' experience, is convinced that women approach the job from an entirely different standpoint because of their role in society. 'Men feel they have the power in this society, which indeed they do, and they tend to operate with that in mind. Private investigators have no power whatsoever so it's an inappropriate assumption to begin with. Women still operate psychologically from an assumption of impotence. We know you have to wheedle your way through life. But we have learned in society that you get what you want by scoping out what's happening around you in what is potentially a hostile and ungiving environment, then developing a path to negotiate through this and achieve your end. And that's exactly what a private investigator has to be able to do.

'You have to be able to go to a door and get a sense of who that person is and make them want to give you what you want to get, as opposed to operating on the assumption that you have a right to it.'

As Sandra points out, one of the results of this pressure on women to be silent and passive is that their listening and observational skills are far more finely honed than those of men. I remember as a trainee journalist in a group of five women and seven men that it was the women who needed far less training in the art of interviewing and translating the product of that interview into an in-depth feature. Women are also better at reading the subtext behind the words, especially if they're mothers. The experience of trying to interpret the demands of a small child whose verbal skills are hopelessly outstripped by their needs and desires inevitably gives a woman a whole new level of skills in the realm of decoding non-verbal signals. And women investigators know this, even if they don't shout it from the rooftops when their male colleagues are around.

'It's my experience that women listen very differently,' Blair states. 'I know that if I go into an interview alongside a male attorney, I will see and hear things that will go straight past him. There are times when there is so much going on in an interview that I'm thinking, I could use an extra pair of eyes, but I might as well be with a blind person! In an interview, you have to get quiet and let your environment work on you for a while.'

According to Pat Storey, women not only notice more, they interpret it better. 'I think women are far more observant than men. If I send a guy to do me a check on a house he'll come back and say it's a semidetached, 1930s style. If I go, I'll see it's a 1930s style semidetached with good quality curtains, the front door is freshly painted, so whoever lives there cares about their property and they're not skint. I look through the window and see flowers arranged in a vase, so it's reasonable to assume there's a woman living there. What's the garden like? Are there kids' bikes lying around on the path? We see out of a woman's eye how a house has been lived in and looked after. There's a lot you can tell from a property. A man will just say that it's a semi. End of story.'

Observing and listening are the keys to the door of getting someone to talk to you. It's one of the first things direct sales crews are taught. Walk into the living room, check out the decor, suss out what their pride and joy is and admire it. Immediately, the punter is on your side, impressed by your good taste and judgement. 'I've always thought the key to this business is being pleasant to people,' Pam Quinney asserts firmly. 'If you're polite and friendly and show an interest in them, people will be equally pleasant in response. It never pays to lose your rag, no matter how aggravated they make you feel. A little bit of persuasion goes a lot further than a lot of aggression. You have to get people to cooperate with you and tell you things, so you get them chatting and lead them on and have a joke. It's surprising the things people come out with then.'

Part of being a good listener is allowing yourself to get involved, not standing back from what you are hearing. 'To get you have to give,' as Blair puts it. Women tend to be sympathetic listeners, but this can make them vulnerable too. Most women eyes have found themselves in a position where male interviewees have made advances to them. It's a frightening situation when you are dealing with volatile and dangerous men, especially when they try to follow you back to your hotel, as once happened to Blair. As Pam Quinney asserts, women have to use all their observational powers in order to judge how each person will react and behave accordingly.

'You've got to be able to assess the person you're talking to and decide what approach is going to work. Some people get very emotional. I find that if the job involves children, emotions spill out all over the place. I remember one chap picked up a brick and he was going to throw it at me because I was serving him with papers to take his child away from him. I really did sympathise with him. It was dreadful. But because I felt genuinely sorry for him, I found it wasn't hard to talk him down and reassure him.'

Pam's comments point to another area where women's social conditioning has a direct impact on the way we live our lives. From childhood, girls are taught to avoid direct confrontation. When we're small, it's often about self-preservation; little boys tend to be stronger and physically crueller than little girls, so we often learn the hard way that there are times when discretion is definitely the best policy. As we grow up, that notion is reinforced as we learn that in direct confrontation with men, women almost always come off worst. So from an early age, we learn to develop subtle means to achieve our ends. We learn our limitations and find creative solutions to overcome the problems that a lack of brute force saddles us with. When it works, it's called diplomacy. When it doesn't, we're conniving manipulators.

Sandra Sutherland talks about this with real feeling. 'I've noticed that a lot of our stunningly successful interviews have been done by a couple of our best women. They somehow manage to spot a little opening, and they're in there. Men are more linear in their conversational styles. When I listen to some of my taped interviews, I think I sound like a complete nitwit but in fact I'm negotiating a series of very hazardous shoals, using my imagination to get by a very devious route to where I want to be.

'There was one which is probably one of the most incoherent sounding interviews I have ever done. This kid had been convicted of rape. He was a middle-class black student at a good university on a scholarship. He had been invited to a party and had got lost and ended up in the cul-de-sacs of some totally white neighbourhood. A young woman was raped by two black guys that night and he was spotted driving through the neighbourhood so he got pulled in and convicted of the crime. There was no forensic evidence, no inkling of who his crime partner might have been.

'For the appeal, I ended up interviewing the victim again, which is a very painful thing to do; this woman had been raped, no question about that, and I was digging all that stuff up for her again. But I was convinced our client hadn't done it. I was with her for about an hour and half and my angle was that I was seeking her opinion on the competence of the defence counsel; I figure, she'll probably feel hostile towards him so she'll probably want to talk about him, especially if he bullied her on the stand, which he almost certainly did. At what she thinks is the end of the interview, we start chatting about where she grew up. I'm talking about growing up in Australia and how different it was culturally. Then I sort of tactfully inserted the issue of race and finally she said, "Well, I didn't know any black people the whole time I grew up." And then she said she couldn't really tell one from the other, they all looked the same to her. The guy got totally exonerated. I'd gone all round the houses to get that admission. Men don't do that sort of thing well. Women do it better. We need to in order to survive in life.'

It is this creativity, the ability to approach a difficult job not head on, but from just the right angle to get it done, that many women find the most satisfying element of their job. Jane Quinney is a great advocate of the imagination. 'You've always got to be looking for a creative way to do things. We were trying to serve papers on the owner of a scrapyard that was patrolled by Rottweilers. We'd tried all ways to get to him, but even if we got past the dogs, we had the mechanics to contend with, and it was a toss-up which was worse. So one day I turned up in an absolute old banger, rust from roof to axle, wearing my tattiest jeans and clapped out trainers. I waltzed straight in. No one batted an eyelid and I just walked right up to him and served the bankruptcy papers right in the middle of the yard. He was gobsmacked!'

Ironically, two of the qualities that have historically been turned against women as insults are two of the key attributes that make for a good investigator. Curiosity—nosiness, when it's being portrayed negatively—and intuition are factors that often mean the difference between success and failure for a PI. Add to that the quality of empathy that women tend to develop in their emotional relationships, and you've got a potent tool for getting to the heart of the puzzles that make up so much of an investigator's workload.

Susan Neary is in no doubt that that's part of what makes women's approach to detecting so different. 'Differences in character affect the way both men and women do the job. Women tend to be more inquisitive. When instructions come in, especially say, on a matrimonial or relating to children, my husband and business partner Brian will read the black and white that's on the paper and that's all he'll see. But I tend to read it and think, why did this happen? What's really going on here? What does this tell me about these people? I do tend to analyse things, what's going on behind the words. I wonder why situations have come about; it's not nosiness, I'm genuinely interested and I think also you can get a different picture. Things aren't always the way that they seem and understanding a bit more about the background can govern the way you go about the job.'

Jennifer Paul agrees. 'I don't regard myself as a feminist but I think that I'm as capable as any man. I'm an equal and I should be treated on equal terms with them. Having said that, there are differences between the way we look at things and how we go about our work. I think women look more closely at life where men take things at face value and don't talk about emotions to each other. I know some women can be conniving and have an eye for the main chance but I think we're generally more interested in what makes people tick. That gives us a head start in criminal defence work, because we're always looking beyond the bald surface of the witness statements.'

Perhaps because women are often denied access to power in many areas of their lives, they tend to empathise with the underdog. And since most of their clients are in a position of powerlessness in some area of their life, it's not surprising that they feel a trust in the women eyes that goes beyond the purely professional. 'It's a clear advantage being a women working child custody,' Joan Beach points out as an example of this. 'I relate well to families. I think they know that I'm serious and that I'm used to working with children. I think the reason I was selected for this kind of work in the first place was because I was a widow and I knew that nobody was ever going to take my children away from me. When I think about it, I think, dear God, my kids could have been taken away from me so many times, we're all human and we none of us act like perfect parents all the time. So I really feel for these people who are struggling to find a solution that's best for them and their kids. And because they sense that I'm sensitive to their feelings, they are able to be more open with me, and that means I have a better chance of coming up with recommendations that are in the best interests of the children.'

A bailiff is the last person most people would expect to be a friendly face in a harsh world. Their image is the heartless bastards who throw women, children and family pets out on to the street without a care for their pain. But for Maureen Jacques-Turner's debtors, the experience is very different. 'Sometimes I feel like an agony aunt,' she says. 'You get the ones that've got six children under seven and wonder why they're in debt. They send you a list of their income and expenditure and they're spending about £20 a fortnight on nappies, and I find myself having these discussions with them. "Well, why don't you use terry nappies, then you wouldn't have to spend all that money on nappies and you can use the same ones for the next baby?"

"I'd have to wash them," she says, like I've suggested something completely unsanitary. Then she says, "And then I've got all this baby food to pay for."

"Why aren't you breast-feeding?" I ask. "It's better for your baby and it won't cost anything."

"You're disgusting," she says to me. "I don't want to talk about it, it makes me feel sick just thinking about it." I feel like saying, have you considered contraception as an alternative to debt? But I just bite my lip.

'I ended up talking about the price of knickers with another one. I said, "What are you spending your money on?"

"I've got me catalogues, I've got to get knickers!"

I point out to her that catalogues are a very expensive way of buying knickers and she ought to go down to Marks and Spencers, a few pairs from there will last her years, and suddenly I hear myself and I think, what am I doing? I'm discussing knickers with a stranger!'

Despite the frustration she sometimes feels with these people, Maureen remains sympathetic and understanding. She describes with affection one of her debtors, a baker. It is typical of her understanding that when he failed to inform her that he had moved house she looked for the reason rather than simply condemning him for not obeying the rules.

'Someone in the office said, "He's not that good, is he, he didn't tell us he'd moved."

'I said, "Have you thought that he might have been embarrassed? He's gone from having a business and a nice house to being on the dole in a council flat, he's not going to breeze in here and say, 'Oh by, the way ladies, I've been repossessed.' He's got his pride, and that's about all he's got left. He still comes in to pay so it's not like he's dodging. He could have just swanned off."

'I try to adopt a friendly approach,' Maureen explains, 'because for a lot of people, their lives have fallen in round their heads and the last thing they need is some hard-faced bureaucrat sitting in judgement on them.'

Lynn McLaren's clients usually face something more traumatic than debt. As a criminal defence specialist in California, a state with the death penalty on the statute books, more often than not she's representing people who will die unless she can find evidence that will either exonerate them or mitigate their offence. 'It's real important that I strike up a rapport with potential witnesses so they will give me the full story and not hold back. I think men probably approach a job from a less emotional and more mechanical perspective. They tend to be quite fixed, whereas women are more flexible. I find I vary my approach and style a lot, depending on the client and the situation. If I'm going in to interview a man who had a hard time because somebody close to him got killed, then he probably would feel he couldn't cry about it in front of another man, so he'd be keeping himself buttoned up tight during the interview. But with me, he would probably feel that he could do that, that it was OK to let his feelings show. Most men go in as an assertive figure, they carry their tape recorder and they have their set routine to get their statement. They know in advance exactly what they're going to be asking, and they tend to stick to that. I don't even use a tape recorder. I don't want to put anything in between me and the interviewee. If I have to take a statement, I take a note pad and write it down.

71

'As far as the clients are concerned, I feel a lot of my job is just being there for them. If I'm working for some guy in jail who hasn't got anyone he can call up and talk to about his case, I'm there. I can metaphorically hold their hand and keep them informed about what's happening with their case, whereas their attorney is probably too busy, or doesn't think it's important enough. You also have to deal with their whole family. They have mothers and fathers, wives and husbands, lovers, kids, and all of those people are scared for the person they love. I relate better to the families because I'm a wife and mother myself, I can imagine how they are feeling. And when I explain what's going on, I talk to them in everyday language that they can understand. I don't dress it up with all the legal double-speak that attorneys use to make themselves feel important. I don't have any need to set myself above anybody in that way; that's not how I define myself.'

René Olsson believes that empathy is an important factor in making a difficult situation manageable. 'Women who do this job calm people down,' she explains. 'I think that every case is different, not for the PI necessarily, but for the other people that are involved in it. It's not a daily occurrence to them, it's something significant and often catastrophic. Their whole lives are being affected in a way that's probably never happened to them before, and feelings are going to be running real high. Sometimes they're on the edge of hysteria, sometimes they're emotionally exhausted, but if you make that jump of imagination and think of how they're feeling, you can take a real calm approach, and that calms them down too. I don't think guys can take a real calm approach. When they try, instead of it looking calming, it looks like they are not giving it their attention.'

Social imperatives aside, there are good practical reasons why women make good PIs. In so many situations, women are invisible. No one pays a blind bit of attention to a woman walking her dog or pushing a pram down the street. If an undercover operative needs to be placed inside a commercial operation, nobody looks twice at a female temporary secretary, whereas a man in the same role would be the centre of office gossip for the entire duration of his assignment.

Susan Neary uses her invisibility as a woman to do 'snoopy shopping', checking up on the staff in large department stores. 'A man just wouldn't be able to do that kind of work,' she says, 'he'd be far too obvious.'

For Diana Middleton, it helps when she is serving process. 'Somebody who's expecting a writ is wary of letting any stranger close enough to serve them, but who looks twice at an older woman walking her dog? They're striding down the pavement towards me, not giving me a second thought, then suddenly, wham! I've served them!'

The Monty Python comedy team used to perform a sketch with the punchline, 'Nobody expects the Spanish Inquisition.' It could almost be the clubhouse motto of the women private eyes. Ask the average person what their image is of a private eye and the chances are you'll get a Humphrey Bogart look-a-like with a trilby, trench coat and a bottle of bourbon in the bottom drawer of the filing cabinet. Nobody expects a woman. If they do, they expect her to look like a cross between Barbarella and Chris Cagney. I met women who might have been mistaken for businesswomen, dress shop managers, social workers, political campaigners or cab drivers. Not one of them looks like the fictional image of a private eye, with the possible exception of Lynn McLaren, a rangy blonde with more than a passing resemblance to Daryl Hannah. It's a major advantage in a job where subterfuge is often as important as building a rapport.

As Pam Quinney says, 'Particularly twenty years ago, I don't think people expected to find a woman coming to serve them. I think the chaps were often quite pleased initially to have a woman coming to see them. That pleasure disappeared pretty quickly if I was serving them with a bankruptcy petition! But at least it gets you in the right place to do what you have to do.'

Susan Neary has no qualms about exploiting people's expectations in order to get the job done. 'It's true that people don't expect to be served papers by a woman. One of the hardest places to get into are blocks with an intercom controlled security door. But everybody knows somebody called Sue. I just never give my surname. I press the button and say, "Hi, it's Sue." Nine times out of ten I get buzzed through. The other classic is, "I've got a personal delivery for you." Which of course is true, a process service is a delivery! You say "personal" delivery because some of them are very cute and if they know someone's after them, they'll try to get you to leave it with a neighbour because a lot of the documents have to physically touch the person. When you serve those ones, you run like hell!

'I think being a woman is useful on traces as well. I love the telephone. I never lie on the phone as such, but it's quite amazing the stuff people tell me. I suppose you could call them idiots because they fall for it every time. If we have a suspect we think is living at an address and they're using the answering machine to screen calls, I'll phone and just say, "Hi, X, it's Sue, can you give me a ring some time?" and leave my number. Nine times out of ten X will phone me back. "Hello Sue?"

'And I say, "Is that X?"

'"Oh yeah," they say.

'I say, "I'd like to make an appointment." Often they just hang up, but at least I've confirmed where they're living.'

Because the face of officialdom is male, it's so much easier for women to get a foot in the door where it will be slammed in the face of a man, as Pat Storey explains. 'Nice Cheshire housewives aren't supposed to be hard-nosed detectives. So being a woman is generally to my advantage. A five foot four, middle-aged blonde in a pair of ski pants and a jumper doesn't look official. I don't carry a clipboard or a briefcase if I go to serve somebody. The papers are always in my pocket, or tucked down the top of my trousers or up my sleeve. So when I walk up to the door they don't think I've got anything on me. If someone other than my target answers the door, I just say, "It's Pat," and they don't think twice about it, they just get the person to the door. A man wouldn't deal with it like that.'

Women find it easier to change their appearance. A quick swap of wigs and that dramatic redhead has disappeared forever. Nobody notices the mousey blonde with the same face and a different pair of glasses. That smart businesswoman sitting in the street yesterday in this year's model executive car surely can't be the same person as that woman in jeans and sweatshirt in the tradesman's van...

Women are also less threatening. In an increasingly violent and predatory society, strange men are automatically targets for suspicion and wariness, and not just by lone women. Not so with women. If a woman sits opposite you on the train and starts chatting, by the time you reach your destination, chances are you'll each know the other's life story. If a man does the same thing, you're instantly on the alert, looking for the hidden agenda. Sad but true.

Like most of her female colleagues, Susan Lauman is in no doubt that the practical advantages of her gender far outweigh the disadvantages. 'Nobody notices a woman, and we're non-threatening. Even in Paranoia City, New York, you can follow someone around for days without raising any suspicions. They might even notice you a couple of times, but they think nothing of it. You're a throwaway because you're female, even if you're an attractive woman. The only problem you sometimes encounter if you're young and attractive and you're hanging around a hotel lobby for a few days is that the house dick might think you're a hooker!' Warm laughter spills out as we both enjoy the irony.

Like Susan Lauman, René Olsson is very aware that being a non-threatening woman makes surveillance work easier. 'We can sit outside somebody's home and nobody feels threatened. If the place you're watching is near a school, a woman can sit there pretty much forever, but a guy will have the police on his neck inside the hour because somebody will have reported him as a pervert.'

As René points out, this also affects juries' attitudes. 'When it comes to testifying, I don't think that we appear to pose any threat at all. We can sit up on the stand and say, "Yes, we followed this person every waking moment of their life. We stood outside their house, we were there when they woke up, we were there when they went to sleep, we know what they eat, we know what they smoke, we know who they visit." When a guy testifies like that and the surveillance target is a female or an elderly person, the jury doesn't like it at all. Their sympathy switches straight to the target; they see the investigator as the bad guy who invaded their life. My sister Anna and I are not big and scary and wild-looking, so juries think it's OK that we've been spying.'

Presenting an unthreatening image can become even more important when a PI is interviewing, whether it's wheedling information out of cagey witnesses or trying to gain a defendant's trust in order to get close to the truth. Kris Kleinbauer believes that a non-threatening image is vitally important in dealing with witnesses and victims in her criminal defence work in Los Angeles.

'The first important step is that people open their doors to you. A lot of the work we do takes us into bad neighbourhoods where people are very reluctant to open their doors to anyone because the level of violence is so high where they live. But they see me, a middle-aged woman in casual clothes, and they figure I'm not going to hold them up at gunpoint and steal all their possessions, and they're curious. When they find out I'm an investigator, they get even more curious, and that overrides their reluctance to have anything to do with the system.

'Sometimes in a criminal case when we talk to the victim, you have to develop a strategy for dealing with them. In rape cases, for example, the thing you have to say to them is, "Anything I'm going to ask you is what you're going to be asked on the witness stand, and you can look on this as a kind of rehearsal." Because I'm a woman, they are more inclined to trust me on that, and so they'll start to open up a bit more. A lot of victims are afraid to talk because they're afraid of the consequences to them and their families. You have to be patient and keep going back over things with them. When a man does that, it's often seen as badgering and aggressive, but a woman does not pose a threat in the same way.'

There is another advantage that women possess over men, but it's not one that any of them are thrilled about. 'There are certain men who think that because I'm a woman I'm stupid,' Jennifer Paul reveals in a tone of depressed resignation. 'They're the stupid ones, because they don't realise that their presumption immediately gives me an advantage. I'm surprised by the number of men who do think that women are fools. It really rankles with me. I hate to be considered a fool.'

Sarah Di Venere points out that the same assumption is made in America. 'There are men who will only talk to a man. There are men who have no respect for women. Period. They just don't want to talk to them, they don't want to cooperate, they don't want to do anything except show their contempt so sometimes you have to accept that it's better to send a man to interview them. Sometimes that arrogance works in your favour, though, because they think you're totally irrelevant so they will almost boast to you. I've played the bimbo on occasion, and it has worked. If I had been businesslike and efficient, the man in question would never have relaxed and told me anything. Doing that is demeaning, but there are times when you just have to bite the bullet and do it.'

It's something many women eyes, with their strong feminist convictions, find hard to do, but most consider it worth it. As Susan Lauman says, being a PI is, 'one of the few jobs where women can exploit the fact that we're second-class citizens.'

Perhaps one of the reasons why women are so good both at developing a rapport and at unobtrusively obtaining information is that they're not driven by ego to the extent that many men are. They are accustomed, by the expectation that they will be self-effacing, to taking a back seat, often to the extent of letting others take the credit for their work. So they are perfectly comfortable with the backroom nature of the work. They don't feel the need to seize the limelight whenever they're involved with a high-profile case, and they can readily subjugate their own ego to the demands of any job they're working on.

Jean Mignolet is in no doubt that that is part of the secret of her success. 'Macho gets in the way of doing things a lot of the time. To be good at this job, you have to put your ego in the back. You take a lot of shit sometimes. I've sat with somebody for two hours just to get the one sentence I needed. Men like to talk about themselves and we let them; that's why we're so good at what we do!'

❧

'Being a woman is the greatest asset a private investigator can have.' Susan Lauman states boldly. It's a view held by almost all the women eyes I spoke to. There are disadvantages to being a woman in a primarily masculine profession, however. Chauvinism, whether it's from men or women, is something almost all female PIs come up against. Most have had to fight to prove their worth ten times harder than their male colleagues.

Vulnerability is another disadvantage for women eyes. 'You have to be cautious,' explains Christine Usher, 'because women are that bit more vulnerable. If I have to meet clients or subjects, I always leave a note as to where I've gone and I'll choose a venue that's a public place because you never know what they're going to turn out like. And I've always got my mobile phone with me. We are physically weaker than men and it would be foolish to ignore that.'

Lynn McLaren agrees. 'I do think some situations would be easier if I was a guy. A guy doesn't have to worry about walking through a dark parking lot at midnight. It's also a lot easier for a guy to walk into a bar and strike up conversation with another guy. If a woman does that without declaring who she is and what she wants from him, it's likely he'll think she's hitting on him, and that leads you into a whole raft of complications that you can generally do without.'

And then there is the disadvantage that every working woman in a relationship has to deal with. It's no different for private eyes than for anybody else, as Pat Storey testifies. 'One major difference between the woman and the man in this job is that we women usually have a household to look after. I've got a husband, two dogs, an elderly mother next door and until very recently, two daughters living at home.' Still, the freedom and independence of the job of PI means that most women eyes can choose their own hours and fit their job around their domestic commitments. Lynn McLaren is typical, 'I got pregnant about six months after I set up as a PI, and I managed to have my daughter in between trials! Luckily she turned out to be a real flexible kid, so I've been able to build up my practice quite successfully. I wouldn't describe the job as fun, because you see the downside of life, but it's a lot more fulfilling on a personal level than anything I've ever done before.'

In spite of the disadvantages of feminine vulnerability, it's hard to sustain an argument that women are unsuited to the job of private investigator. On the contrary. It seems clear that because of the roles society assigns to us and the qualities we are taught to value in ourselves, we are in fact better equipped to penetrate the mysteries of the human heart and untangle the puzzles that strew our lives. Presented with so much evidence by the women eyes, I found it hard to resist their conclusion. Women do make better detectives.

While the Balance of His Mind . . .

Cases are memorable for all sorts of reasons. One tragic incident thrust me into the glare of publicity, very much against my wishes. A millionaire farmer who was convinced he was going to be a target for murder was killed by a booby-trap he had constructed himself. Days before, he had been in my office, asking me to breach my code of ethics in exchange for cash. The last thing he said to me after I refused was, 'Time is running out. I'm going to be dead by the end of the week.'

You're lucky to be hearing this story. At the time, I was besieged by journalists wanting interviews, and I said no to the lot of them. The local TV station were so desperate they resorted to filming the front door, which I was really annoyed about. I want to be discreet, I don't want people to know about my clients and cases.

It was a very mysterious case. He was very odd and very sad. He told me he was in fear of his life, that he was going to be murdered. He wanted me to go to the police and give them a false name and address which supposedly belonged to this female who he said had been threatening to kill him. I said, 'Ethically, I cannot do that.'

I felt a bit sorry for him, I could see that he was very unbalanced. When he said he'd be dead by the end of the week, I took it with a pinch of salt, but when I heard about his death on the local radio I thought, Oh gosh, and I thought of what he'd said to me and I felt terrible that I hadn't been able to do anything to help him. What made it worse was that at first the media were suggesting it was murder. Of course, I spoke to the local police and told them what he'd said to me. My statement was read out at the coroner's court, but they found that it was death by misadventure. They thought he had rigged up this equipment to shoot foxes or deer in his wood, but the gun went off and killed him. The whole thing was weird. He'd built this whole fantasy around himself. I'm sure this mystery woman who was supposedly threatening his life never existed at all. I think it was suicide to be honest, and probably nothing I could have done would have changed that. There's nowt as queer as folk.

CHRISTINE USHER
Hampshire

5

Playing with the Big Boys

Investigators are always in the news and it really pisses me off that it's always the sleaze that hits the headlines. When do you get anything nice reported about an investigator?

JANET WILSON
Dover

There are a lot of slimeballs in this business.

RENÉ OLSSON
Seattle

Hearing the women talk about their male counterparts, it's not surprising that private eyes have such a sleazy image. Many of the women investigators express extreme unhappiness with a lot of the things that go on in the business, and point out that it is men who are largely responsible for this. They're not holier than thou about it; they simply discuss it with regret and a degree of anger that it reflects badly on the profession as a whole.

By and large, women don't do illegal bugging; they don't lie to clients about the work they've done on a case; they don't pay off their old buddies in the police department in exchange for information; they don't hack into other people's computers and steal their data. I asked them all if they'd be prepared to break the law for a client, and not one of them said they'd be willing to risk their reputation or livelihood for any client. The only exception was the issue of confidentiality. There is no client privilege for private investigators. If they are called as witnesses and asked to disclose what their clients have revealed to them, they cannot refuse to answer without risking being found in contempt. Like journalists, most private eyes accept that they would go to jail rather than betray their clients' confidences.

Sarah Di Venere's experience illustrates that male operatives really do bend the rules in order to deliver what the client wants. She served her apprenticeship in Chicago with one of the premier agencies in the city, but finally left after a case that put her in an impossible situation. 'I was never real comfortable there, because it was clear the boss did not like having a woman on the team. He took me on because having a woman on the staff made it look like he was real equal opportunities orientated, but he never treated me the same as he did the guys. The case that finally did it for me there involved a very wealthy man who was having a custody battle with his wife,' she explains.

The man claimed that his wife was an unfit mother so Sarah was sent to investigate. After several days trailing the woman, she had discovered nothing incriminating, in fact quite the reverse.

'My report was so complimentary to her, her own attorney could have used it in evidence! But that's not what the client wanted to hear. I got flak for that and my boss put a lot of pressure on me to change the report. I refused point blank. We had a huge row about it, but I was not prepared to alter my report. They had wanted to make a case against her instead of finding out what she really was like. They didn't care about the truth, only what the client wanted to hear. I realised then that when there is a great deal of money involved, there are investigators who will play along. I wasn't prepared to be like that, so I got out of there soon afterwards.'

Sarah believes that this kind of greed and corruption is widespread among male PIs, an opinion that is supported by other women eyes on both sides of the Atlantic, most of whom have come across similar cases in their work. Once, an agent she had employed tried to charge Yvonne Twiby double mileage for the journey to visit an interviewee. Unfortunately for him, she had made the same journey the week before. That was the end of him.

'Over the years, you get to know almost every other PI in Chicago and how they work and their techniques,' explains Sarah Di Venere. 'Years ago, this city was so corrupt you could buy licences and a lot of cops retired and went into the business. They were lazy, they were prepared to sit back and take money from people without doing the job. If a lawyer wanted a case to go a certain way then they'd do the report that way.

'One time, I was working with a couple of other investigators at the company where I did my training. We were supposed to follow this guy who was apparently going to Wisconsin on a business trip. These two guys weren't even going to go. I said, "You mean to say you'd put in a report that you went when you didn't go? What if something comes up, what if he gets a car problem or something, you can't go to court and lie!" But they acted like I was crazy, because theirs was the common way to do things. I know this kind of thing still goes on, and that's one of the reasons I set up my own agency. I didn't want to be associated with that kind of sleazy behaviour. I'm real careful about who I hire to work for me, but if I suspect one of my staff is behaving in any way unethically, they're gone. They're history.'

Sometimes a reputation for honesty can actually work against a PI. Joan Beach was once offered a job by the aides of the discredited ex-mayor of Washington, Marion Barry. Joan quoted them a price for the work they wanted done but never heard back from the mayor's office. She later heard that they had asked around and found out that she was straight and couldn't be paid off to provide a report that would say what they wanted to hear. 'It seems they were scared I might uncover things they wanted to stay buried,' she explains. 'They way things turned out, I wasn't sorry that I hadn't got the job.'

This strong sense of ethics, and determination to do the best possible job, even if it means doing more than you are paid for, seems to be a universal trait shared by women eyes. For them it's a matter of self-respect and compassion, not making a quick buck.

'A woman comes to you and she's going through a tough divorce and child custody case, so you go over the top, because you feel for her,' explains Jean Mignolet. 'You have to look yourself in the eye in the mirror.'

Nancy Poss-Hatchl reckons that being a woman means she turns down business that male operatives would seize upon. 'I don't like to feed off other people's misery,' she says. 'When women come to me with marital problems, and they want me to follow their husband, sometimes I say, "I'm a stranger. If I tell you that he's certainly not cheating will you believe me?" And usually, they hem and haw. "Well, I know he's cheating."

'"But what if I tell you he isn't? You'll sit there saying you don't believe me, that I haven't done my job properly." So I tell them to watch the guy themselves. Get in the car and follow him. Put on a different wig. You can make yourself look different. You aren't going to believe anybody else, so use your own eyes, go do him yourself. It's empowering. It's saying they have control of the situation, they have the right to go follow this man. They don't have to pay me to do something they wouldn't believe anyway. I think it's important to give people a sense of dignity and a feeling of power rather than helplessness. I have done some counselling of troubled people through a mental health clinic when I was younger, and that made me realise there are different approaches other than just doing what people are prepared to pay you for. We're not magicians. But there are people in this business, and I'd say that most of them are men, who would take the money of any woman who wanted her husband followed, regardless of what the outcome was going to be for her.'

For Susan Lauman it's helping people that the job is all about, not making money. 'People are in this business for a variety of reasons. For a lot of them, principally the men, mostly it's about the commercial side of things. They never lose sight of paying the rent. My partner and me, we often seem to forget about paying the rent, because we do this job for different reasons. I do it because it is a way of showing compassion. Sometimes the most important thing a private investigator can do is listen to a client. I do this job because I like to help people, and when the case works out you can see clearly the difference you have made in their lives.'

It's not just men working the sleazy end of the street, giving PIs a bad name by exploiting their clients, that drives the women eyes crazy about their male counterparts. The institutionalised sexism that has characterised police forces on both sides of the Atlantic spills over into the world of private eyes. When the men leave the force and go private, they carry all the old attitudes with them. Add to that the macho culture that still operates in most law enforcement agencies, and reinforce it with social conditioning, and you get an environment that at best is unhelpful to women and at worst hostile. Jean Mignolet, based in South Florida where the Hispanic culture still arrogantly shuts women out, knows all about it from bitter experience.

'I started working in partnership with two men. About four years later, we took in another partner who was the macho, Cuban type. And I was gone. He just did not want me in the business, and it was clear to me that I had to get out of there if I was going to maintain any kind of self-respect.

'When I started up on my own, I had a lot of problems getting the kind of high-profile criminal cases I'd been working routinely when I was working with the guys. The criminal defence area was still a man's league in South Florida. Attorneys who have the big money cases want a male investigator. It's the macho thing.

'But women are really better investigators, and in recent years everybody has begun to realise that, including the men that run the agencies. So they figured they needed to exploit that fact. But we're still second-class citizens in this business. The men tell their women employees they don't need to bother getting their own licence, that it's an unnecessary expense. An investigator told me the other day that whenever he is working in a area for a protracted period of time, he just gets himself a little girlfriend and he trains her in the basics to help him out while he's there. That is exactly the attitude I hate. That just doesn't improve our status.'

Determined to fight this kind of sexism, Jean now organises seminars for women investigators, trying to elevate women in the profession, making sure they have support and sharing useful information. 'They still don't take you seriously when it comes to money. The attorneys don't give you the big money cases. I've even had attorneys trying to get out of paying me a retainer up front! A person like me who works solo has to do all ends of it; I've had to learn to get my money up front. Otherwise you get in situations where the attorney just doesn't pay up and thinks he can get away with it because you're only a woman.'

'There are a lot of slimeballs in this business,' admits René Olsson. 'That's why I'm glad of groups like the International Council of Investigators. They set standards, and you know that if you've been elected to membership there, you're doing something right. But even in the Council, I've had my disappointing moments. I had such hot ideas about this group. I figured I'd be hanging out with international detectives with really high ideals. When I arrived at my first conference, Nancy Poss-Hatchl, whom I'd never met, had left me this really warm message inviting me to a reception, and that made me feel really welcome. But the minute I walked in this room I realised I was a lot younger than anybody else and I was one of very few females. One guy hit on me within the first hour there and I said, "Hey, I know you have a wife."

'He said, "I have a hamster too, what's the difference?" I told him it sure as hell made a difference to me. One other guy was pestering me all night to dance, he was a real slime-ball, and he was a total slob too. Eventually, I got up to dance, and I'm thinking, all right, you old geezer, I'm going to dance you right off the floor and I hope you have a heart attack!

'It was such a disappointment to get right to the top of the private investigators' tree and find the same old sexist crap.'

Even the most generous spirited women have to admit they're somehow regarded as second-class citizens in the PI world. Sally Isted and her partner Pat Wingate found the line between being helped and being patronised hard to define. When they first started out as PIs they attended a number of ABI seminars on different aspects of investigation in order to learn the ropes. Although they found the male PIs they met helpful, they had their reservations. 'They're a bit like little boys with their toys, and there's no question that they feel superior to us women. It does seem a bit patronising, and an awful lot of them are pretty chauvinist, but I suppose their world, the police, was like that. However, they're having to realise that this isn't an unsuitable job for a woman these days.' Whether the boys like it or not, the women are here to stay.

Short and Sweet

Silly little things give me a real buzz sometimes. An old lady came to see me once. She must have been about seventy. She had cancer and although she'd managed to survive so far, she was obviously still quite ill, and thought she was going to pass away quite soon. While she'd been in hospital she'd been going through a list of people that she wanted to see before she died. She'd found everyone on this list except one old boyfriend. She knew he'd moved to this part of the country, so she came all the way down from up north on the coach to stay locally.

She wanted to hire me to trace this man for her. She clearly didn't want to disrupt his life, but she would dearly love to see him again before she died. We managed to find this chap without too much difficulty. He was married and had grandchildren and great-grandchildren and he was a gardener at a local big country house.

We found out what time of day he went there and she got the bus and went to this large country house. She walked up through the gardens and there he was. They sat on this little bench which overlooked the woods and reminisced and she felt so good. Afterwards, she just walked away down the road, caught the bus and went back to wherever she came from. She sent us a postcard to say how delighted she was that she'd got to see him. It was like a real Mills and Boon story.

Little things like that stay with you.

CHRISTINE USHER
Hampshire

6

On the Job

*My parents always said one day they'd get a proper job
because this isn't like work! Now I know what they meant.*

SUSAN NEARY
Gloucester

I can work fifteen billable hours in five hours.

JANETTE ESTRELLA
Los Angeles

Faced with the idea of a women private eye, most people think either that the job entails following unfaithful husbands, or that it involves a lot of glamorous running around in fast cars with guns waving. As is often the way with myths like these, the truth does not fall somewhere in the middle; it lies so far away from these extreme notions that they're not even kissing cousins.

However, it is true that there was once a time when private eyes lived up to the image of spies lurking in bushes or bribing hotel chambermaids so they could bound through bedroom doors, flashgun popping, to cause instant impotence in errant husbands. Zena Scott-Archer is one of the few who have been doing the job long enough to remember the golden age of in flagrante.

'Up until 1970 when the divorce laws changed I would say almost seventy-five per cent of my business was divorce,' Zena admits. 'It was often simply a matter of checking out the suspicions of one person about their partner and a classic one that comes to mind concerns a chap who wanted his mistress following to see whether she was being faithful to him! She went on a cruise and I had to go along too. Whether she would have had an affair with anyone I don't know, but she tripped and fell as she got on the cruise ship and broke her ribs. She spent the whole of the journey in her cabin. But I had a very nice time!

'It wasn't usually so dramatic. We weren't always lying in wait with a camera in order to leap out and take photographs. The majority of it was just interviewing people and getting confession statements. It sounds so antediluvian now, because you can get a divorce on shirt buttons these days, but back then you had to prove it up to the hilt.'

When the divorce laws changed, Zena thought that would be the end of her business, but she quickly developed other work to fill the vacuum. 'It's very diverse now, I've even taken photographs of a piece of pavement which someone tripped over before the council came along to mend it!'

That diversity is the keynote to private investigation in the 1990s. Variety is the spice of their lives. As long as it's legal and ethical, there is almost nothing these women won't do, from tracking down a missing aeroplane to going into therapy to expose patient abuse. For every one who refuses to act for rape defendants, there is one who takes their cases because she believes the justice system would not be served otherwise. For every woman who avoids surveillance jobs because they're too boring, there is another who thrives on the challenge they present to her creativity. Several of the women I interviewed specialise in particular areas—criminal defence, child custody, process serving. But not even they are averse to doing something off their usual beat provided that the job grabs their imagination. When I asked what they liked best about their work, there was a surprising degree of unanimity. The constant variety, and the freedom to schedule their time to suit them, were mentioned by everyone.

Once she became a detective, Zena never again considered another career. 'I love the variety,' she admits, her eyes shining with a zest that most people wish they still had at forty, never mind in their seventies. I've been to an extraordinary number of interesting places that I'd never have gone to otherwise. You get people who come to you saying that they're having a problem with their warehouse, a lot of merchandise is going missing, and it turns out to be a wool factory so you learn all about wool. It's of no practical use to me but I always find it interesting and I've learned things about various aspects of life which I wouldn't have learned if I weren't on a case. If you can do a good job and turn out a decent report and get paid, that's fine. But I like to have my own personal gratification, and a lot of that is about the challenge of trying something a bit different.'

Jean Mignolet's business runs the gamut of cases. The main criterion for her on whether or not to take a job is whether she likes the attorney who's offering the case, so her caseload is as diverse as the area she lives and works in. As Jean explains, South Florida is full of transients. People drift there from all over the country, from drug dealers to the retired elderly to the celebrity circus. For the outsider, arriving in Miami Airport is like leaving the USA without going through Customs and Immigration. Most of the faces around are Hispanic and

Caribbean, English seems the language you're least likely to overhear and all the airport announcements are bilingual. It did nothing to calm my nervous apprehension about being in the land of the midnight gun.

We pile into the air-conditioned haven of her BMW, and Jean gives me the tour of Miami Beach, hang-out of the beautiful people. By day, they're bronzing on the beach, by night they're spilling out of the pastel Art Deco cafés and restaurants, posing and being seen on Ocean Drive. It's the sort of place where you perfect your Clarins tan before you even get there. Nobody here would dare to peel.

The sights Jean points out are different from the ones in the tourist guides, however. Every block holds a memory. 'That's the Steven Talkhouse, where the rich and famous supposedly hang out. I was undercover there, posing as a customer, on an investigation. That's the block where I was threatened by a bunch of black guys.

'That gallery on the next block is where I had to sweet-talk a witness in a scam I was investigating. Took me a week. That hotel is where all the Colombian drug dealers hang out. I haven't worked for the Colombians in I don't know how long. That fancy restaurant is where I served court papers on one of the property developers who revamped South Beach into the beautiful people's paradise it is now. Over there is the house of a client I worked for, right next door to one of the BeeGees.'

She points out a beauty parlour which she investigated when the gay couple who owned it split up and disagreed about the division of money and property. Her client's ex-lover claimed his beauty parlour business was barely keeping its head above water. Over the next few months, Jean went there for manicures, pedicures, face masks, so that she could find out how many customers the business had. 'I've never been better groomed in my life—the guy was running a really good salon there!'

Because she works for a big agency, Janette Estrella is another who is accustomed to working on all sorts of investigations. She works in Los Angeles, the city of the fallen angels, where the myth of the private eye and the mean streets was born with Raymond Chandler's Philip Marlowe. Janette has found her range of work expanded as her experience grew. She started by serving subpoenas, then moved on to neighbourhood enquiries which lead on to background investigations. Now she does everything except surveillance work.

Janette enjoys the variety of experiences and environments she encounters in her job. It's the reason she likes insurance, background and workers' compensation investigations best. 'You can be in a shampoo factory one day, a Hollywood studio the next. One day I'll be interviewing a prisoner in jail, the next day I can be in a mansion in Bel Air talking to a scriptwriter. I don't really mind what the case is about, I just enjoy the process of investigation.'

From script writers to prisoners, being a PI certainly brings you into contact with the widest possible variety of people. It's not just the diversity of people and places that keeps the woman eye on her toes, however; the circumstances and outcomes of the cases they investigate are incredibly varied. Even in the seemingly straightforward cases there is no room for complacency; things aren't always what they seem.

Janette describes just such a case. 'I did one case where this girl claimed sexual harassment. She said that the guys at work were bringing in Playboy magazines, putting calendars on the walls which were offensive to her and making suggestive remarks. When I investigated, I found out that she's the one that would bring in nude male magazines, and say to the guys, "Oh, is this how big you are? Are you like this?" She had been coming into work wearing clothes that were very revealing and she provoked them. She would always instigate everything. As I dug down, I found out that she had been on this TV show called Studs; there's two guys and three girls and they all have to go on dates. It's kind of sleazy, the girls are very voluptuous; you only get on if you're real attractive and real aggressive. So that blew her claim out of the water. I guess she was trying to set up a situation where she could get a profitable sexual harassment case going. You have to keep an open mind in this job and go with the facts; in this instance, against the expectations, it was the woman who was at fault.'

At the other extreme the jobs themselves can be utterly bizarre. Diana Middleton has been sent in search of everything from a buried body to a Boeing 707. And then there was the case of the counterfeit Paddington Bears....Perhaps it's this variety that gives these women their sparkle. Diana seems to confirm this view. 'You never get the chance to get stale in this job. Just when you think you've seen everything under the sun, a case comes in that gets the adrenaline going again, and off you go!'

There's no doubt that the women PIs find their job mentally stimulating. They're the kind of people who love a mystery and a puzzle—and there's no shortage of those in their jobs. 'What has always interested me about the job is putting all the bits of information together and getting a result,' explains Pat Storey. 'It's a bit like a jigsaw puzzle, especially with fraud inquiries or an in-depth investigation where you're getting information in from lots of different sources and you put it all together and read the file and suddenly two identical telephone numbers jump out at you and you think, aha! It's magic when it comes right, especially if you're doing surveillance. You've sat there for five hours and absolutely nothing is happening and then in ten seconds, it all comes together. The adrenaline is absolutely brilliant!' Pat's eyes light up at the very thought of it. It's clear she gets a real kick out of her work.

'It's the best job in the world, for my money. There's no such thing as a typical day. We deal with a wide range of cases, we come up against all kinds of people. Posh or poverty stricken, virtuous or villainous, we get them all. There's never a dull moment, your brain's always buzzing. I wouldn't swap it.'

The variety of BJ Seebol's cases is restricted by one factor. She's not actually a licensed private investigator. She is a para-legal and a registered process server, which allows her legally to do many of the things a licensed investigator can do—interviewing witnesses, serving legal papers, skip tracing, asset searching, heir tracing. For her, it's a compromise that works.

'I don't really care if I can't sneak around in bushes and take surveillance film of unfaithful lovers and other crap like that. You take these two hats that I wear and a lot of what I do looks like private investigating work, sort of like the difference between love and lust—the acts are very similar but we all know it's not the same!' She grins, an attractive toothy smile that accompanies her self-deprecating humour.

The other side to the equation is that BJ's legal knowledge gives her specialist skills in some areas of the private investigation field. She does a lot of work on litigation matters because her clients know she will spot things in a case whose importance might not be recognised by somebody who doesn't have a law degree. 'When I'm conducting an interview, in the back of my mind I'm running a checklist of possible different causes of legal actions that we can maybe develop as fall-back positions if the road we're going down dead ends.' This specialisation doesn't mean that her job is less interesting than other PIs'; the variety is still enormous. 'I've done real estate stuff, personal injury cases, heir tracing, criminal stuff—anything and everything, really.'

When it comes to paying the bills, process serving is one of the most reliable, bread and butter sources of income. At one time or another, almost every one of the women eyes has kept the wolf from the door thanks to the unreliability of a sizeable chunk of the population. Process serving is an umbrella term that covers a wide range of legal documents. Subpoenas, domestic violence injunctions, court judgements for debt, warrants to seize goods, mortgage foreclosure, injunctions relating to child custody. Whatever the paper that's being served, the chances are that the person on the receiving end is less than delighted to get it. Small wonder, then, that most PIs are relieved that their practices encompass a lot more than that.

Receiving instructions from the court or solicitor is only the first step in serving process. Next, the investigator has to check that they've got the right address and that the person they're trying to serve still lives there. If they've done a runner, the investigator has to find where they've gone to earth. And the police are seldom willing to pass on information to PIs, as Jackie Griffiths outlines.

'Sometimes when I go down the police station and I'm looking for something they'll be helpful, but in a roundabout way. They won't tell me what I want to know but they might point me in the right direction as to where I might find it and then it's up to me to dig up what I'm after. But there are no tame coppers any more. Definitely not!' She laughs, shaking her head regretfully.

This means it's up to the PI to find the person to be served. Jackie gives an example of a recent case. The last address she had for the man was in Chester, but he was no longer there. After talking to his neighbours she finally tracked him down to a pub in Rhyl. 'That's fairly typical of what happens when they're not there,' she explains. 'Mostly, people haven't deliberately gone on the missing list.'

Some have, however. And they know only too well that someone is out there looking for them. It's a scenario that can cause problems for even the most enterprising eye, especially if they've already successfully breached their target's defences once. Jackie recalls a case in point.

'I had to serve a writ on a chap who was a car dealer over Manchester way. The first time was easy, he didn't know who the hell I was and I had a photograph of him. He was doing up this old mill where he lived, and he stuck his head out of the window upstairs. I just shouted up to him that I had a writ for him, and I was serving it. "I'm not him," he shouts. I said, "I've got a photograph," and I pushed the writ through the letter box.

'Subsequently, I had other papers to serve on him, but do you think I could get near to him? He knew who I was so he just hid. In the end, my son-in-law, who's a mechanic, went down in his working overalls. He drove up and strolled over to this chap and said, "I've a writ for you, mate," and ran like hell. You do it all ways. You play all sorts of games. It gives you a buzz in the end, you think, yeah, got him, he's not getting away!'

Pam Quinney finds a similar satisfaction in the job of process serving. 'Although a large part of our work is process serving, every job is different. They're all some sort of a puzzle; if it was easy, you wouldn't get sent it. Solicitors send us the difficult stuff because we can commit the time and the expertise to it.'

A lot of Pam's work involves debt but she has found herself involved in some serious cases, including murder. She's currently working on a big criminal defence case that has involved travel to Holland. Even when the case itself is simple, it often leads her to the peripheries of something far more dangerous. She once served a straightforward matrimonial process on a man and later discovered that she was the last person to see him alive, apart from his murderers. He had been killed by a gang whom he'd got involved with and his body dumped in a nearby lake.

Another side of Pam's work is repossessions on behalf of building societies, an area of the business that really grew in the eighties. It's something that needs careful handling by the PIs because the last thing their building society clients want is adverse publicity.

Repossession is not a job that earns much sympathy from the general public. What could be crueller than throwing people out of their homes or taking their belongings? It's a reaction Pam often feels herself, but she also sees another side of the story.

'You can't help feeling sorry for some of the borrowers. But then we see other places that are absolutely filthy, where they've left their animals starving. It's very distressing, because animals have got no defence.'

Fortunately repossession isn't always such a painful job. Pam's favourite case was the repossession of an old Cotswold manor house. It was full of beautiful antiques, furniture and paintings which Pam and her daughter Jane had to catalogue. 'It was in a beautiful part of Gloucestershire, it was September, the weather was lovely and we spent a whole week sorting out all these beautiful items. We couldn't have been further away from the mean streets!'

But even that job had its unpleasant side. At one point, the owners turned up and the two women found themselves confronted with a man waving a hammer at them. The threat of violence from irate owners is a constant danger for women eyes who take on repossession work.

Maureen Jacques-Turner also deals with debt and repossession. She's a licensed bailiff, but she doesn't actually serve the papers on the clients herself. Her job is office-based, dealing with debtors who come in to pay, processing the paperwork and, if payment isn't made, deciding when someone must be sent in to remove goods. Like Pam, she takes a pragmatic view of the job. 'It's harrying people for money, I suppose, but you get this buzz out of collecting what is owed. There are some horrible cases of poor people who through no fault of their own have been made redundant and debts just accumulate, and yes, you feel very sorry for them. But you get an awful lot of people who say, "Well, that's the best rate of interest I've had all year, see you next year when it goes to court again."'

As Maureen points out, 'If your video gets seized and it's one you bought for ten quid down the pub anyway, you've got a result.'

Getting hold of the goods is probably the most difficult part of the job. The word goes round the estate as soon as the bailiffs appear and all the decent, portable goods get ferried into one safe house.

Even when they can't hide the goods, Maureen's debtors will try to find a way out of giving them up. 'The excuses people come up with leave me gasping. We had these people that brought in a scrawled receipt on a little piece of exercise paper and said, "I've sold all my goods to Mr and Mrs John Jones for £200, they don't belong to me now so you can't take them away from me, can you?" Well, I think we need a little bit more proof than that, lovey! They're up to all sorts of tricks.'

Sarah Di Venere has also grown accustomed to fairy stories over the years. One of her agency's specialities is investigating Workman's Compensation claims. She gets the hardcore cases, where the insurance company is already convinced that the person making the compensation claim is trying to defraud them. 'The people we end up investigating are almost all lying to some degree,' she reveals. 'Ninety-nine per cent of these people are claiming they're more incapacitated than they truly are, and often they've got another job going on the side. They are not showing up for therapy, they're refusing to go into a work training programme. To hire an investigator is expensive so unless the insurance company really feel that there's something there, they don't do it.'

In order to sell her services to insurance companies, Sarah has compiled a video of cases she has worked on and the evidence she has uncovered—a man who had a hand injury playing a saxophone, another with major whiplash playing football, somebody with a back injury playing golf. It's an amazing catalogue of deceit.

Like most private eyes, Sarah is paid by the hour. For the insurance company, time is money, so they'll only authorise her to work on the case for a limited time— perhaps as little as eight hours initially. It means using all her intelligence to find the quickest way to get the information she needs. 'You have to try and figure out how you can get some relevant information with a couple of hours here, a couple there. So you come up with ruses that will let you talk to their neighbours and find out if they're working or not.' Fewer hours on the job might mean less pay for Sarah but it's worth it for the business. 'I always try to do these kinds of cases as fast as I can, because I know that if they get a fast result they'll mention my name to other people.'

Nancy Poss-Hatchl has been impressing insurance companies in Southern California with her services in sudden death inquiries for years. Forget all those preconceptions about insurance being boring. The kind of work Nancy does is anything but. Because of her masters degree in chemistry, and the kind of objective research she learned studying anthropology, Nancy very quickly found herself right at the sharp end of claims investigation.

'I've become something of a specialist in sudden death. I've had cases I've suspected to be murder. Many, many, many of them. On more than one occasion, I've shown a case to be murder when everybody else was prepared to write it off as accident or suicide.'

A classic example is a case she investigated in which a man had fallen to his death from a balcony. The police thought it was an accident and the apartment house owner was being sued by the widow because the balcony broke. Nancy was brought in by the landlord's insurance company and she spent a lot of time talking to the neighbours and looking at the scene.

She learned that the dead man had driven up in a brand new Rolls-Royce, although the crime took place in a a low to moderate income neighbourhood. He'd left the engine running and the lights on and run up the stairs. There was a loud noise like an argument, and after he fell, one of the neighbours saw the upstairs tenant come down and take something out of the dead man's pocket.

Then Nancy found a piece of the balcony rail and some wood shavings on the ground in the bushes and realised that the balcony hadn't broken, it had been sawn about ninety percent of the way through. The tenants had hung a little tapestry rug over it so the visitor wouldn't notice. Then when they pushed him, it simply gave way. The 'accident' was murder. It turned out that the dead man was a dope dealer making his run. The tenants were small-time dealers who decided they were going to get his money and drugs for themselves.

The police were not pleased with what had been uncovered. That's a typical response according to

Nancy. 'They do not like private investigators scooping them and making them seem dumb. They are not cooperative and it's not like it is in the movies where you call the police and they send a super-duper detective to liaise with you. The day a policeman will be a buddy, the pigs will be flying.'

Part of the problem is that there is just too much work for the police in the high crime area of Southern California. In effect Nancy is often left making the inquiries that they don't have time for. 'If a person dies with a bullet hole or a gaping stab wound it's usually ruled unnatural death. Anything else, you've got a good chance of getting away with it because the police just don't have the time to investigate anything that looks like it could be written up as accident or suicide. It's a great place to get away with murder,' Nancy adds wryly.

It's fortunate there are people like Nancy about, who still feel that the truth is worth finding. For her there is an integrity in the job she does. 'I like what I do, I like to seek the truth. Most of my work is on the civil side; they are prepared to pay investigation fees and you're not defending the guilty, which is what criminal defence work feels like to me.'

Luckily for the criminal population of America, there are plenty of women private eyes who don't feel the same way Nancy does about criminal defence work. For them, it's a way of making a living that also makes them feel like they're doing something worthwhile. Also, they're never short of cases. Crime in America isn't something that only happens in a handful of notorious, high-profile neighbourhoods like the Bronx and Watts. It's everywhere.

Nobody ever mentions the cities by the Bay when they talk about America in the grip of violent crime. Unlike most American cities, where the danger zones shade into the tourist areas so closely that visitors walk warily, infected by a mild paranoia, San Francisco keeps the shit far away from the glitz. As they wander round Fisherman's Wharf, Ghirardelli Square and Alcatraz, as they ride the cable cars down streets lined with charming pastel-painted bay-windowed houses, and watch the fog roll in to obscure the Golden Gate, the nearest most visitors ever get to the realisation that there's another world lurking behind the Victorian skirts is the street beggars, and even they are unusually polite. Yet the Bay Area is no stranger to violent crime. Just across the Bay Bridge from downtown San Francisco, Oakland boasts the highest per capita murder rate in California.

It's an aspect of life in the laid-back, liberal Bay Area that only ever breaks the surface in mystery fiction. And its role in that arena is unique. Dashiell Hammett chose the San Francisco area when he blazed the hard-boiled trail with Sam Spade and the Continental Op. Forty years on, Marcia Muller followed his lead with Sharon McCone, first of the feisty fictional women eyes. Now, dozens more have followed, making this urban swathe round the bay the capital of crime fiction that features women investigators. As if to reflect that, there are no shortage of real women eyes operating in what Florida's Jean Mignolet calls 'the gourmet PI belt'.

Blair, from Berkeley, outlines the process she goes through in her criminal defence work. 'Once you get a case, you get the discovery material, which is the most important source initially. Sometimes the defence is in there, sometimes a client's innocence is in there, so it means reading things very carefully, making notes. You're only talking about physical evidence that might exonerate your client if you're going in on the first trial level. Some of our cases are ten or fifteen years old. There are ones where photographs haven't been taken, evidence lists are only what was entered into evidence in court. Sometimes what wasn't even bagged as evidence is the key factor here. Often times that stuff is gone. We have to rely on paper when I'd much rather go to the scene and figure out what occurred here, what's possible, what's not possible, what's likely. By and large, I can't do that.

'We look for discrepancies; why wasn't this picked up, how is it possible that this happened, how can you square this witness saying this with this cop saying that? I build a picture.' She describes a case in which her client was found guilty of a murder charge on the assumption that he was the only person in the apartment apart from the victim during the whole of the critical three week period. With a bit of background research, Blair discovered that the victim had previously gone to a neighbour and said she was sick and tired of all these people in and out of her house all the time and she named those individuals. Two weeks later they found her body.

Next Blair found a witness who had been on the scene and could name four or five people who had been living there. All of them were now prosecution witnesses. 'I wonder, did the District Attorney know these people were living there? How come I found out and he didn't? And what about the fingerprints? They had a party there and there were at least fifteen people who were in that place. Where were the fingerprints? Why wasn't it brought up at the trial that there were fifteen different sets of unidentified fingerprints? And how can they be unidentified if they are prosecution witnesses and they all have records? Excuse me?' Blair's voice rises in ironic ridicule.

After she's ploughed through all the paper, Blair goes to see the client, which usually means a trip to jail. It's one of the hardest parts of the job, walking into a jail, being locked in a cell with somebody that you've never seen and who is accused of a crime, often murder. It takes some getting used to, even for the toughest PI. That's something Blair knows all about. 'The first time I went to see a client who was on Death Row, I was locked in a cell in the county jail with him. I came out thinking, well, I got through that. Wrong! I was sick for two days.'

It's one of the downsides in a job where the rewards are great and so are the difficulties, as Blair admits. 'The excitement is from the chase, it's in the hunt. You're looking for a needle in a haystack, you're looking for a way to see information, a way to understand the crime, a way to go into your client. I love finding people. I love identifying people, I love identifying angles, reading the discovery materials, finding out what's in there, finding out who did what, how they looked at it, what false assumptions were made, doing chronologies; setting up the case is really exciting. What I like least is that the job is so dismal. I didn't know how long anybody could look at the world through its anus. I'm a small-town girl suddenly on the big city streets, talking to murderers, drugs abusers, abused individuals, and just society's dregs. Disenfranchised is a popular word, but most people never hear, never see, never understand life on the streets. I did not imagine I was going to end up doing this kind of work!'

Francie Koehler also works the same criminal defence beat in the Bay Area. There are more than enough felonies to go around. Like Blair, she starts by reading up all the files on the case, then talks to the defendant. She explains how her work differs from the investigation the police make. 'You're conducting your own inquiry, but you're also reworking the police case. You're going to everybody they talked to and you interview them to get their independent memory of the facts of the case and then after you are satisfied that all these questions have been answered you go through the police report again and verify that the two things tally. Often they don't. Not necessarily on purpose, maybe it's been misinterpreted because they have a prosecution viewpoint. The police's job is not to exonerate, it's to convict. I don't see myself as trying to provide a good defence; just to verify the facts, evaluate the credibility of the witnesses and report back to the attorney and let him or her decide what to do with it.'

Mostly it's the detailed research that uncovers discrepancies in the prosecution case, but Francie relies on her instinct too. She describes a child molestation case where something told her things weren't right, even though the evidence was extremely powerful. The mother and grandmother were charged with prostituting a five- and nine-year-old. The children were able to give detailed information to the police on the men who were accused of abusing them.

Initially Francie was horrified by what seemed to be going on. The prosecution claimed that the girls made appointments with men to have sex with them, that they even had a price list on their bedroom door, that their mother drugged them so they'd go along with the racket. But when they started naming celebrities and TV stars who had supposedly molested them, alarm bells rang for Francie, who decided to re-evaluate every scrap of evidence.

'When I started charting the descriptions and the names, I started to see a pattern. For example, this little girl was describing men by age and weight and height and tattoos. From a time when she was supposed to have been drugged and it was semi-dark in the room. I couldn't even remember all that information with my mind at its sharpest. And how can a kid estimate height? When mine were nine, they didn't say a guy was six feet tall. They'd say, "Taller than X," or "Smaller than Y."

Gradually the hidden agenda emerged—a custody battle. The mother's sister wanted custody of the two children and she had orchestrated the whole thing. She coached the kids in what to say, fed them horrifying lies. Once she had guessed what was going on, Francie started to put pressure on the sister and finally she cracked. Francie's instinct had proved correct 'I'd had a feeling really early on in the case that all was not as it appeared. I'd kept thinking, I know strange things happen but I don't think all the child molesters live in one small place!'

That trained instinct for spotting when something is not quite right is what drives Byrna Aronson in her criminal defence inquiries. Byrna works on all areas of the defence case, meeting lawyers and discussing legal strategies, investigative strategies, even media strategies if the case is high profile. However glamorous this may seem, the job still involves a lot of legwork, driving from place to place, knocking on doors, making telephone calls and and ploughing her way through reams of paperwork. Sometimes what she discovers tells less about the case than about the police investigating it.

'I've gotten very good at reading medical reports, forensic reports, and police reports and finding out what's missing, what's wrong with them, where they might have been altered and unfortunately, in lots of cases with police reports that's true. Different typewriters, different signatures from the ones that should be on the report; so-and-so says that these five police officers responded to the scene and this report's written by a sixth one who wasn't supposedly there. Those little things can really turn a case around.'

Sadly it's evidence like this, rather than evidence about the defendant's actual guilt, that can make the difference, especially in appellate work. As Byrna sees it, in the American justice system the courts are not interested in guilt or innocence, only whether someone has had a fair trial in terms of process. Susan Lauman agrees that criminal defence work is often a struggle against the system. 'Criminal defence work is tough, and often dispiriting. The system is not geared to maintaining the presumption of innocence.'

The work Susan pursues embraces the extremes of an extreme city, New York. At one end of the social scale, she does criminal defence work, often working for clients from the ghettos and the housing projects who have never known anything other than the culture of drugs and violence. At the other end she deals with middle-class families where children become pawns in the vengeful games adults play. What these twin strands have in common is that they constantly bring her face to face with the worst things human beings can do to each other.

The constant grind of working with the seedy and downright evil is hard, which is why women eyes who choose criminal defence work are often driven to do it by strong personal convictions. That's certainly the case for Sandra Sutherland. 'I think that an absolute guiding principal in my life is hatred of abuse of power, which is why I have always done criminal defence and really liked it.'

Sandra cut her teeth on high-profile political cases in the early seventies. She felt strongly that she was on the side of right and truth. One incident always stays in her mind from this time as justification of her view. 'I interviewed this black guy in prison who became a friend and he said, "I wondered why a nice little white girl like you was messing around in this. Then I got it. You're the peoples' pig." I have never forgotten that. In a sense, it's the way I feel about myself.'

But even Sandra sometimes gets depressed by the sleaze and depravity she encounters. She recently worked on the much publicised Michael Jackson case, for the lawyer of the young boy at the heart of the allegations against the superstar. Sandra remains convinced that the boy was genuinely abused and felt very evangelical about the case, particularly when she saw the thuggery on the part of Jackson's lawyers. What also horrified her was the number of journalists that she discovered had known about or had seen things over a period of time but had been forced to keep their stories quiet, because of the corporate power behind Jackson. But Sandra's feelings changed when the huge financial settlement was made. 'It was a professional triumph for me I suppose, in that we got this unbelievable settlement for our client but I had this sense that something really sleazy was done under the table.

'The kid's not testified, the charges have been dropped. I don't blame the kid. He's now about fifteen. That's an incredibly sensitive age, he's not going to want to talk in front of the world's press about what went on between him and Michael Jackson. God only knows what's going to happen to this kid's sexual sense of freedom now. He has to be contaminated by events; probably least by what Michael did to him, because Michael was not violent, only manipulative. And after all, an awful lot of boys have similar experiences when they're thirteen. But the attention that surrounded it must have an effect. I don't know that there's an answer, but I felt like a tool more than anything, a tool in somebody else's dirty game.'

Most women eyes agree that cases involving children are the most distressing, whether they are criminal investigations of child abuse or messy custody battles. For Susan Lauman, searching for kidnapped children is the most wearing work she does. Usually they've been snatched by their fathers, looking for leverage against the mothers. Sometimes it's less about the child than it is about persuading the mother to settle for less alimony or child support. The child gets snatched as a kind of bargaining chip. It's not a scenario that provides a very positive view of human behaviour.

Getting things to work out for children makes Joan Beach's work valuable to her. She came to private investigation through her work in the child custody field, and it is that work which has established her reputation in the nation's capital. The day the phone rang in her office and a voice said it was calling from the White House, she knew she'd really hit the big time. 'It was a real kick to get a call from the White House, I have to admit,' she confesses. 'That was very satisfying. It related to a child custody dispute involving senior White House staff. I had to go there to meet with the client, and I'd be lying it I said that wasn't a thrill. I worked with both the mother and the father. They didn't want to go to trial, they wanted me to find out how they could find some solutions.'

Looking at Joan, it's not hard to see why she's so effective in child custody cases. She's fifty-two but looks at least ten years younger, in spite of the odd thread of silver in her thick, light brown hair. An unthreatening five feet tall, she's chirpy and friendly, her engaging grin never far away. She looks like she should be running the friendly neighbourhood mystery bookshop rather than battling cases that outdo any of her fictional counterparts. No father could feel threatened by her, no mother judged, no child ignored.

Criminal investigation, child custody battles and kidnapping cases; much of the PI's work is on a very personal scale, dealing with relationships, the mistakes that people make and the price they have to pay. But there is also the commercial work, often involving mistakes and crimes on a much larger scale.

Sandra Sutherland has recently moved into environmental work, another area which she feels very passionately about. When a corporation has been accused of causing environmental damage, their insurance company will often call on a PI to investigate where the blame really lies. Sandra was recently hired by Lloyds on a case involving the aerospace company which put the men on the moon. They'd managed to poison the Sacramento Valley water supply and were looking at a $300 million clean-up bill. If it had been simple negligence that caused this toxic pollution then the insurers would have had to foot the bill. But if it had been wilful and malicious negligence, then it would not be covered by the insurance and the company would have to pay. After a major investigation, Sarah eventually showed that the negligence had been wilful, so the company was liable.

It may seem that if the damage has already been done, then who pays the clean-up bill is irrelevant, but as Sandra explains, 'It was a major victory for the environmental movement in general because it hit this company where it hurt.' I'm not surprised by the momentary note of triumphalism in her voice.

Nancy Barber works the other side of the environmental street. She acts for major corporations threatened by litigation from people whose lives have been damaged and often destroyed by their activities. She's particularly involved in the area of asbestos litigation. But it's not because she believes her clients are the guys in the white hats and it's right to screw the plaintiffs. Quite the opposite. Although her clients are mostly corporations, she sees her role as developing information that means cases will be settled while the victims are still alive to receive their settlement.

As well as the asbestos cases, she does a lot of what are called Potentially Responsible Party searches. New legislation in the USA means that polluters now have to clear up their mess. When the Environmental Protection Agency informs companies that they believe they have contributed to the environmental damage at a site, those companies usually form a defence consortium and hire investigators like Nancy to find out what really happened. 'The reason I respect my clients is because what they say is, "Did we do it? How much of it is down to us?" They don't know what happened thirty, forty, fifty years ago and they say, "Just tell me if we did it so we can settle." When my clients say that, it's music to my ears. That's the kind of people I choose to work for. I don't work for companies who want to weasel out of their responsibilities.'

One of the biggest cases Nancy has worked on involved tracking down truckers from over forty years ago. 'They'd worked for a company that had been a front for the Mafia in Oakland,' she reveals. 'Oil waste had been taken to a tip in a central California town and just dumped. This stuff was seeping down into the underground water table and so the object of the game was to find out what this particular company had been doing, starting in the 1930s and going up to the 1950s. 'Generally, thirty years ago, companies were a lot smaller. It's a little bit easier to get a hook because all you need is one old retired guy who worked for the company. In this particular case, I found the book-keeper for the company and he consented to an interview. He remembered the names of every single trucker because he'd had to write out their pay cheques. He gave me the names of nine people.

From that, I tracked down this one trucker who had kept all his logs for the whole thirty years he'd driven trucks. He's living in this little mobile home and he's got this whole shelf filled with his logs. He had been interviewed by the Environmental Protection Agency and nobody asked him the right questions. He had details of every job he had been to, date, amount. It gave us a big part of the picture. Here's some guy who's really bright. His memory was unbelievable. Interviewing him was pure pleasure. People think, oh, truck driver, dumb. But during the thirties a lot of people who today would be professional people lacked the opportunity because of economic circumstances. And I took the time. That's the other thing. By the time you get to what you want to ask them about you know their whole life story. All about his second wife and her rotten little dog that was very smelly!'

René Olsson finds herself doing similar background research in her financial investigations. She concentrates on one aspect of what is known in the USA as due diligence work. René analyses loan portfolios to find out their worth to a potential buyer by assessing how much of the money outstanding could be recouped. This allows her clients to make accurate bids when the portfolios are auctioned. Because she is a private eye rather than a financial analyst, René believes nothing unless she's seen the physical evidence herself, so she doesn't just read the files, she actually goes out to look at the collateral cited in the loan file. A building may look like a valuable asset in a photograph but a carefully cropped picture doesn't reveal what the building next door is like; it could be a burnt-out crack house or a sanitary landfill.

After the loan has been acquired Rent will help negotiate with the debtors. Though she is working for the creditors, she feels sympathy for debtors and she does everything she can to work out a repayment scheme acceptable to both parties. For Rent, working with people in financial difficulties is a welcome change from criminal investigation. 'After years of talking to the victims of criminal cases about all the horrible, horrible things that have been done to them, talking to people about being upside down financially is a lot easier.'

Nevertheless there's no escaping the criminal element when you're working as a PI, even in financial investigation. Part of René's work is to investigate the conmen trying to exploit the loan business. This might involve long hours of surveillance and research but it brings its own satisfaction. 'It's a great feeling when you nail somebody like that!' René reveals.

For Christine Usher, the commercial world also provides satisfactions. She offers an anti-bugging service, vital for large corporations in these days of industrial espionage when bugging equipment is easy to come by and needs little technical ability to exploit. Industrial espionage can completely destroy a company, so there's always a demand for the kind of counter-measures Christine's company can provide.

The first thing Christine does on any commercial assignment is to sweep the office for bugs. There's no point setting up an undercover investigation if the offices are wired for sound. She quotes an example. The managing director claimed the office had previously been swept for bugs but during the course of the enquiry it became quite apparent that an insider knew that the investigation was taking place. Christine insisted on sweeping the office herself and discovered bugs everywhere from the boardroom to the MD's telephone.

The managing director's complacency is typical of the arrogance that the women eyes often come across in the commercial field. Sarah Di Venere has found a way to use it to her advantage. If a company thinks their security does not need improvement, she'll prove them wrong by talking her way into supposedly secure areas. It's an effective selling tool, even if it doesn't always make her very popular!

Even when she has been brought in by a company to investigate internal problems—usually involving narcotics or staff theft—Sarah often finds that they are far from grateful for her work. 'The trouble with large companies is that they want to be told it's only the underlings that are doing all the bad things. But often it's people in management. Sure, there might be somebody that's sneaking a joint here or there on the factory floor, but the main people making the money, doing the deals are management. The bosses don't want to hear that because now they have to make major decisions, they're going to have to go to their stockholders and other partners and admit one of their main guys is involved in cocaine dealing. It's a real love/hate relationship. All of a sudden, it's my fault! So then they try to bury the investigation because they can't handle the information.'

Private eyes may not always be popular with commercial companies but they are always needed and it can be a very profitable aspect of the business of private investigation. And profit is what keeps the private eyes out on the mean streets. Especially if they want to do any pro bono work, they have to keep their overheads covered. So how good is the money for the women eyes? It seems to vary almost as widely as the range of work the women do. Byrna Aronson is certain that it's not a job a person takes on if they want to get rich quick. Or even slow. 'Most PIs either have other sources of income or they're hard-scrabbling it,' she maintains. 'There are a few that make big money from corporate clients and famous names. And then there are the rest of us....'

At the other end of the scale are women like Sandra Sutherland and Joan Beach. Sandra charges herself out at $125 an hour, though she admits that slides downwards if she's working a case she cares passionately about and she knows the client hasn't got the cash. For Joan, working in DC, she charges $100 an hour for her own time, and $75 per hour per operative if she's using other staff investigators. Most of the other women I interviewed have hourly rates of between $40 and $65.

In the UK, £25-£35 an hour seems to be the average rate, though there are some women who charge a fixed fee of around £40 for certain categories of process serving. Pat Storey has firm views on a professional approach to fees. 'I talk to new PIs quite often and I say to them, "Every minute that you're on this job you should be making money. Even if you're stuck in the office making phone calls that must be logged on your sheet."' As Pat explains, it's not just the hours involved but the overheads, everything from petrol to paying the expensive database charges.

It's not a price structure that's going to turn women PIs into overnight millionaires, although they seem to be rather better at managing their money than most of the fictional private eyes, who nearly always seem to be teetering on the brink of some financial crisis or other, probably because they spend so much of their time working cases that feed their egos or principles rather than their bellies.

Janette Estrella is one woman eye who certainly knows how to make the most of her time. 'I have to schedule my time geographically to maximise my effectiveness. I have to be home by two thirty because I have to get my daughter from school. If I have more work to do I can leave her at her grandparents', but usually I have everything done in a span of five hours. I can work fifteen billable hours in five hours.

'Say for example I've interviewed someone in Inglewood, I would bill the client three hours; travel time back and forth, plus the interview. But if I'm down that way, I'll go to the court at Santa Monica and maybe work four cases—review two cases, look up something in the criminal court, do some research on a civil court case. So then I'd bill each case for two or three hours work, and there you've got your fifteen hours of work already. Or I can make a trip to the courthouse downtown and work on eight files and I can bill my travel time eight times.' I bite my tongue and refrain from pointing out that where I come from, lawyers who do that get charged with defrauding the Legal Aid Board.

Other women eyes choose to make extra money by developing sidelines. One PI, Francie Koehler, is working on a prototype for a new generation of bulletproof vests. The concept cropped up in the course of something completely different. Janet Wilson is another who has come up with an idea she hopes might turn into a money-spinner for her—Hercule Hound.

Hercule Hound is a dog with a deerstalker hat and magnifying glass who started life as Janet's company logo. She is now developing a soft toy of Hercule, and speaking to toy companies about manufacturing. The next step will be a children's investigation club and maybe even a board game. Her enthusiasm is irresistible as she talks about the project; I feel I'm listening to the birth rites of the Next Big Thing.

But is it ever as glamorous as the TV and the movies make it? Jean Mignolet, a woman who could pass as Barbra Streisand's body double, shouted with laughter. 'Glamorous? Working in this job, how glamorous can it be?' Certainly the work can take PIs like Jean to some glamorous places—charity balls, smart parties, restaurants and clubs—but if you're there to work, you don't have time to enjoy the scenery. Even when the case involves celebrities, the work is still the same old grind, as Jean makes clear. 'There's nothing glamorous about sitting outside a house in your car, no matter whether the house cost fifty grand or a couple of million.'

Over in England, Pam Quinney and her daughter Jane are equally dismissive of the idea that their job is glamorous. To them the image of female private eyes presented in television dramas, 'all short skirts and arms waving' as Jane puts it, is a joke.

But there are women eyes who do find glamour in the job they do. 'I travel a lot and to me that's glamorous,' Joan Beach confesses. 'That's probably the best part of the job, having someone pay me to travel and meet people!' Sarah Di Venere doesn't agree. Her job has involved following targets all over the country and she gives a very different picture of what the work involves. 'People think it's a great job; you get to go in all these really nice hotels, eat in restaurants and everything. What they don't realise is that it's work. You don't enjoy yourself, you can't relax. You're really riveted all the time to what you're doing and you have to make sure that when the cleaning girl cleans that room you're there to see what's in the garbage; you have to wait till she's gone into another room and you have to pull it out and haul it into your room and root through all their used tissues and stuff. You have to eat alone, you have nobody to talk to, you sit in your hotel room watching stupid things on cable TV that you'd normally cross the street to avoid. You do not have a good time. Ask anybody whose job takes them out on the road. Glamorous is not the word, believe me.'

Eventually, even a job as varied as private investigation can become repetitious. Jackie Griffiths admits that she found it glamorous at first, but now it all seems very ordinary. Whether she's chasing someone across the country or digging for clues, for Jackie it's just another job.

It's not the money or the glamour that attracts the women eyes to the job. So what is it? Partly it's the enjoyment of solving the puzzle, finding the needle in the haystack, revealing the truth behind the lies. Then there is the satisfaction of doing something that can make a real difference to the clients' lives, whether it's help to resolve their matrimonial difficulties or keep them off Death Row. It means that they develop strong relationships through their work, as Janet Wilson explains. 'I treasure my clients because they're also my friends. There aren't many parts of the country now where I don't know someone I could drop in on and feel welcome. There aren't many jobs that put so much back into your life.'

Memories Are Made Of This

I had to serve an ex-Naval Officer with an injunction order. When I went to see him, his mother said he'd nipped out for some cigarettes and invited me in to wait. I was sitting having a cup of coffee with her and in he walks. As soon as I said what I was there for, he pulls out this big machete. It took me two hours to disarm him. Not disarm him physically, just to talk him down. Finally he puts it down, then he reaches down the front of his trousers and pulls out this bloody revolver. I couldn't believe it! So I had to start all over again with the gentle persuasion. Another hour goes by and he eventually puts the gun down and settles down.

I have to admit I felt sorry for the chap. He'd been through a lot, and he wasn't a bad lad at all really. It was just that his life was in bits and I was the last straw. This was not long after the Hungerford massacre, and this chap was wearing this army type jacket and camouflage jeans and he had whiskers just the same as that Michael Ryan guy. His hair was lank and filthy. He was disgusting, he'd lost his job and he'd turned into a bit of a drunk. But in spite of all that, I did feel for him. I told him that if he got himself straightened out, had a wash and a haircut and smartened up for the court, I'd leave out of my affidavit that he'd threatened me.

When I turned up at court, I was looking out for him. Then this smart lad came towards me in a beautiful blue blazer, with naval insignia on it. I couldn't believe it was the same chap. He behaved exactly as I'd told him to, good as gold, and he got through the hearing OK. After the court case I rang his old boss at the council and put in a good word for him, so he got his job back. That helped get him back on his feet, and he got himself a flat up in Gateshead. He'd turned the corner, he was putting his life back together again.

About six months later, his mother rang me up late at night. She was worried because he hadn't rung her at the usual time, and she'd been trying to ring him at his flat for a couple of days and she couldn't get any reply. So I picked her up in the car and drove her up to his flat. We found him lying dead in the sitting room. He'd had a heart attack. He was only forty-two, but he'd gone, just like that. I helped to organise the funeral and helped them out, did all these little jobs that I probably shouldn't have been doing, sorting things out. Then one night his mother rings me and says, 'We've been clearing out his flat, and we've got his machete and his handgun and we wondered whether you would like them as a reminder!'

You think you've heard everything. You think you've seen everything. And then something like that happens and you think, is it me, or is the world mad?

BRENDA BALMER
Sunderland

7

Target Practice

A *gun is either a good friend or a true albatross.*

SUSAN LAUMAN
New York

*I do not carry a gun because I'm not willing to die for a pay cheque
and I'm not willing to take somebody's life for a pay cheque.
There are issues for which I would put my life on the line and I
have. In my political work I have been shot at and had death
threats and had my car run off the road. But not for money.*

BYRNA ARONSON
Boston

A *bridle's a beautiful weapon.*

SUSAN BALMER
Sunderland

The fear of street violence or home invasion is something that most women live with. For the majority of us, it's distant, a low background hum that informs the way we behave. We don't walk down inner-city dark alleys on our own at midnight. We have our lamps on timer switches so that the house looks inhabited when we're late home. We have peepholes in our front doors and we keep them on the chain when we open them to strangers. We lock our car doors when we're driving anywhere dodgy and we keep our handbags slung across our bodies when we're in busy shopping centres.

But for private eyes, the danger is immediate. It's a constant, there in the foreground. Their work regularly forces them to confront the violent, the unstable and the angry. When they knock on a door, they can never be certain what lies behind it. More often than not, what they are bringing with them is unwelcome, whether it be an injunction or a series of questions. Facing already aggressive people with the unwelcome is a recipe for danger.

Add to that the vulnerability of almost always being smaller and weaker than the other person. It's not a combination most people would feel sanguine about dealing with on a daily basis. Speaking as someone who gets twitchy driving through certain areas of Manchester late at night, I've got nothing but respect for women who deal with these potentially explosive situations day after day.

It's an issue that is seldom dealt with realistically in crime fiction. The women private eyes who pound the fictional mean streets seem to take an extraordinary amount of physical punishment in their stride. Not only do they manage to make incredibly swift physical recoveries, but they don't suffer the kind of psychological damage that real victims of violence know all about.

Sandra Sutherland agrees. 'I used to enjoy Sara Paretsky, but I don't like the way VI Warshawski gets beaten up in every book and leaps back into action almost like nothing's happened. I am one of the few private investigators who has been beaten up and pistol whipped and stuff and you never quite get over it.'

The incident took place when Sandra was on her way to do an interview on a murder case. It was unrelated to the case; she just happened to be in a difficult neighbourhood because of the job. Determined that she wasn't going to let anyone get the better of her, she carried on with her work. 'I had this sense that no little creep is going to interfere with my life any more than is necessary so I went and knocked on these people's door and said, "Could I have a glass of water, I've just been beaten up." And then I burst into tears. The woman gave me a drink of water and sympathised but then I went ahead and did the interview. I went back to the office and reported it to the police. They said, "You've got to be off your head, we wouldn't send armed uniformed officers in that place on their own!"'

It was a lesson in reality for Sandra, whose strongly held convictions had made her something of an idealist. 'Before that, I always had the sense of invulnerability. You just do. You think, I'm a nice person, I'm here doing good work, I'm out to save somebody and you just assume that the world knows that when you're young and stupid. But after you've been physically attacked, so often the hair on the back of your neck raises up and you wonder if it's going to happen again. I'm walking down the street, the cadence of someone's footsteps alters slightly and I think, I'm going to get jumped, and there's just this sense of horror. We're talking over fifteen years ago, but I still pay attention on the street. If someone is walking close behind me I am always aware of who that person is and I take evasive action even if that seems to be a bit nuts.'

I can relate to that. When I was a national newspaper journalist, I was beaten up once by a twenty-stone professional wrestler. These guys really know how to hurt without leaving a mark. I was lucky not to suffer any broken bones; I ended up with deep bruising round the spine and kidneys. For about three hours after the attack, I kept having fits of uncontrollable shaking; for days afterwards, I kept bursting into tears for no reason at all. I had no desire whatsoever to leap out of bed with one mighty bound and settle my score with this man.

All I wanted to do was lie there with the duvet over my head until the world went away.

More distressing than all of this was the effect it had psychologically. My bottle went completely. This attack had come out of the blue; I had simply knocked on this guy's door and identified myself. I hadn't even had the chance to say what I wanted to talk to him about. What I didn't know was that the tabloid dailies had been doorstepping him all week to confront him with rumours that his wife had run off with another woman. I happened to be the unlucky one who got someone else's kicking. But because it had been so unpredictable an onslaught, I no longer had any conviction that knocking on a stranger's door was a safe occupation. For years I'd been blithely doing my job, fearless and intrepid as the next hack. But after the hammering I took from this guy, every time I knocked on a door I felt my stomach contract and cold sweat on my back. It took me between three and six months before I felt comfortable doing a job I'd always enjoyed and knew I was good at. So perhaps more than most, I admire women private eyes for the way they not only face the fear of confrontation, but also manage to defuse potentially violent situations without getting hurt. But how do they do it? What steps can they take to protect themselves?

It's a truism that society is growing more violent, both in the UK and the USA. But the danger has always been there. Nearly forty years ago, Zena Scott-Archer had her one and only brush with violence. She had served papers on a man who swore she had got the wrong person. Determined to return the papers to her he chased her around Liverpool in his truck. Eventually she stopped to face him and he shoved the papers down the front of her dress. More angry than frightened, Zena slapped his face and the man had the audacity to call the police, threatening to have her charged. Zena was humilitated to be caught in such a situation but it turned out to her advantage in the end. When the police arrived the man had to give his name, and thus admit that the process had been for him all along.

The story finally ended in 1993. 'I was at the station, waiting for a train, and this chap came up to me and said, "You don't remember me, do you?" And I said, "Oh yes I do!" Even thirty-five years later, his face was etched on my memory. And he said, "I just want to apologise!"'

All the women I interviewed were alive to the perpetual danger of the work they do, and were at pains to talk about the importance of appearing non-aggressive and sympathetic. Paradoxically, although women are more vulnerable, there is still a reluctance on the part of most men to hit a woman. Sometimes that reluctance is far from a powerful restraining force, but it usually gives the investigator a breathing space that lasts long enough for them to use their verbal skills to defuse the situation. An aggressive attitude is the last thing an investigator needs when she's out on the street; that's fine for hustling lawyers when fees are overdue, but face to face with the punters, charm is the best fashion accessory a woman eye can have. None of them have bothered with martial arts skills, figuring that if they can't talk their way out of a situation, they're not going to be able to fight their way out of it either.

This doesn't always have to mean backing down or running away. As Zena's story shows, the women eyes are quite capable of standing up for themselves and taking a firm stance against the threat of aggression. Sometimes, showing you're not afraid is enough to defuse a situation. Bailiff Maureen Jacques-Turner has had people storming into her office threatening violence more than once. On one occasion a man yanked her computer from its socket and threatened to walk out with it. When he threw a punch at one of her male colleagues she immediately dived between them and told him firmly to stop it. It worked. Now, her office is protected by bullet-proof glass and closed-circuit TV!

One of the lessons women learn quickly if they are to survive in this job is to develop a sixth sense for danger. They need to know when to make a stand and when it's sensible to be scared and necessary to back off. This sixth sense is vital when they are forced to go into dangerous areas. 'It's an inescapable part of the job,' as Blair explains. 'This is not a job where you can sit in the office and theorise. We have to go out on the street and find the whole story.'

For Blair this often means going to gang neighbourhoods on a regular basis. In fact she was scheduled to go to South Central LA, home of the most notorious street gangs, the day after it was torn apart by riots. Discretion won out, and she waited a week! But it's not enough to be cautious and alert to the possible dangers, it's vital for the PI to have a good knowledge of the area—where the danger points are, who to avoid. In areas like South Central that means understanding the gang culture, knowing the gang colours for the various turfs so you don't accidentally wear the wrong colour clothes in the wrong neighbourhood. You have to think about what car you're driving. There are some cars that are just too visible, too brightly coloured, flashy or new. If you're black like Blair, and you're driving a brand new car in the ghetto, the police will use that as an excuse to stop you on the basis that they suspect it's stolen. You don't want other people to like it too much either or you'll lose it to thieves.

Even with this kind of knowledge, there is a chance that the PI will be caught out. Yvonne Twiby works regularly in the inner-city areas of Birmingham. She has learnt where the flashpoints are and how to dress appropriately to avoid attracting attention. But recently she was jammed—a new kind of car crime where a driver, usually a lone female, is trapped between two cars at traffic lights. The criminals just open the doors, or smash the window if the doors are locked, and take whatever they can—handbag, mobile phone, purse—before running off and disappearing into the night. Often it's over and done with before the lights have even changed.

Yvonne reported the incident to the police but their response was unhelpful. As far as they are concerned, women shouldn't be visiting such dangerous areas, and if they do they only have themselves to blame if things go wrong. It's an attitude that women eyes come across on both sides of the Atlantic and it doesn't make their job any easier, or their opinion of the police force any higher.

Treading the mean streets might be dangerous enough, but the reason that women eyes are there in the first place is usually because they have to visit a witness, suspect or someone to be served papers. This means entering an unknown house with a potentially volatile and violent person, often alone. It is a situation that Jennifer Paul often finds herself in, although fortunately she has never been the victim of violence.

'I feel like I lead a charmed life, but the reality is that almost without thinking you behave in a way that protects yourself. If I go to interview someone and it's clear they've been drinking or using drugs, I always make sure I sit nearest the door.'

Jennifer describes a recent visit she made to a witness. Although it was only ten in the morning she found the man with two others drinking strong lager and vodka. Although they tried to be hospitable, these men were obviously no strangers to violence, as they made clear by showing her their array of wounds and battle scars, some still fresh. It was an awkward and potentially dangerous situation, a woman alone with three drunken men, which Jennifer had to handle with diplomacy and caution, finding a quick exit without insulting the men's egos and sparking off the very trouble she was trying to avoid.

Sometimes, however, the intrepid PI's determination to get the job done properly sets natural caution and an awareness of potential danger aside. Jennifer recently found herself climbing through the kitchen window of a witness who she had been trying to talk to for days and who claimed to be locked in his house. She got the statement she'd gone for but later discovered that the man was a convicted rapist. She had put herself in considerable danger even entering the house alone with him, never mind when the front door was locked.

Many women investigators have experienced the terrifying reality of what happens when situations do turn nasty. It takes courage to deal with that and then continue doing the job. In spite of being a fifty-nine-year-old grandmother, Brenda Balmer is surprisingly philosophical about the dangers she faces. 'Getting hurt is an occupational hazard in this job,' she maintains.

Brenda works in the north-east of England, an area with a strong culture of violence. 'There's an awful lot of matrimonial fighting going on between men and women and I think that the men just don't care whether the person they're thumping is a woman or a man. That's what it's like in the north-east. I just have to tell myself, I'm not going to let myself be scared by these people. I tell myself I'm in the right.'

Only recently Brenda was attacked when trying to distrain goods. She had ignored the householder's threat to throw her out so he had done just that, picking her up and hurling her down the steps. Her response was to get up and go straight back in. By the time the police arrived she had been thrown out three times and had a chipped ankle, torn ligaments and bruised back and wrist.

'You cannot just turn round in the middle of a job and bleat that you're hurt,' Brenda says firmly. 'You get on with the job. I've been faced with violence dozens of times. I've had my nose broken more than once.'

On this occasion, however, Brenda has decided to charge the man with assault, a decision partly precipitated by the fact that her client decided to let the man off the money owed despite all Brenda's hard work and suffering.

Each violent encounter, or threat of one, teaches the PI a lesson for the future. When doing what she thought would be a quick process serving job in rural Cheshire, Pat Storey once left her keys in her car. Unfortunately, while she was talking to the man's wife he sneaked round the house and stole the keys. Pat called her office for a spare set but as she sat waiting in the car she saw a JCB coming towards her, a forty-foot steel girder hanging from a chain, a very angry man in the driving seat. Moments later the girder was slowly descending towards the roof of the car. Knowing that she had nowhere to run to she sat it out. By the time the cavalry arrived with a spare set of keys the girder was inches from her roof. It taught her never to leave the keys in her car.

Pat also got a locking petrol cap after another man stuffed some unwelcome papers into her petrol tank. It's typical of the kind of abuse process servers come across in their work. Yvonne Twiby has had her car damaged, coffee thrown over her, not to mention the endless verbal abuse. Although in her experience it is the male PIs who are more likely to be physically assaulted, while women will calm things down with some diplomacy, she believes that being a woman sometimes makes matters worse.

'Those have been situations where men have been served an injunction; they've already terrorised the wife and kids and think women are the lowest form of life.

What they can't take is that they've actually had an injunction served on them by a woman who's not frightened of them. They can only express themselves physically and they haven't got a brain. In potentially violent situations like that, I just rely on crucifying them verbally, being a Gemini!'

The private eyes of fiction have no qualms about using more than words to defend themselves against violence. The Americans pack a pistol, know how to use it and don't suffer from angst every time they tuck it into the waistband of their jeans. Linda Barnes' Carlotta Carlyle makes great play in *Hardware* of her need to upgrade her weapon from her trusty .38 to an automatic with more shots in the magazine. My own Kate Brannigan is a Thai boxer. At a mere five feet and three inches, she knows she's not going to out-fight most men, but the sport keeps her fit and she knows in a crisis she can land one good kick, then leg it.

Jean Mignolet is a member of the Brannigan school of thought. 'When I was working undercover in law enforcement, they stuck a gun in my hand and said, "We're going to teach you to shoot." I said, "Never mind teaching me how to shoot, teach me how to run in high heels. That would be a damn sight more useful." Legs be loyal now, that's my motto. Now, I'm the only PI in Florida without a gun!

'When I was a cop, I carried a gun twenty-four hours a day for five years and it comes to rule your life. You go into a restaurant and you can't have a drink because you've got your gun and you might have to use it...I've had it with letting anything control my life.'

Jean demonstrates her argument with an incident that happened to her recently. She was working in a bad area when she returned to her car to find it broken into. Suddenly she was surrounded by a group of men. 'I started screaming like a lunatic, "How dare you! I come in here to help you people and you do this? I want my files back!" There were seven of them. If I'd had a gun, I could have shot how many? I would have been killed or raped or indicted. It's better to use your brain than a gun. Besides, I think I'd be too quick to pull a gun because of my law enforcement experience. I don't want to be in that position.'

Jean's views echo a surprisingly large number of her American colleagues'. Hardly any of them are licensed to carry a gun, and of those who are, I only met two whole-hearted advocates of pistol packing. Most of them broadly support Byrna Aronson's opinion. 'I do not carry a gun because I'm not willing to die for a pay cheque and I'm not willing to take somebody's life for a pay cheque. There are issues for which I would put my life on the line and I have. In my political work I have been shot at and had death threats and had my car run off the road. But not for money. Only for something I believed in. You don't carry a gun with the idea that you're not going to kill another human being. I cannot imagine being willing to kill someone in the course of a job.'

Janette Estrella and Helen Kliner are both licensed to carry a gun, and they do occasionally take it with them when they know they're going into dangerous neighbourhoods. After her years in the police, Helen is comfortable with a gun. She's used it when she was a police officer, but she prefers not to carry one now. Janette too prefers to use other methods to deal with danger. 'I carry my gun only when I feel I really need to. Not just because I'm going into a bad area, but because I know I'm going to interview people who I think may be dangerous, based on the information I've already got.'

For Sarah Di Venere and Susan Lauman, having a gun and knowing how to use it are part of the process of handling themselves out on the street. Sarah's snub-nosed Smith and Wesson is her best friend, though she's never had to fire it in anger. 'I've had it out of the holster, and I'd use it if I had to,' she says firmly. 'If I'm in a situation where it's him or me, I want to be damn sure it's me.'

For Susan, danger is something she's stared down too many times to take chances with her life. 'I carry a gun,' she states baldly, with no hint of apology. 'For a woman, a gun is a great equaliser. The bottom line is that I will never be as strong as a man. No matter how much martial arts and self-defence training I do, in a confrontation, a man is going to be heavier than me, stronger than me. I only weigh 120 pounds so my weapon is a really nice thing for me to have, to know it's there. I would never shoot an animal—only a human being in a situation where it was them or me.

'Also, knowing you have a gun and that you are prepared to use it gives you a lot more control in interviews. It can make you polite, calm and confident when the people you are talking to are being threatening and hostile. You don't have to be afraid. I don't use my gun to threaten people with; it's there if I need it. I would never take my gun out unless I was going to use it then and there. It's crazy to take a gun out and wave it around and say, "Hey, stop that, I have a gun," because chances are someone is just going to take it away from you.

'If I have to get my gun out, it's because the next thing I am going to do is to use it. I have never had to kill anybody, but I have had to shoot somebody to stop them. It's not something I like to boast about.'

But the protection of a gun comes with a price tag. If you carry a gun you owe it to yourself to be an expert with that weapon, as Susan explains. 'Forget everything you've seen on the movies. Life is not like Hollywood. A gun fight lasts maybe seven seconds, maybe ten, maximum. That's a very short space of time and if you don't practise a lot, you won't hit the person coming at you. If you don't know what you're doing, you can empty your gun without hitting someone, even if they're only seven, eight feet away. It's the adrenaline. Once that starts pumping, your knees shake, then your hands shake. You have to look at it like driving a car. You train yourself to drive so that everything comes automatically. Then in a crisis, you just do the right thing to get yourself out of it in one piece without thinking. You know almost by instinct when to brake, how to steer, when to hit the gas so you get out of that situation in one piece. You have to be like that with your gun.

Susan practises target and combat shooting regularly. It's not something she enjoys doing but she knows its value. 'Without the practice, you're just asking for somebody to take it away from you. A gun is either a good friend or a true albatross.'

Even if you are not willing to take the responsibility of a gun, Susan believes that all women should be ready to protect themselves. 'Women are vulnerable in so many ways that it's not paranoid to take every care of yourself. I tell women that if you drive in the city or on the highway, a car phone is as important as a gas tank to you. You can never tell when you're going to break down or get a flat, and too many women have been raped or killed that way. To be aware of the reality of danger is not to be paranoid. I also suggest women carry an axe handle down by the driver's door. Then if anybody comes after you while your car is stopped, soon as they reach in you can smash that piece of wood down on their wrist. That is going to cause them enough pain and injury to get them to back off.'

As well as her gun, Susan has two Dobermans which she finds a very useful deterrent. Nancy Barber, another Doberman owner, agrees, and as she points out, someone can take a gun off you and turn it on you, but no one is going to take your Doberman and turn it on you!

Of course the other side can also have dogs and Susan Neary, who admits to being terrified of the animals, carries a tool for just this eventuality. It's a gadget which looks like a remote control but when aimed in the direction of a dog will stop them in their tracks with a high pitched whistle that humans can't hear. The gadget is illegal in England but for Susan it's worth the risk of carrying it. In fact she sometimes wishes that she could use something similar on the men she has to serve with injunctions. 'In this job, I'll do anything reasonable to err on the side of caution,' she says in justification.

A gadget to calm dogs is not the only unusual weapon carried by the women eyes. Yvonne Twiby always carries a fish whacker, a tool more usually used by fishermen to stun fish with. She also keeps a can of white car paint in her handbag. If you spray it without shaking it the first thing that comes out is thinner. Get that in your face and you're not going to be doing much for a while. As Yvonne sees it, if the police carry a truncheon with them, why shouldn't she have protection too?

Susan Balmer has discovered an even more unusual weapon, a horse's bridle. A keen rider, she often serves process while out riding. 'The amount of times I've walked up a path brandishing my bridle! One time, I was on my way back from the stables, and I'd flung the papers at this guy who was giving me a really hard time. He picked up a brick and went to hit me and it missed. I swung round and I had my bridle on my shoulder. I turned at such an angle that I knew it was going to swing, and swing it did. The bit got him right in his gob. He was some mess! Beautiful weapon, that bridle.'

Sometimes, though, the constant fear of violence inherent in the PI's job can get too much. In spite of the satisfaction Pat Wingate and Sally Isted have gained from their work, they have decided they don't want to continue, following threats made against them. 'I went to see a woman to ask her a few questions in connection with a mortgage fraud,' Sally explained. 'She must have had something to hide, she got so worked up about it. She was abusive and threatening to my face and then she left this really frightening message on the answering machine. She was threatening violence. She ended up by saying, "I wouldn't like to be in your shoes when I get hold of you." It really shook me up and it seriously worried me for a couple of days. I even sneaked out the back way whenever I left the flat. It unnerved me and made me realise how very vulnerable we are. I'm fifty-three and I don't want to live in fear.'

Once Is Unfortunate...

I had a very strange case recently which tied in to the very first murder I ever did. The dead man was the brother-in-law of the accused and there had been a feud between them for a number of years. Apparently they really hated each other. There had been an incident three or four months previously when the two of them had met on the street. They had a row and the brother-in-law was carrying a can of petrol which he proceeded to open and pour on our client, then went into his pocket for a match. Our client was with his three year old son, so you can imagine how pleased he is when this happens. So he ran to his car, jumped in and drove the car at his brother-in-law, who jumped over a hedge into a garden. He wasn't injured, wasn't struck. But when it came to the murder case about three or four months later, our client was also charged with an attempted murder for the incident when he'd driven at him. You can imagine how bad it looks on paper.

What had apparently happened on the night of the killing was that the deceased's wife had been noising up. She didn't get on with her brother and she was winding up her husband, goading him, going, 'You're frightened of him. Get over there and sort him out,' and all this stuff. He gets tooled up with hammers and what all, and went over to the accused's house at three o'clock on New Year's morning, up to the eyes with drink. He threw a starter motor through the front window, shouting and bawling, 'I'm going to burn you and your house down, and all your fucking weans are getting torched.'

Our client was sitting in the house having a quiet New Year drink with his wife when suddenly all this goes off. He rushes out and there's a fight at the front door. His wife is afraid for herself, for him and for their five kids, so she gets a knife from the kitchen and gives it to her husband. In the ensuing ruckus, the deceased got stabbed. The statements I took painted a very different picture from the police's case, and when it came to trial, our client was found not guilty. That happened five or six years ago. That's the history to this recent case.

I got a set of papers in relating to a culpable homicide [manslaughter]. You can imagine my surprise when I saw it was the same man who was accused. It had always stuck in my mind because it was the first murder I ever did and at the time I was chuffed to get a job like that. Anyway, by this time, he and his wife had separated. This time, it's the live-in girlfriend who's dead. He and she had been having a drink in the house and they'd also been smoking cannabis. It was quite late, and the girlfriend decided to go out and get more drink in even though she's already guttered. He's sitting in the living room and it dawns on him after about ten minutes that he hasn't heard the front door close. So he goes out into the hallway and she's lying on the floor, dead. That's his story.

What she had died of was a subarachnoid haemorrhage. It's a rupture beneath the ear, just behind the corner of the jaw. It's the one place where the main arteries that come up through the spine are exposed to some extent to the outside world before they go up into the brain. If you hit somebody on that area it doesn't actually sever the arteries but it jolts the head and that can cause this kind of haemorrhage. It's very similar to a ruptured aneurysm.

There have been test cases about this and there have been convictions. But the pathologist told me it's a very difficult area to strike. If you aim to hit that area, it's very difficult. If I did it to you just now it's very unlikely that you would suffer that injury because you're sober; you brace yourself for a blow when you see it coming and you automatically protect yourself. In cases where it has occurred it tends to be when the person has been drinking. Well, on paper this is a classic case. She had a bruise in this area, she had been drinking heavily, she'd been smoking pot.

Apart from the bruise, the only evidence they had against my client was one witness upstairs saying that he heard someone downstairs shouting, 'Stop it, you bastard.' During the course of my investigations, I spoke to the client who told me they had a dog called Buster, a young pit bull terrier who was very boisterous. The dog went everywhere with the girlfriend.

Picture the scene. She comes out into the hall, she's getting her coat on, the dog sees her and thinks, I'm going for a walk! And what does the dog do when he's going for a walk? He jumps up. With his wee head solid as a brick. And her already drunk enough to be bouncing off the walls.

The case was eventually abandoned because we made the prosecution look at the possibility of the dog. It could have been the dog head-butting her, or the dog knocking her into the door jamb that caused the bruise and the fatal jolt to the head. What the neighbour almost certainly heard was her shouting, 'Stop it, Buster,' not 'bastard'. I think the police were desperate to have him because he'd got off on the previous murder charge. There is an element of that with the police. I must be that guy's guardian angel—twice he's been charged and twice he's walked away.

JENNIFER PAUL
Glasgow

8

Criminal Elements

What I like best about this job is getting the truth and the bad guy.

SARAH DI VENERE
Chicago

*I think probably the most grisly things I've been associated
with have not been down in South Central LA.
It's been white folks in the suburbs*

KRIS KLEINBAUER
Los Angeles

*I've been really really fortunate in that I've had a few defendants
who were actually innocent and because of my efforts they're not
in jail. I have always said that if I had one of those that would
make a whole lifetime worthwhile. Just one. But I have been
fortunate enough to have had several and that's really rewarding.*

FRANCIE KOEHLER
Oakland

*Some of the criminals I do defence work for, I wonder
why we're spending taxpayers' money defending them.
It's hard not to get cynical in this job.*

YVONNE TWIBY
Solihull

Most nice middle-class people don't know any criminals. Not proper criminals, that is. Sure, they know someone who's lost their licence for drunk driving. In these days of middle-class protest, they might even know someone who's been arrested for trespass or breach of the peace. It's possible that they've even encountered someone who's been done for some nice, clean white-collar crime like fraud. But things like that don't count. They're not real criminals, after all.

Most crime writers don't even know any criminals. Not the hard-core villains who pull armed robberies or deal drugs on a major scale or counterfeit thousands of pounds' worth of branded items or sell automatic pistols in pubs. Or kill people, sometimes for money. Generally, we make it up, based on what we have read or seen on TV, because hard men like that send most of us running for cover.

Private eyes, on the other hand, encounter criminals all the time. It goes with the territory. Either they're helping to catch them, or they're serving papers on them for their civil misdemeanours, or they're helping to defend them. Whatever the job, it's an alien world that they have to learn to cope with. They need to be tough and streetwise, which are not qualities that middle-class women aged between thirty and sixty are supposed to have in great measure. What they do have are highly developed people skills and the ability intuitively to read a situation and work out the best approach. I guess that's why so many of them place such a high premium on common sense and empathy as key tools of the trade. The full wisdom of the streets is something that only comes with experience. But if you don't have the common sense and intuition to start with, you're not going to last long enough on the street to make it as a PI.

Sarah Di Venere told me about a young woman who had come to her for a job. Sarah sent her out to carry out surveillance on a particular target out in the Chicago suburbs. An hour later, the woman called up to report that she didn't know where this address was, could someone please give her directions. Had she brought a map, Sarah wondered? No, came the answer. 'I gently put the phone down at that point,' Sarah says drily. 'Somebody who doesn't have the nous to have a map in her car sure as hell is not going to make it in this business. I get a lot of young women coming to me for work, acting like they think they're going to be running round the streets in short skirts shooting at men. They haven't got the faintest idea of how tough these guys are. Sending them in to deal with some of the people we have to tangle with would be like throwing baby rabbits into a lion's den. Sure, you learn the job as you go along, but if you haven't got a little bit of street smarts to start with, you are never going to cut it.'

One thing is certain; it's not like it is in the movies or the novels. In real life, private eyes don't get hired to solve murders when the police have failed. They almost never work hand in hand with the police to put the bad guys behind bars. Currently, Helen Kliner is working a case that is the exception to this rule, however. She has been hired by a family that were the victims of a robbery and are worried that the police might suspect them or their employees of being involved. It's an interesting case which is still far from completed, but Helen is convinced she'll get to the bottom of it. 'I'm used to the waiting game from my time in the police department. I've got real patient over the years. Sooner or later, criminals make a mistake, and we're ready and waiting for these guys when they do.'

More usually, solving crime is incidental to the PI's major task, which is to establish a defence for a client facing criminal charges. Occasionally, private eyes are employed to uncover crime, but it's almost always white-collar crime or employee theft, where confidentiality is an issue or where the police don't have the resources or the incentive to dig deep and find out what's going on inside a company.

The other area where private eyes operate against criminals is in the growth area of fraud. Usually, insurance companies are the victims, and they call on PIs to protect their interests and establish a case against the defrauders. Janette Estrella often works cases like this on behalf of automobile insurance companies. 'Sometimes these cases can be really frustrating because you just know people are lying to you, but proving it can be very difficult. You know you can read people well enough to know that you're not being told the truth. I use that frustration as an incentive to spur me on to greater efforts to nail those liars.'

There are a lot of different types of auto insurance fraud, but one of the most common is something called ghost passengers, in which the claimant arranges for a friend to deliberately rear-end his car. He then makes a claim, saying that several people were in the car and suffered injuries. The claimant will be in cahoots with a crooked attorney and a crooked medical facility, and between them they will cook up medical reports and send them on to the insurance company, along with bills from the doctor these ghost passengers are supposed to be seeing.

If the insurance company is suspicious, they will call a PI to investigate and interview the supposed passengers. Janette explains how she finds holes in their story. 'Obviously, these people will have collaborated on a story about the accident, and they're probably all going to be word perfect on that. So what I do is I ask all sorts of questions that don't really pertain to the accident. Where were you going? Where had you been? Who was sitting where? Was the radio on? What station was it on? What was Mary wearing? Once I've got all that stuff, I move on to the medical side. Can you describe your doctor? Now, I've done my research before, and I know what this doctor really looks like, but they're stumped because they've never seen this guy in their life. So either they give me a totally bogus description, or they say they can't remember, which gives me the perfect comeback. "You saw your doctor every single day and you cannot say whether he's black or white or Asian?"'

Once she has got statements from each ghost passenger, she compares their answers. 'By the end of it, we've got Mary saying they were going to the ice-cream shop, Sally saying they were going to pick up pizza, David saying they were on their way to visit his brother and the driver saying they were just out cruising. Plus the doctor is black, Asian, male, female and has a moustache. So now I've got all this conflicting testimony and I just turn on the attorney and say, "This is fraud. You going to carry on colluding, or are you going to make it go away?" Usually they drop the whole case. Mostly the insurance company doesn't prosecute; they're just happy they've saved the money they would have had to pay out.'

Sometimes the stories are perfectly consistent, but to an experienced investigator, this can be just as much of a giveaway. Then it's a matter of grinding away at the story 'til you find a crack. These cases may be hard, but they are the ones Janette enjoys most. 'I like to do those cases, because I get satisfaction from knowing I have stopped somebody profiting from crime.'

Listening to the stories of the women who do criminal defence work, it's hard to believe that anyone still thinks the supposed profits of crime are worth the aggravation, especially in states like California where they still have the death penalty as well as their new law that sends people to jail for life when they steal a slice of pizza, just because it happens to be their third offence. The more I heard of their working lives, the more I marvelled that not only could these women do this on a daily basis, they could still bring enough conviction to the job to go the extra mile for clients who are at best social misfits. No matter how strong the passion for justice, it can't be easy to go into work day after day batting for people who have murdered, raped and robbed. It gives a whole new meaning to the expression, 'It's a dirty job, but someone's got to do it.'

What keeps most criminal defence specialists going is a firm commitment to an ideal of justice that the reality falls far short of. They hold tight to the idea that everyone is entitled to a fair trail, however appalling the crime they're accused of, and that means they're also entitled to the best possible defence. In reality, what also sustains them through the grim mill of process that passes for justice is the knowledge that every now and again, maybe at most half a dozen times in a career, they will prove someone innocent of a crime that would otherwise send them to Death Row.

Marion Smith had just such a case involving some real Perry Mason style courtroom drama. Her client was accused of killing a dope dealer and his girlfriend. He'd supposedly taped their hands behind their backs and shot them both in the head. His fingerprints were on the tape so a conviction seemed certain. The client and his girlfriend claimed that the real murderer had come to his house and ordered him to take the tape off the roll in order to incriminate him. When Marion examined the tape closely she realised that her client's fingerprints were on the wrong side of the tape. Their position was entirely consistent with his story, and at odds with the prosecution version.

Marion tracked down the real murderer and by luck he was in custody over something else. There was a dramatic moment when he was brought to court and the girlfriend pointed to him and identified him as the killer.

It's cases such as these that make it worthwhile for Marion and her colleague Kris Kleinbauer. 'A lot of what we do, some of the clients are pretty unsavoury, and some of the crimes are really disgusting,' Kris acknowledges. 'It's very easy to say these guys are monsters and they should be put away or executed, but deprive them of a defence and who's going to help you and yours when you get arrested? My take on this is that everybody is entitled to a defence and what we do is find out the facts. It's then up to the attorney to put it in the best light.'

The truth is, once the police and the prosecution have a suspect, they want to do everything possible to prove their guilt. They are not interested in an alternative suspect or clues that don't add up. As Jennifer Paul says, 'The police are only looking for what substantiates their belief. Maybe that's a bit harsh but I do think it's true. A case in point is a murder I did. The victim died of head injuries. He was with his wife in the pub and he'd had a tremendous amount to drink. They were being chucked out by the publican, and the wife was winding him up, saying, "Are you going to let him put us out?" So of course the guy felt obliged for the sake of his manhood to make some sort of stand about it. Now, he was a big man, about six foot three inches, and the publican was quite a small guy even though he was an ex-boxer. In the doorway, the husband, very, very drunk, turned round to have a go at the publican, so the publican punched him once in the jaw and the man fell against the door, hitting it with his shoulder, and slid to the floor. It's not clear whether he was unconscious or whether he was just dead drunk.

'He'd been punched, he fell to the ground and he had a head injury. That was the prosecution case. What didn't come out in the prosecution statements was that the wife and the other chap that was with them tried to lift him up and get him into a taxi. But he was too big for them and he fell, and his head hit the pavement. There was a man across the road doing some deliveries and he saw all this happen. His words were, "His head hit the pavement like a brick." The lights are flashing in my brain; he died of a head injury and his head had hit the pavement like a brick, that could be very important. When it came to court, our client was found not guilty, and I think that was right. If he'd been relying on the police evidence to show the whole picture, he'd have got a very different result.'

Sometimes it's the pressures of police work—the desire to close the case and see that someone pays—which cause miscarriages of justice, but sometimes it's laziness and bigotry, as Marion Smith explains. In gang cases, where it's black on black, or latino on latino, the police just put it on the first guy they get their hands on. They'll intimidate witnesses into saying the suspect did it when they really didn't do it, and that becomes the basis of their case. Then these guys will languish in jail for two, three or four years before their trial comes up.'

Marion recently worked on a case that involved just such abuse of power. Her client was a gang member but not a hard-core criminal. The police had charged him with two counts of murder and, since he was well-known in the neighbourhood, had no trouble finding witnesses they could lean on to give a positive identification in a line-up. Marion found enough evidence to feel strongly that they could beat the case but her client wasn't willing to risk it. Instead he took a plea bargain, pleading guilty to manslaughter and serving eight years.

'He decided going to trial was too much of a lottery. He was going to have to depend on his friends to come to court and depend on the jury to believe them, and I guess he just felt that the odds were stacked against him. If he'd lost the gamble, he could have gotten twenty-five to life. The eight years was a sure thing; he's done three waiting for his trial to come up, he only got eight so he only has to do another two and a half years as opposed to twenty-five to life. And because he's already done three, he knows he can do another two and a half. And this was a case where we had evidence that the guy was innocent.'

Although Marion is obviously depressed by the case, without her evidence the defendant wouldn't have been in such a good position to bargain. All too often this is the case for the PI in a system in which only a tiny number of cases actually go to trial. With the huge number of cases and the pressure this puts on the courts, there is enormous pressure to reach an agreement out of court through a plea bargain. Establishing mitigating factors may mean the defendant gets twenty years instead of fifty. As Lynn McLaren explains, for the client it is still worth it. 'I know it sounds strange to say that getting twenty years is a victory, but believe me, my clients know the difference.'

But plea bargaining can be a dangerous game to play especially with the new law that means anyone convicted three times automatically gets life. You have to think twice now about a plea bargain when you're not guilty because if you get into trouble again, you're going to go away forever. Another recent law in California means that the defence now has to make a full pre-trial disclosure to the prosecution. Lyn McLaren is bitterly opposed to this. The burden of proof should lie with the prosecution, she argues, so why should the defence help them out by giving them advance warning of the holes in their case?

Such weaknesses and pitfalls of the system are what drive the women eyes. Sandra Sutherland's career case, the defence of John De Lorean, involved a struggle against some very powerful forces within the system, including the FBI.

Once among the most successful executives in the American automobile industry, John De Lorean achieved overnight notoriety when he was arrested in 1982 on drug-trafficking charges. He'd headed nationwide divisions in the General Motors empire, quitting in 1974 because, he claimed, he was frustrated with General Motors' management. He formed his own company to develop and produce a revolutionary luxury sports car built from stainless steel, instantly identifiable by its trademark gull-wing doors.

Hugely subsidized by the British government who were desperate to attract industry to the troubled province of Northern Ireland, De Lorean went into production in Belfast. But not enough of the people who wanted to buy the car could afford it, and the company descended the downward spiral of debt. The plant went into receivership early in 1982, and the British government closed it down permanently later that year, tired of pouring money into a bottomless sump. One of the few surviving examples of John De Lorean's dream became a dream machine of another kind when it was chosen to star as the time machine of the Back To The Future films. But for De Lorean himself, the future was grim. The same day his factory was closed down for good, De Lorean was arrested in Los Angeles and charged with conspiring to import and sell large quantities of heroin and cocaine, in an alleged last-ditch effort to raise funds for his company. Following a tip-off from a supposedly reliable source, the FBI had set De Lorean up in a sting that blew up in their faces. After a twenty-two-week trial and thanks in no small part to Sandra and her partner Jack Palladino, De Lorean was acquitted in August 1984 when a jury believed his story of having been set up by the FBI.

'John De Lorean,' Sandra sighs. 'That was an unbelievable set up. De Lorean was a shit, but he wasn't a drug dealer. He just didn't look too closely at where his investment money was coming from and at the very last, he probably suspected that it was drug money. But when these two FBI agents posing as investors turned up, De Lorean called the bank and said "Are these people serious businessmen, do they have this money?" Now, if you think it's drug money you don't call the bank and draw attention to yourself. He just didn't want to think about it. He just desperately wanted money for investment. It's like people who sell another person a Mercedes for cash; no one is hauling them off to prison for twenty-five years for laundering money. I suspect we've been paid with drug money more than once, we've worked for our share of sleaze-buckets. But you don't know.

'De Lorean was victimised in a really cruel way. It ruined his life. His wife left him. He had his own little robber baron dream of selling his stupid cars, but whether he was really bad or not, it was appalling the way the FBI just did unbelievably shitty things to him. They falsified investigative reports and gave a murderer a free ride and a few hundred thousand dollars because he made an ordinary little dope case into a star case for the prosecutors when he implicated De Lorean in drug dealing.

'When people first saw the famous video of De Lorean in the hotel room with the cocaine, all they saw was what the FBI had engineered that they would see. Oh boy, can the camera lie! The reason there was cocaine in that hotel room was that the FBI had spent a lot of time and resources trying to tie John De Lorean to cocaine dealing. But they'd got nothing. They'd got all these taped conversations, all this surveillance, and they'd got absolutely nothing to take into court, nothing that suggests De Lorean was a drug dealer. There was a lot of pressure on the agents to get a result and close this thing down.

'So they come into the room with this bag of cocaine and literally throw it at him while they're filming through the wall. De Lorean just doesn't know what to do. If you look at the video-tape, you see he's looking more than a little bemused. All he says is, "Better than gold." And he's thinking, "These guys are off their heads, but they're going to give me all this money. I better not offend them." And that's really the way it was.

'John De Lorean wasn't the nicest guy in the world to be defending, but the bottom line was, he didn't do it. There's a lot of pleasure for me in watching the innocent walk free, but I have to admit there's even more pleasure when we've given the powers that be a bloody nose in the process!'

The De Lorean case was a high-profile media event involving the rich and priveleged, but far more often it is those at the other end of the social scale that become victims of the system. Many of Marion's clients have come from family situations full of neglect and abuse. The end up in juvenile court and instead of receiving the therapy and support they need, they go to Juvenile Hall and then graduate on to the long road to becoming a hardened criminal. They have no positive role models and little experience of a straight life. And as an ex-con, they've got even less chance of a job than they do as a ghetto kid.

'It starts in school,' Marion adds. 'They are failed by the education system. I get clients all the time who talk really well, they're bright, they're logical, and then you discover they literally cannot read or write. There's a guy I came across recently who's just got out of jail. He was one of the great success stories of drug dealing. He had a really solid, complex business going. He clearly had a phenomenal head for business because he'd confessed to deals all over the country. He'd been wholesaling with the Colombians, in direct contact with the drug lords, and he was completely illiterate. In prison, he learned how to read and write. Now he's out, he's thirty-four years old, and he wants to do things differently this time around. If he can do it, he'll be a millionaire. But it's going to be so hard for him not to get sucked back into that criminal mentality that says being straight is weird and boring, and who wants to pay taxes?'

Not all PIs can show such sympathy and understanding to their clients, and as Kris Kleinbauer admits, even the most sympathetic PI sometimes finds the job a struggle. 'Sometimes even with our mind-set it's hard to motivate yourself to work for the client because the crimes are so heinous. But the death penalty is just as grotesque as any crime that's been committed.'

For many women eyes working in criminal defence, one of the hardest jobs is to work on cases of rape and sexual assault. Some are simply not prepared to do it. Lynn McLaren is one of the exceptions. It's not just her belief in the right of everyone to a fair defence that motivates her in these cases. 'I've learned to be a good judge of people, and I can usually tell when a woman is telling me the truth. So I often go back to the attorney and say, "This woman has been seriously traumatised, and she knows it was our client who did this, and she is going to be very damaging in the witness box." Then the attorney can go to the client and persuade him to accept a plea bargain, which means the victim never has to go to court and testify and go through all that stuff again. When the evidence is presented to the accused by their own investigator rather than the police, it's often more compelling. Of course, some of them are so arrogant that they think they can beat the rap and they insist on going to court. I can't say I'm sorry when they get what's coming to them.'

René Olsson also believes that the PI can play a positive role with the victim in a sort of damage limitation exercise in such cases. She would rather take on a difficult case of rape or sex abuse, knowing that she would do her best to protect the victim from trauma, than leave it to another PI who might be far more ruthless and insensitive. In many cases she has worked on the victim has trusted her so much that they have phoned her for support and she has had to explain that officially she is on the other side.

Working for the supposed bad guys is especially hard when you come from a background in the police force. Having been a police officer for nearly twenty years meant Helen Kliner had some serious thinking to do before she could work in criminal defence with conviction. 'I tell myself the system has got to be safeguarded. While we may assume that most people charged with criminal offences are guilty, in my experience, there are always going to be some that aren't. I've had kind of a hard time with this because I worked on the other side of the fence for so many years. My husband is a police sergeant, my friends are police officers, my friends' husbands are police officers or retired police officers. But I do have a strong belief in the constitution and in the justice system. As long as I keep my own personal code of ethics, which is to be an honest interviewer and reporter, then I can square it with my conscience.

'I don't falsify anything. If the witness says something that's going to hurt the defendant then I will report it that way to the attorney and if I have to take the stand and testify in court and I'm asked a question that's going to hurt the defendant, I just have to tell the truth. I probably wouldn't be able to live with myself if I had to lie and twist the truth. There are people in this field that would do that and there are defence attorneys that would ask for you to do this so that they might win a case. I can't do that.

'Sometimes in some of the criminal defence cases I feel like I'm only being hired to go through the motions because when a lawyer is hired to defend someone, even if they know in their heart that they have a losing case and there is nothing that they can do, they still have to do their best and show the client that they are doing something. If that means hiring a private investigator to go and interview people, at least it looks like they are trying to do something. Even at the start of some of these cases I know they are losers. I know I'm being asked to find something that doesn't exist, evidence that will get a guilty man off. That's not a comfortable feeling.'

Blair is another PI who has obviously thought hard about the reasons she works on criminal defence cases. Blair feels that you have to believe in your client's innocence, no matter how cynical you may feel about it. One case she worked on proved her theory. Her client had confessed to murder five times but she was able to produce experts to explain why an innocent man might do that under certain circumstances. She also found discrepancies in the prosecution's version of events which supported her client's story.

Needless to say, the police weren't happy with her investigation and did everything they could to disrupt it. She discovered that her client's partner in crime had been bragging in prison in Florida that he'd got away with murder by putting the blame on him. Ten witnesses were transported from Florida State Prison across the United States on a bus. On the way there was a minor insurrection and they were beaten up by the police. Blair wasn't allowed to see them until their bruises had healed, though the police claimed that the injuries were a result of all the witnesses falling down some stairs while chained together.

Blair's managed to get her client off Death Row after ten years, but it is not just for the few cases like this that she works. 'Because the cases do mean Death Row, I had to get rid of that "I'm working to save somebody's life" routine. That really doesn't work for me. You lose too often to live with that,' she explains. 'I take the position instead that in all likelihood our client has not had a fair trial. If he had, he wouldn't be on a re-trial now. Almost certainly he had no investigators running around doing what I'm doing. He had no attorneys looking from a distance at the legalities of what went down in court and nobody looking at the angles of the actual plot. We have to go out on the street and find the whole story. And that's what fascinates me; the search for the truth, no matter how sleazy or unpalatable it is.'

Despite the sleaze and the tragedies they encounter everyday it seems that the women eyes who do criminal defence work genuinely enjoy it. Francie Koehler loves the feeling when one of her clients walks free. 'I've been really really fortunate in that I've had a few defendants who were actually innocent and because of my efforts they're not in jail. I have always said that if I had one of those that would make a whole lifetime worthwhile. Just one. But I have been fortunate enough to have had several and that's really rewarding.'

But as Blair points out, not every case can work out this way and there are other things about the job that give the women eyes a feeling of satisfaction. 'What I like about this job is the fact it allows me to be creative, resourceful,' Francie explains. 'I use every inch of my powers to get a result. You dream about it, you wake up thinking about it. It consumes you. I've had to develop new areas of expertise. Every new case is a new area, and you just learn by asking questions, and each time you meet somebody, you learn some more.'

Kris Kleinbauer agrees. 'People ask me how can you defend a killer? But that's not what it's about. It's about trying to get some justice out of the whole system, not just the legal system. That's what keeps me going. I like the work. Don't ask me why.

I guess it's the variety. I like being out there at the sharp end. You see all kinds of things. I think probably the most grisly things I've been associated with have not been down in South Central LA. It's been white folks in the suburbs.'

In order to prove her point, Kris describes one of her most gruesome cases.

'There was one where I represented this woman, back when I first started as an investigator. She knew this guy because they both worked at the same hospital. He was picking up hookers in Hollywood and he would stab them and then he would cut their heads off, make up their faces and then have sex with the head. Then he'd put the heads in the freezer. My woman was an unhappy lady who got too involved with him and finally turned him in. Then of course they charged her because one of these headless bodies was a man and they reckoned she had confessed to his killing, which I never believed. The killer is out now, supposedly all cleaned up and healthy. I actually saw him on a talk show blaming it all on her. Nice middle-class white folks.'

It's been said many times that all it takes for evil to triumph is that the good people do nothing. Doing nothing is not an accusation that can ever be levelled at these women investigators. Whether they're out there catching criminals or clearing the innocent, they are all going above and beyond the call of duty, committed to combating the flaws in the criminal justice system so that we can all feel happier that in spite of the shortcomings we can't fail to recognise, it's not a lost cause. It sounds corny, I know, but I sleep easier in the knowledge that if I ever fell foul of the system, there are women private eyes out there who would go the extra mile to safeguard me against the worst that fallible human legal systems can do.

Charles and I . . .

Gloucestershire's got more Royals per square mile than any other English county. Since they started buying houses down here, all these up and coming idiots with money and pretensions have followed, swamping the traditional county set. Some of them are real chancers. They all feed off each other's backs. If you're not in their gang, they close ranks, which makes our job pretty difficult when we've got a case that involves any of them. The Tetbury Mafia, we call them, because they seem to be centred around Highgrove, the Prince of Wales' house.

We did one case recently that brought us right up against the Tetbury Mafia. We were hired by an elderly German man who had met this woman at a Rolls-Royce rally. They got together, and she made it clear that she wanted a serious relationship, she wanted them to set up house together. He wanted to take it a bit more slowly, so she gave him the cold shoulder. He then went back to Germany and pined for her, and she said that if they had somewhere to live in England where he could come at weekends, they could get back together.

He said, 'Well, find somewhere in England. I will send you the money and we will live happily ever after.' He'd sent her the money and she'd promptly bought the property in her sole name. Meanwhile, he had also discovered that she was married with children, which he didn't know. He also suspected that she was seeing somebody else while he was in Germany.

He hired us to find out all we could about her. He was after evidence that would back up his claim against her so he could either get his house or his money back.

We found out that she had left her husband. We found the 'little' place that she had bought, which was half a village, I should think. It was beautiful. We found the boyfriend that she was seeing, a self-made millionaire character, married with kids, one of the Tetbury Mafia. He had an antiques business, and we discovered that he was clearly doing some very dodgy deals, either with stolen property or fakes. We got all of this through observations. It was a nightmare trying to get any information, because that lot just close ranks. I spent a lot of time wandering around with my toddler Samantha in the pushchair, trying to get people to gossip, but it was an uphill struggle!

We discovered that she had a china and porcelain repair business, which I knew a bit about because I used to work for Royal Doulton. So I made an appointment to go and see her and take a piece of china for repair. The night before, Brian and I decided to go out there and check out the lie of the land. We drove into this little courtyard where she had her shop among other little craft shops.

Suddenly we were surrounded by armed police. Brian goes, 'Oh, shit.' And I'm going, 'Don't panic!' as I panicked quietly. Three of them were standing in front of the car with guns drawn. There was one on either side of the car too. We wound the windows down, looking at each other, wondering what the hell we should say, because we can't really tell the truth. The police said, 'What are you doing?'

I gabbled, 'Well, I heard there was a china repair shop around here, we were just looking for it, we'll come back in the morning!'

The policeman said, 'Just sit there for a minute, don't move.' I suppose they were checking out the car. I only found out later that we were on the Prince of Wales' land at Highgrove, and that the Sultan of Brunei was over to play polo and this little courtyard of shops was close to where the two of them were that evening! Talk about cardiac arrest!

This poor old German lost out in the end. We couldn't really ever prove conclusively that his girlfriend and the antique dealer were having an affair because their properties were impossible to stake out. You can't do much when the house you're trying to watch is at the end of a dead end lane a mile long and there's no other houses for miles around. And we couldn't get people to gossip to outsiders like us, they're all so close round there.

We were working on it over a period of three months. It was costing the client an awful lot of money and there's got to be a point where you draw the line. We got so engrossed in uncovering the truth, I'm sure we billed far too little. My parents always said one day they'd get a proper job because this isn't like work! Now I know what they meant.

SUSAN NEARY
Gloucester

Val McDermid

9

I Spy...

I hate surveillance. But I know PIs, ex-police officers, mostly the guys that did vice, that love surveillance. That's all they want to do. If they weren't PIs they'd be psychos!

FRANCIE KOEHLER
Oakland

The popular image of the private eye is someone who spends half their life lurking in the bushes waiting to catch some hapless husband with his trousers down in the bedroom of another woman. The other half of their time is spent tearing up and down motorways and freeways keeping tabs on suspicious characters. While it's true that surveillance is an inevitable part of the job, the reality is quite different from either the seedy or the exciting experience people imagine it to be. For one thing, the bulk of surveillance work has nothing to do with marital suspicions. And car pursuits are nightmares.

These days, most surveillance work is related to fraud. Commercial scares and insurance cons are the biggest earners for private eyes willing to wait and watch for something to happen. Most women eyes hate this aspect of the job, but they accept it's a downside that they have to live with. Having done my share of surveillances as a journalist, I know exactly what they mean.

There's nothing glamorous about a stake-out. Often you're stuck in your car alone for hours on end with nothing to tend off the boredom except the car radio. You can't read a book, you can't do a crossword. You can't do anything that might distract your attention from the building you're watching, waiting for your target to make a move. You're either freezing because it's dead of winter and you don't want to attract attention by running your engine to get some heat into your icy limbs, or you're sitting in a puddle of sweat because the sun's beating down and your car is hotter than the fires of hell. Boredom is the enemy because boredom leads to tiredness and tiredness leads to dozing off. You can't swig coffee to stay awake because then you'll need to pee, and sure as God made little green apples, the moment you leave your post to find a toilet will be the moment when everything happens, and you've missed it.

Sometimes you have to abandon the relative comfort of your car because it's impossible to park it in a place where you can carry out the surveillance. Then you're stuck in a shrubbery or a field, and sod's law of surveillance decrees that as soon as you step into the fresh air, the heavens open. I once worked with a photographer who was the most determined operator I ever knew. Jobs with him were a nightmare. We were once doing a story that involved him sneaking a photograph of a man who lived in a small village. We couldn't park outside the house, because we'd have stuck out like a pimple on a bald head. The house was surrounded by a high wall, and when our target left, he usually drove his car straight out through the electronically controlled gates. Eventually, my colleague spotted a small clump of young trees and rhododendron bushes across the village green which gave him a clear view of the gates through his long and heavy telephoto lens. Every day at dawn he pushed his way into the bushes, armed with soft drinks, sandwiches, camera bag and tripod, and stayed there in the rain. It took three days before the target finally emerged from the house on foot and he got his pictures. Glamorous? Exciting? I don't think so.

Car chases are the other nightmare. It's always so easy on TV and in the movies. The target never spots the tail. They never slip through a traffic light on amber, leaving the tail stuck on the red; or if they do, the tail always picks them up at the next junction. Real life isn't like that. More times than I can count, I've lost someone that I've been following on a journalistic job. The first thing that goes wrong is they emerge from their drive or the car park at work and turn in the opposite direction to the one you're facing. If you manage to make a U-turn fast enough, and without a screech of tyres that alerts the target and everyone else within a half-mile radius, you can bet your life that they're going to turn right at the end of the road and by the time you get to the junction, there will be a solid line of traffic preventing you from following. If you stay right on their tail, they'll soon notice that the same car is behind them all the way, unless they're so absent-minded they never check their mirrors. But if you hang back, leaving a few cars between you, you know you're going to lose them at the first set of lights or roundabout. Say for the sake of argument you manage to stay with them as far as the motorway. Chances are they're driving a powerful car, while you're in some insignificant workhorse chosen for its anonymity rather than its horsepower. They head straight for the fast lane and disappear over the distant horizon while you're still trying to gun your engine above sixty.

The other problem with surveillance is the curiosity of the rest of the world. These days, chances are if you sit in a street in your car for a few hours, someone from the Neighbourhood Watch will call the cops. Even if you are a woman and they're not convinced you're a burglar. Next thing you know, you've got a uniformed bobby leaning on your car asking politely what exactly you're doing there. So much for being unobtrusive. I remember one occasion where a photographer and I were staking out a private clinic, checking out which doctors were working there. The clinic was on the first floor above a row of shops, which included a jeweller's. We were holed up in the doorway of the Job Centre across the street. My photographer was standing behind me, his long lens resting on my shoulder. We'd been there about an hour when a police car screeched to a halt in front of us, blue light flashing. Someone in the jeweller's had spotted us and thought we were a gang of armed robbers staking out their shop....

Inevitably, things go wrong on surveillances. Because it's so difficult to get right, there are even more potential pitfalls than in the average job a PI does. And operatives have to take that into consideration right from the start. 'If somebody phones up wanting observation work, I tell them I want paying so much up front because sometimes you don't find anything because there's nothing going on,' Jackie Griffiths explains. 'You can be sitting out there for hours on end and then the client turns round and says, "He didn't do anything. You haven't told me anything. I'm not paying for that." Well, I'm sorry, I was there. I can't make them do things and I'm not going to invent things either just to make the report sound interesting. I report what happens, and if nothing happens, that's my report. Some observation work can turn out to be very expensive and there's nothing to show for it at the end of it. But the work still has to be paid for. I also insist on meeting them first. I want to know why they want this person followed and to get as much information as they've got. But I tell them up front, there are no guarantees.'

In spite of all these drawbacks, some women eyes admit they enjoy surveillance because of the challenge it offers in terms of skill and creativity. Ex-police officer Christine Usher has even chosen to become an expert in the field. But surveillance is almost never a single-handed job, and getting a strong team together can be a headache. 'It's difficult to find people you can rely on, because it's a position of trust. I suppose what I worry about is that they're projecting me. They represent me outside the office and so I want it done my way. My way works. That's the reason I've got so much work, that's why I don't need to advertise, because the insurance companies like it done the way I'm doing it. They know they get an honest report. If we haven't achieved any-thing they still get a report on it, and if we have, well and good. You can't make things happen on a surveil-lance, but that's an area that's open to abuse. I know agencies who take the money and do nothing. They say, "Oh sorry, he didn't move all night," but then they haven't been there all night. How does the client know? They don't, do they? So when I employ people they've got to be trustworthy, they've got to know the law, criminal and civil, and work to my guidelines and the moral code that I stipulate,' she says firmly.

As Christine explains, surveillance is exhausting and often frustrating work. It is incredibly hard to follow someone in a moving vehicle and demands constant concentration, particularly if you're dictating a commentary. Is the subject going to stop, is she going to go shopping, is she going to get on the bus, go on a train? It can also be expensive—if you abandon your car, you get a ticket or towed away. And if you skip a red light you're in danger of getting stopped by the police and given penalty points, not to mention losing your target. On cases in London, Christine often uses a motorcyclist because it's easier for them to weave through the traffic after a target and since there are so many couriers about, a motorcycle is inconspicuous in the city. Unfortunately they are much more noticeable in the countryside and cannot be used if video evidence is needed.

'You have to develop patience. I remember one January day where I was sat in the back of the van in London from about five in the morning until gone seven at night. It was pouring down with rain all day and I was absolutely frozen, but I wasn't moving until I had seen this bloke. I think most people would just have gone home at lunchtime. But that's where my police experience comes in handy. When you're doing surveillance on serious crime you can sit there for days, weeks and months. It might be twelve months before you get a result. So I don't find it difficult just to sit there. You can't leave to go to the loo; that's where the good old Tupperware comes in useful I'm afraid.' Christine gives one of those stiff upper lip smiles that the British Empire was built on.

It takes more than patience to make a good surveillance expert, however. Before any of that begins it is vital to do the homework, make sure you have the right person and the right address. The more information you have, the more likely you are to get a result, and the less time you will have to spend sitting waiting. Getting the information without alerting the subject isn't always easy and many of the women eyes have developed clever tricks to get what they need.

If you can't be imaginative, you might as well go home, as Jean Mignolet has discovered. Although it's not an area of work that she enjoys, she believes that some of the most creative opportunities in the business are surveillances. Like the time she was hired by two women to check up on their boyfriends. The men were supposedly on a fishing holiday and had hired a huge yacht. Their girlfriends suspected that they were going to use it to pick up girls. To hire another boat and follow the men up the waterways would have been expensive and conspicuous so Jean tried a different approach.

'Myself and another girl, who was very attractive, dressed up in our sexiest outfits and went out to one of the bars where they were and basically picked them up. We found out their schedule for the entire week! So we knew exactly where they were going to be on any given day. That way, I could have my surveillance guy posted wherever they were. You have to think of ways of achieving a result for the client when you're on a budget!'

Chicago's Sarah Di Venere is the undisputed queen of the surveillance ruse. She adores the challenge of using disguises, cover stories and ruses to carry out the surveillances that are a key part of her work in exposing Workman's Compensation cheats.

'I think that being an investigator is fun because you have to figure out how you're going to get information where a policeman uses a badge. They can automatically expect respect and cooperation. In theory, at least. Investigators have to think, how am I going to get this stuff, and that's why it's interesting. It's one of the things I love about good mystery novels—I see the characters looking for a way to get some information, and it's exactly the kind of process I go through too. You can have something in your mind that you're going to do and when you walk up to that door you may have to switch just like that.'

One of Sarah's oldest ruses involves keeping a dog leash and pictures of her cat and dog in the car. 'If I want to find out whether somebody is going out to work, I'll walk up to the next door neighbour's house with a picture of my dog and say, "I was visiting somebody in the area and my dog got loose, have you seen this dog around? Somebody down the street told me that this guy next door was seen patting a dog like this. Do you know where this guy is? Can you tell me what time he goes to work? Do you know where he works so that I can call him?" I've even got tears in my eyes! With a dog leash and a photograph, you can go anywhere. You can walk in back yards, you can peer through windows. And the neighbours will not be suspicious, they'll tell you exactly what you want to know and more.'

Sarah generally uses women agents for surveillance but will sometimes use a man and a woman together. 'I think that sometimes the job is like a dance. They can complement each other and I think that as couples they're useful; they don't cause as much attention when they're following somebody.'

Being inconspicuous is the name of the game in surveillance and this has become doubly difficult since the beginning of Neighbourhood Watch schemes. On short jobs, sitting on the passenger side makes the PI look much less conspicuous, especially a woman eye. People generally assume she is a patient wife waiting for her husband!

On longer surveillances remaining unnoticed becomes even harder, although sometimes this isn't the disadvantage it might seem, as Pam Quinney discovered. 'People will always suss you out eventually. We had one a few years ago where we had to keep a house under surveillance for about fifteen hours a day for a fortnight. Well, the neighbours soon spotted us and they loved it. They used to bring us out cups of tea! We got quite friendly. We even had people lurking about in the bushes taking photographs of us because they'd never seen real private eyes before!'

On another occasion, Pam got chatting with a woman who ran a shop close to her surveillance target. The shopkeeper was so fascinated by the idea of being a detective that she began to help out, noting down movements in and out of the house and filling Pam in with all the details.

On a long surveillance in a residential area, Sarah Di Venere often deliberately befriends a neighbour. The first thing she will do is go to a house where there are children's toys outside. She talks to the mother, telling her that she is a private eye watching for a teenage runaway, a story which will gain sympathy from any mother. Usually the woman will be more than happy to let Sarah sit in her driveway, which makes her much less conspicuous, and also means that she is less likely to attract attention from the local Neighbourhood Watch group.

To help with such ruses, Sarah always brings a gift, and has discovered that chocolate chip cookies work particularly well. 'Doormen are great with cookies. If it's a locked building and you take them chocolate chip cookies that you make yourself, I guarantee that you'll get in. With pets and food you can get a lot of information!'

Photographs of animals and tins of cookies are not the tools usually associated with the PI's work. If the movies are anything to go by, they all use high-tech equipment and clever disguises. Christine Usher fits this image more closely, using the latest sophisticated electronic gadgets. Among the surveillance equipment she uses there is a jacket which incorporates a video recorder with the lens in the lapel. Designed for men, the jacket is cumbersome for her to wear, but she's been so impressed by its usefulness, she's having one tailor-made for herself!

The video camera is an important tool for Christine. Normally she uses ordinary hand-held cameras which record the date and time, a great help when providing evidence in court. Christine takes pride in providing the best possible standard of evidence. 'I approach every job with the idea that I might have to stand up in court and back up my work. I'm doing what the client requires, but at the same time, I have my own mental standard of proof that I know will stand up in court. Some investigators just want to do the job and get their money. Not me. I want the job done to the highest standard.'

For surveillances in offices, bugs are a vital tool. Because Pat Storey's company is a general business that takes all sorts of cases, she is used to running surveillance in a wide variety of cases. 'We're doing more commercial fraud inquiries these days. We've been involved where a company employs a guy and they've got suspicions he's thinking of setting up in the same line of business elsewhere. We have to find out what he's up to, and one of the first things we do is to put a hard-wired bugging device on his office phone. We can tape his calls inside the office perfectly legitimately because we're being asked to do it by the person who is paying the phone bill, i.e. the company. It's amazing how much information that produces. It certainly points you in the right direction. Then we do observations on where he's going, what he's doing, who he's seeing. Suddenly you've got a picture of what's going on here, and within weeks you've got enough evidence to get rid.'

Pat points out the importance of obtaining evidence legally. 'When you stand up in court to give evidence, which you may well in any surveillance case, you've got to tell them how you got that information.' If the methods are illegal the information is inadmissible, however damning it is to the defendant. Courts are becoming increasingly aware of the tendency by some agencies to act as agent provocateur, particularly in insurance fraud cases, and now if there is any suspicion that a target has been set up, for example by letting down their car tyres to see if they are capable of changing a wheel, the court will throw out the case.

On surveillance jobs that involve following the subject's car, Sarah Di Venere will use several agents in different cars, communicating by two-way radio. That way the subject is less likely to get lost or spot the tail. Since most subjects are alive to the idea that they may be followed it is vital to swap the tail car regularly to avoid being spotted.

'It's not like on the TV,' explains Jackie Griffith. 'Everybody looks in their rear-view mirror, they see the same car and you're spotted; you hang back a couple of cars and you lose them at junctions, especially at night. It's not easy.'

Like Sarah, Jackie has sometimes used two cars for surveillance, like the time when she was hired to keep tracks on a philandering husband. On her first attempt, the man spotted her, so the following night she parked in an obvious place outside his home and allowed him to think he had lost her by setting off in the opposite direction. Little did he know that her own husband was poised to pick up the tail. He was able to follow the man to a hotel where he was meeting his mistress. Jackie's husband phoned her and she passed the information on to her client, who headed straight out to the hotel to confront her wayward partner.

Of course it's not always possible to have more than one agent on the case, or to use sophisticated equipment. For some women eyes, a false wig and a pair of sunglasses are as important tools of the trade as video cameras or telephone bugs.

Sarah Di Venere carries wigs, glasses and spare clothes with her in her car. She uses disguises regularly and points out that a quick change of appearance is much easier for women than it is for men. 'We can change our height really easily by changing our shoes from flats to heels, we can switch from jeans to a skirt and look completely different. There's only so much that a guy can do, and he can't do it in thirty seconds crouched down in his car.' One of Sarah's favourite items is a long wrap-round skirt. It takes a matter of seconds for her to throw it on and roll up her trousers to completely change her image. And she has discovered that it has other uses on long stakeouts, too. 'This skirt is real handy if I have to nip into the bushes to pee; it just spreads out round me and keeps me totally private!'

Another favourite of Sarah's is a pair of sunglasses that sound like they were invented by James Bond's Q. They have silvered mirrors on the inside edge of the lenses so that the wearer can see behind her. 'I literally have eyes in the back of my head. I add to that a genuine blind person's cane and a white stick. Nobody thinks they're under surveillance from a blind person!'

Disguises aren't always quite so successful, as Helen Kliner has discovered. The only time she used one—a black wig—she was immediately spotted in the street by an old friend! It was an embarrassing moment that has put her off disguises for life.

Whether they are kitted out in a wig and sunglasses or simply wearing their own clothes, the most important thing about a woman eye's appearance while on surveillance is that it shouldn't make her stand out. 'Being Ms Anonymous didn't come easy to me at first,' admits Susan Lauman, 'because by nature I'm a pretty flamboyant personality. On my very first surveillance job, I turned up wearing red, white and blue. My boss winced and said plaintively, "Don't you have anything in tan?" Now, I go out to work looking like an Italian widow; people in New York City wear a lot of black!

'You spend so long being self-effacing that sometimes it's hard to remember who you really are. The way I feel rooted is to hang on to the things I believe in, and remind myself that what I see in the mirror is only a surface.'

Trying to blend in becomes even more difficult when you don't know where the client is going. An outfit that is perfect for the street might stick out like a sore thumb in a smart restaurant or club. Knowing what the target is planning to do can sometimes pose problems of its own, however, as Susan Lauman knows from bitter experience. 'One time, I was keeping surveillance on a doctor. I knew he was going to come out of his office and go to a fancy restaurant, so I was dressed to fit in with the restaurant. I was wearing a thin cocktail dress and high heels, and I was out on the sidewalk for three hours with the temperature around freezing point. I thought I was going to die of cold. But I couldn't dress up warmly, because rich women in New York don't. They never go anywhere that isn't a temperature controlled environment. They go from their centrally heated apartment into the warm car into the cosy restaurant or the warm shops. If I'd turned up at the restaurant in a heavy winter coat, I'd have stuck out immediately as somebody who didn't belong there. You have to blend in at all costs. You have to be non-memorable. Even if you're not average looking, you have to work at making yourself look that way. You just can't afford to stand out.'

Visiting smart restaurants and clubs might be seen as one of the perks of surveillance work. Janet Wilson made it her speciality. She works as a pub spy, a hired gun whom breweries send in to check out what was really going on in bars where they suspected all was not running according to the book. Having worked in the pub business, she has a real insight into the world and found she had a natural flair for investigation. 'You have to know how to act, how to react, how to interact with customers and staff, how to mix in, what excuses to use. I was used to being in all sorts of places because of having done relief work where you don't choose where you go, you're just sent. We've done pubs that have very, very bad associations. I don't want to go into detail, but obviously we are talking about the criminal fraternity. I've done places where we've come out of the premises and I've made sure we weren't being followed by diverting from one tube line to another, not going directly to the railway station, always moving around, checking that we're on our own.

'We've had situations where the manager has obviously been forewarned that spies were coming in, so obviously they're going to try their damnedest to make it look as if everything is straight. Roger and I went into one pub where the manageress made a grand entrance, I've never seen anything like it. She was wearing a long silver evening gown. And this was in a basic community pub, council houses, slightly upmarket of the Rover's Return. And there she is in this gown! The bar staff were running around like lunatics emptying ashtrays and collecting glasses. She was looking round, desperately trying to spot the spies she was expecting, but of course we'd been in before on a preliminary reconnaissance, making the excuse of looking at a house down the road which was for sale and wanting to see what the local pub was like, so we weren't entirely new faces. That made people feel comfortable with us. It's important that you don't stand out. Well, you can imagine the report that went in from us! A lot of couples are dismissed as a result of the reports we produce. It reached the stage where when the unions saw our reports, they recognised our name and they would just back down.'

Janet proved so effective at scouting out misdemeanors in the pubs she visited that she had to start taking on more staff to cover all the jobs that were flooding in. She ended up with teams ot agents all over the country, as organised as a KGB network. As her reputation grew, Janet expanded her business to include restaurants and nightclubs and began to get international assignments, travelling around Europe checking out bars and restaurants for their owners. A trip to Paris for Janet might mean visiting three restaurants a day, followed by a visit to a top nightclub or two every evening, while a visit to Ibiza might might mean checking out the local disco, or even a gay bar.

'People say what a great job, you can go to pubs, clubs and restaurants every night! But they don't realise it's work. When we have a day off, we'll go anywhere to get away from them!' Of course not all the clubs and restaurants Janet visits are glamorous hot spots; often they will be grotty dives where the staff are ripping off the punters or the clientele are all dangerous criminals. If she's not enjoying an expensive French meal Janet could just as easily be photographing a stinking blocked Spanish toilet.

Still, photographing lavatories is a mere bagatelle compared to some of the difficult and uncomfortable surveillance assignments the women eyes have taken on. Pam and Jane Quinney once had to keep surveillance on a refuse tip. It was the kind of job that would put many off private investigation for life.

'We were in a hedge, under all these bushes, and the ground was moving with rats. There was a field of pigs behind us. These pigs were inches away from our faces, so we had the rear ends of these boars to contend with as well. You can imagine! We were convinced they'd all had baked beans for breakfast! I just couldn't believe what I was doing, lying around with cameras and binoculars under this smelly hedge. There were guys with guns and dogs patrolling this tip, and we're stuck there, praying they wouldn't spot us. It was wet and foggy as well. And people think this job is so glamorous!'

...And Never Called Me Mother

There's one adoption case that sticks in my mind because of the powerful emotions it stirred up. My client was adopted when she was a few days old. She's forty now. Adoption records are sealed in this state, so in adoption cases, you start with your client. How much information they know. Bits and pieces they've picked up over the years that they're not sure about the accuracy of. How much they've been told by their adoptive parents, bearing in mind that may not be true. What they know of their adopted family's history, where they lived before. That has something to do with where the adoption procedure took place, unless they went to China or someplace! I try to put some of those pieces together to figure out where to start searching.

This woman had been told that the doctor who had been her paediatrician had also been the paediatrician for her biological mother. First step was searching down that doctor. Dead. So I went to probate court to find out who had control of his assets and see if they still had the files. Too long ago. They'd been destroyed.

I went back to the forty-year-old street lists for the town where she'd been born, figuring if they both had the same paediatrician they probably both lived in the same part of town. Then I moved forward year by year through the street lists to see if any of the old families still lived there. No dice. Town's changed much too much.

My client only had a wallet-sized birth certificate that her adopted parents had given her. So I went down to Vital Statistics to look at the full-sized copy in her adopted name. There wasn't one. As far as the State of

Massachusetts was concerned, she didn't exist. If she lost that piece of paper, she has no way of getting a birth certificate. So I went back to the town she was supposedly born in. I went to the hospital. They'd had a major fire and all their records had been destroyed. I went to the town hall. They'd had a fire and they had no record of this person, period, end of story. So there are absolutely no official records of her birth.

My client had one other relevant piece of paper. There is a face sheet on court records called a docket and it has a minimal amount of information on it: case number, the name of the Plaintiff and Defendant. Her adopted mother had given her that. So we knew the name that her biological mother had used. So I started tracing that last name back through old telephone directories, through old street directories in the general geographic area we were looking in. We came up with a bunch of possibilities. I called every one of them but none of them worked out. They were not connected to my client's mother. By this time, I'm starting to wonder if my client really exists!

As a last resort, I went back to Vital Statistics and looked up birth certificates in the name her biological mother had used. Now, it shouldn't have been there. It should have been stapled to her adopted certificate and the whole record should have been sealed. But there it was, the certificate in her birth name. Because somebody had screwed up somewhere along the line, I found it.

The birth certificate gave the name of the paediatrician, which confirmed what she had been told. Now we had names for the father, the mother, their parents' names, street addresses at the time of birth, and place of birth of both the father and mother. The mother was born in Cambridge. So I went down to Cambridge records to try and find this mother's birth certificate. I found it and then looked for other birth certificates for siblings and found some. I checked whether any of them still lived in Cambridge. All gone.

Then I started trawling through the Family Court records and what I finally found was a divorce between the mother and the father. The divorce record had lots of information in it, and eventually that led us to the stuff that really moves an investigation along—social security numbers, last known address, that kind of thing. At that point, it just becomes a missing person trace, which is pretty straightforward.

I knew then I was either going to find the mother, or find that she was dead. I managed to track down brothers and sisters of the mother. I told my client, and she decided she didn't want to go any further. She didn't want me to contact them.

In a case like this, you know that you're opening up somebody's whole life, and every step you're taking has repercussions for them, because that step can never be undone. It really sticks with me, that sense of responsibility. You can't be wrong. You can't come up with the wrong person. And every piece of information that moves you a little closer has to be right so that even if you get hit by a truck tomorrow somebody else should be able to take over. There is a level of responsibility at every stage of adoption searches that is different to other cases where you can pick up the pieces, you can backtrack if you say the wrong thing, or you can retrieve the situation if somebody gets wind of something.

It took her a couple of years to decide to continue and finally go through with it. It turned out that she had this huge biological family, lots of brothers! She asked me to make the phone call to set up the meeting and to go with her. She didn't want to go alone. She wanted me also to do most of the talking for the first hour.

When my client and I pulled up to the house, her half-siblings were there with their families. They knew right away which one of us was their sister because she looked just like other people in the family. It was remarkable. They all ran to her and she said, 'How did you know it was me?'

And they said, 'Come in the house and we'll show you, you look just like us!' There was this amazing mixture of human emotions. The biological mother had to explain why she hid this secret and why she never told anybody. A lot of things fell into place for the kids that they hadn't understood before, little bits and pieces in a kid's life that they somehow feel ill at ease with, but don't know why. The siblings were thrilled to find this person, but they were furious with their mother who had lied to them their whole life. The mother was thrilled because she had wanted to know what had happened but had never known how, but was not happy at having to sit there and be in the hot seat and to answer questions.

My client was just numb and wasn't absorbing half of it, I was taking notes. It was really remarkable to watch everybody's lives change at that minute. Everybody in that room, their lives changed when we walked in the door. There's not much you can do in this life that changes fifteen or twenty people's lives immediately, and I got to sit there and watch it happen. Most cases I work on, I change a dynamic in a case, I might change somebody's freedom or I might get somebody a piece of information they need to know. But in these cases and in this one in particular, to watch this roomful of people was really mind blowing. All these feelings, good and bad, anger and joy, knowledge and distrust; it was really very powerful. That will stay with me always. It was like watching lightning hitting somebody else's house.

BRYNA ARONSON
Boston

10

Human Elements

*A lot of funny things happen in this job. Even in the
heaviest cases, things happen that crack you up.*

PAT STOREY
Birmingham

*When you go out on a job, to you it's just another case.
But you have to remember that this is the probably the biggest
event that's ever happened in these people's lives. You have to
be really sensitive. Caring and also a complete bulldog. You
have to go out there and work every case like it's your last.*

RENÉ OLSSON
Seattle

Taking the decision to become a private eye means that
your life will never be the same again. It's one of those
occupations that it's impossible to treat as just another
job. You'd have to have a heart of stone to remain
dispassionate and emotionally distant faced with other
people's life crises on a daily basis, in the same way that
doctors never see their patients when they're healthy,
private eyes never get hired unless somebody somewhere
has a problem.

Most of the careers where human misery is such a major part of the daily grind have in-built support systems of some kind. The Fire, Ambulance and Police Services all have the camaraderie of teamwork, as well as counselling services specifically tailored to their needs. Doctors and nurses have a similar structure. They have people to share the horrors and the black humour that flows alongside the human tragedies. Journalists have the rest of the pack to relax with in the pub at the end of the job, swapping stories and slagging off the rest of the world. Not private eyes. They tend to work solo, and even if they're active members of an organisation, they only meet occasionally. They're like writers in that sense. But for us writers, the horrors only happen inside our head. For private eyes, they're all too real.

They serve injunctions on people whose dreams of a happy marriage have turned into a bitter and violent nightmare. They sit in scummy apartments in desolate neighbourhoods ravaged by drug wars and hear the hopeless stories of the dispossessed. They deliver the papers that prove people's hopes and ambitions have finally drowned in a sea of debt. They sit with clients who are looking down Death Row and seeing their face under the helmet of the electric chair and they try to find a chink in the prosecution's case that might make the difference between life and the long walk. They listen to children sobbing out the stories of their abuse. They watch grown men cry because they're not going to see their children again. And somehow, in the teeth of all this pain, they have to maintain a professional facade. They have to swallow the emotions that rise up inside them and not only deal with the person who's suffering but also get the job done.

It would be easy to become hardened, to adopt cynicism as a defence. I saw little evidence of that among the women I interviewed, and even those who professed to have become cynical in their job clearly had gaps in their armour a mile wide where cases sneak in and lodge themselves deep in their consciousness. It's obvious from the clarity with which they recall traumatic cases they have dealt with.

It would be easy too to have contempt for the weak and the gullible, to despise them and label them 'natural born victims', but I saw no evidence of that either. Women like Maureen Jacques-Turner and Jackie Griffiths, constantly faced with a procession of people who have got into debt entirely through their own fecklessness, do not condemn; they may feel exasperation, but they also feel sympathy.

What seems to keep the women PIs going is the successes they score. It's a kind of trade-off against the misery that they achieve results that have a profound effect on people's lives. They do prevent clients from being sent to the electric chair. They do manage to get children out of abusive situations. They do trace the missing person whose absence has made an aching hole in the lives of their clients. They do uncover the evidence that gets cases settled so that claimants can start to rebuild their lives.

They also find elements of the job that give them particular satisfaction. For Zena Scott-Archer, report writing was the key to keeping the job in perspective and staying in touch with the human aspect of the work. 'I've always found doing my reports was a real challenge. I approach them as if I were writing a novel, where it's vital to convey the whole picture to the reader. I did a job once for a woman whose baby had been snatched from her by her husband, who was Indian. He had taken the baby back to India and she didn't see him again. She divorced the husband and got married again but when the boy was seventeen years old she began to wonder how he had turned out and where he was. She didn't want him back in her life, she didn't want contact, she just wanted to know how he was doing.

'I made inquiries and tracked the young man down. When my secretary typed up the report she said, "The man just grew in front of my eyes. His colour, his height, right down to his fingernails and the way he did things. It was wonderful!" I think my client was pleased, but my secretary was delighted. She said it was better than reading a novel!'

It's not always quite so satisfying, however. Being a PI certainly brings you into contact with the seedy side of life, the secrets that most people keep hidden from public view, from the bizarre to the disgusting to the downright comical. 'People are extraordinary,' Zena states knowingly. 'Once, a colleague and I were installing a bug behind the headboard of a bed at the client's request. When my colleague moved the headboard away from the wall, out fell what looked at first like a collection of dead mice. On closer inspection, they turned out to be mouldy used teabags! What you might call the unsavoury side of the job....But we were making up all sorts of bizarre stories for a long time afterwards, trying to come up with some sort of explanation as to what they were doing there in the first place. Some strange sexual aid, perhaps?' She laughs wickedly.

Oh yes, the weird sense of humour. They've all got it. Sometimes, it's a bitter gallows humour that to outsiders can sound cruel and exploitative, like the sick OJ Simpson jokes which sprouted like weeds within days of the former football star's arrest. But it's the kind of defence mechanism psychologists tell us we'd go crazy without. I'm with the psychologists on this one.

Certainly the women eyes can find humour in the strangest of circumstances. 'Even in the heaviest cases, things happen that crack you up,' Pat Storey acknowledges. 'Probably because the cases are so heavy, you're more desperate to see the funny side.' She recalls a particularly horrible surveillance case she did. A husband and wife had parted company and the husband had taken the four children to go and live with another woman and her four children. They had told their mother that they were forced out of the house at six a.m. and had to dress and have breakfast on the doorstep. Pat was sent to investigate and sure enough, at six o'clock on a cold February morning, four children appeared on the doorstep in their pyjamas, got dressed and waited there until it was time to go to school.

Pat was furious with what she saw, but she remembers the case so vividly because of the strange incident that happened on the third day of the surveillance. 'While I'm sat there watching them, some woman had clocked me, seen I'm a blonde—not natural these days! The third day, she tapped on the window and asked if I was Myra Hindley! I was gobsmacked. I've been taken for lots of things in my time, but never a mass murderer. I said of course I wasn't and she went on her merry way. I was sitting there on pins, waiting for the fuzz to arrive—I was sure she was going to ring them up and say, "Myra Hindley's escaped and she's stalking a bunch of kids in Birmingham!" Completely bizarre!'

Pat can laugh at this story now, but at the time it was no laughing matter. Not only was she genuinely concerned about the children's welfare but she had to worry about being exposed by the attention of one interfering old lady, which would spoil the work she was doing. One of the problems with a high-stress job like this is that you don't always realise how strung out you are until you stop. René Olsson found that after she switched from general investigations to her financial speciality. 'When I changed course, I started sleeping again. I suddenly realised I hadn't slept very well for six years, and a lot of it was the stuff that I was taking home with me.

'I was dealing with thirteen-year-old abused kids that would decide I was the one they were finally going to spill their guts to about the terrible things that had happened to them. People do rely on you, it's like you've got their whole life in your hands. They think you're God for solving their problems. It's a lot of responsibility and you don't have as much control as you think you do.

'When you go out on a job, to you it's just another case. But you have to remember that this is probably the biggest event that's ever happened in these people's lives. You have to be really sensitive; caring and also a complete bulldog. You have to go out there and work every case like it's your last. There's so much heartache in this job that you just think sometimes, for the money you make it's not worth it.

'Sure, you gain a lot of satisfaction from general investigative work, but your life changes completely. I know the difference between my life before, my life when I was doing the all-purpose investigations and my life now, and you don't realise what a toll it takes on you until you step away from it. And I'm someone who really loved the work. At least now I get to sleep nights.'

The cases that stick in the minds of the women eyes are not always the most spectacular or the ones they dealt with most brilliantly. Often, it's the human element that turns an otherwise routine case into something that stays with an investigator forever. Zena again; 'Overnight successes come and go; the ones I remember are the ones that took time, that made demands on me and that worked out in a positive way.'

One such case involved an Australian man who wished to track down a former girlfriend. He knew that she was married and had a son but not what her married name was. Zena went to her former address and was told that her married name was Rutter and that she was living with her son, who was a solicitor. It seemed an easy job to track down a solicitor called Rutter but after months of work, Zena had got nowhere. In frustration she returned to the original source of information. When she explained her problem the woman realised that she had made a mistake. The name was Nutter not Rutter. A simple error had cost Zena three months' work, but at least perseverance paid off and she was able to wrap up the case in a matter of hours.

Another case that sticks in Zena's mind was memorable not for her own hard work but as an example of how devious people can be. Her client's father was virtually senile. His housekeeper was determined to marry him and inherit all his wealth. She had taken him along to the register office and told him that he was to be a witness to a wedding when in reality it was his own wedding. He clearly didn't know what he was doing and was hardly even able to sign his name on the register. The bride had even asked the registrar if she could guide his hand when it came to the signing. Thanks to Zena's work, the marriage was dissolved and the woman's plans failed. 'She was a villain,' says Zena firmly, 'not an obvious villain committing burglary, but a villain none the less. I've always remembered that case because it shows how devious seemingly respectable people can be.'

Inevitably, some cases burst through the Chinese wall PIs build between their work and their private lives. Susan Neary found herself befriending the widow of a gambler, who suddenly discovered that her husband had hocked everything from the house to the car to finance his habit. The woman had no idea how to cope with the debt mountain that threatened to engulf her, so she turned to the private eye who had served the debt collection papers on her. They became quite close, with the widow calling Susan regularly, sometimes for help, but sometimes just to chat. Brenda Balmer felt so sorry for one family she'd had dealings with that when the son died, she organised the funeral. But generally, the women try to keep the individuals they deal with at arm's length; any other course of action would swiftly swamp their lives.

'There are cases occasionally where one is affected by something and it sticks in your mind, but that's the exception,' Diana Middleton says. 'You have to learn to treat it as a job, no matter how harrowing it is at the time. In the police force you learn to cope with everything; back when I was on the force you had to. There was none of the counselling that they get now. You went out and dealt with a nasty murder or a fatal accident where you were scraping bits of somebody off the ground, and you went back to finish the shift and go off home, end of case. But some things do penetrate that shell you construct. Occasionally something happens and you worry about it.'

A tragedy involving young children has proved impossible for Diana to forget. 'The case involved a couple who were divorcing. The issue was the father's access to his two daughters and the judge directed that we make enquiries. I took statements from both of them, and from the maternal grandmother who sounded fairly neutral. That of course told in his favour, because you'd expect her to be biased against him. The judge decided that the father could have access to these two little girls.

'A short while later, the father had his daughters staying at his place. He was alone with them and he drowned one of them in the bath. Luckily the other one managed to get away. My involvement was indirect, but I've never forgotten it. That case has always stuck in my mind, and every time I deal with children, it comes back as a flashback.'

It's not surprising that the case that stays so firmly in the front of Diana's mind involves children. Many of the women I spoke to talked of these cases as being the ones that distressed them, whether or not they have children of their own. There is something about damaged children that speaks to us on a deep level and provokes an anger that nothing else does. One of the prime motivations for Joan Beach in her child custody work is to prevent children being hurt any further by the break-up of their family.

Joan is considered an expert witness in child custody evaluations. 'I do a neutral report, no matter who my client is. But it's only neutral in the sense that I don't take sides between the parents. In reality, I'm on the side of the children, and I'm totally focused on discovering what would be the best outcome for them.' To make her report, Joan meets both parents and the child and with other witnesses like schoolteachers, neighbours, friends, so she can make a full appraisal of the child and parents. Over the years Joan has become adept at seeing the signs that show if a child, or parent, is unhappy and disturbed. 'I have my own standard format after all these years. Tell me your name, where you were born, tell me about your parents, are they still living, tell me about school, your education. I find that if the parents answer the questions in the first part of the evaluation within an hour, we're probably looking at a fairly straightforward situation. When they take two hours to do it, I know right away that something is troubling them. Often they're so bitter and unhappy that you can see why their children have problems. That's a dead giveaway.'

Another giveaway is the attorney that the parents have selected. Some attorneys have a reputation for pugilism. They will do anything to see their client wins the case, no matter what the rights and wrongs are. A difficult attorney usually means a difficult client and a difficult case.

Despite Joan's years of experience, she hasn't yet learnt to completely cut herself off from the cases she works on. 'When I've done a custody case, I'll think about it for a long time and wonder if I'd added one more piece...sometimes I don't get closure right away. Other times, it's over and I'm out.'

There are far worse things that can happen to a child than being trapped between warring parents and private eyes see those things too. Francie Koehler still can't get out of her head the very first child molestation case she did, right at the start of her career as a private investigator. The victim was a four-year-old girl called Gina. Francie was working for the defence. Her client was the father of a little boy who was a neighbour of Gina, and the cops said that's how he had come into contact with her.

Gina lived with her mother, her stepfather and her three younger siblings in a two-bedroomed apartment in the projects. The truth was that she was being molested by her mother and stepfather. But there is a phenomenon called transferable trauma where, because what's happening is so close to them that they can't handle it, children transfer the blame to somebody else. This is what Gina had done. She told her little girlfriend who was five, who then told her mother who reported it to the deputies.

By the time Francie came on the case, her client had already been in jail for three months. The breakthrough came when she went with Gina's little friend and her mother to the back-yard where the friend had supposedly witnessed the abuse.

'I had her walk through what happened.' Francie explains.

'She said, "But that's not what Gina told me."

'I went, "What?"

'And she said again, "That's not what Gina told me." I looked at her mom, and she looked at me. Then the whole story comes out, the real story. The little girl hadn't witnessed anything directly. She said, "Gina said that they would kill her if she told." Then all the pieces that had made me uneasy started fitting together. I had been to see Gina, and her mom let me take her in my car to get an ice cream cone. Yet I was a stranger. And Gina had wanted me to buy her mum some cigarettes, which made me feel that her mom was evidently using her.'

Her client was exonerated, but that didn't mean Francie ended up feeling good about the case. 'They took the kids away from the mom but they couldn't find a place for them. Their real father wouldn't take them, his parents wouldn't take them. Finally, their maternal grandmother took them to live with her in Bakersfield. A month later Gina's mom moved to Bakersfield and probably the same story is being repeated there. Tragic.'

Pursuing cases like this is often more harrowing for private investigators than it is for other professionals, not only because they lack the formal support systems, but also because in order to be a good PI, you have to have imagination and empathy. Faced with the horrible things that happen to children, those qualities become a massive handicap. Many women spoke to me of the depression that can follow cases like this, especially when things haven't worked out the way they had hoped.

'Losing a case is the hardest thing,' Blair says wearily. 'We lost a case last year for a number of reasons. We'd been working on it for three and a half years. And my boss and I both wanted to go home and fall into bed and just never get up again because we felt that this man's case was defensible, and nobody, nobody got behind us.

'Like so many of our clients, he had been grievously brutalised as a child, and that had certainly contributed to what he'd done. Child abuse has become one of my pet things. If the stories I've heard from my clients are representative, and I have no reason to suppose otherwise, well over ninety per cent of inmates on Death Row have been savagely abused, many of them from infancy.

'When people actually treat children like this and live the way these people live, how the kids survive in any reasonable capacity is beyond me. Women get to be multiple personalities. Men get to be killers. But it's hard to make a defence out of it because you always get people on the jury who are thinking, that happened to me, and that happened to me, and that happened to me, and I'm not a killer. So they distance themselves from it and everybody can wash their hands of it. Across this nation it's a hideous problem and if it's not stopped, we're going to hell in a handcart. No one is taking responsibility for abuse, because if they allow themselves to think, "These things are happening because children are abused," that would mean they'd have to accept that these things are going on in their world.'

Blair describes a recent client whose family background gives a horrifying example of the effects of childhood abuse. He had a twin brother who had been in prison for molestation murder, he had an older brother in prison for molestation, he had a sister who married a cousin, another sister who had married an uncle. It was clear that he was raised in a family where abuse was routine. The girls were raped by their father, the boys were sent out to bring home children for the adults to abuse.

'This man was raised to do what he did. When you were a kid, you learned to play, you learned to tie your shoes, you learned to open a bank account. That's not what our client learned. He didn't even learn how to read until he was in prison, forty-two years old. That's not how you build a healthy society.'

Blair did not find her view shared by mainstream child abuse experts, however, who seemed more interested in the politics of the issue than really understanding the case. 'They turned round and said, "Well he's a man, and his victim was a woman, and we cannot allow ourselves to be attached to saying he was a victim too. Not in the current political climate."'

Blair openly admits that child abuse has become a pet subject for her, something that will make her choose to take a case on. She's not alone. Several of the women eyes I spoke to give up their own time to help such victims. For Sarah Di Venere, one of the plus points in running a successful and profitable agency is that it allows her to do the pro bono work she chooses for battered women and abused children.

Sarah is in the middle of such a case, in which a wife is accused of attempted murder. Her husband was physically abusive and even after he had walked out on her, leaving her alone with no money in a freezing apartment, he would return regularly to harass and beat her. The woman visited her husband to beg him for some money for food and heating and he threatened to kill her. She always carried a gun, since her job as a nurse had led to some frightening encounters, and in fear for her life, she pulled the gun and shot him.

The defence needed to prove that the man really did threaten to kill his wife so Sarah was sent to interview him. 'I told him that I was trying to get his side of the story and buttered him up. Now, there are men who have no respect for women. Period. Sometimes that works in your favour, because they think you're totally irrelevant so they will almost boast to you. So I played the bimbo. Sure, it's demeaning, but it's in a good cause. Pretty soon this guy is telling me everything, how his wife likes to be roughed up, and what he does to her to turn her on sexually and before he knows it, this guy has hung himself. Yeah, he did have a knife and yeah, he did go after her. So now I know for sure she shot him in self-defence.'

Sarah believes she has enough evidence from the interview to get the woman off. Making a positive impact on a case such as this is what makes the job worthwhile for her. 'I think my work makes a difference in people's lives, that's what's so satisfying. You can stop people's lives being ruined by abuse or by drugs.'

Diana Middleton shares this awareness of the difference the PI's work can make in other people's lives, positive or negative. She believes that this gives them a special responsibility to be caring and sympathetic. 'My policy is to try and get the person that you're serving on your side, and sometimes that means sitting with them crying on your shoulder. Strictly speaking, that's not part of our brief but that's how I believe we should do the job. A lot of the people we are dealing with are in trouble and they open their heart up to us and we listen, which makes it a lot easier if we have to go back a second time. I get a certain amount of satisfaction when I think that perhaps by letting that man cry on my shoulder it's relieved him and by doing that it may also have saved his wife from getting another beating. You have to show them some compassion because they are in terrible trouble, often through no fault of their own.'

Perhaps the cases which strike the deepest chords with the investigators are the ones where they haven't been able to make a difference, where no resolution has been reached. To be a private investigator, you have to be in love with finding answers and solving puzzles, so frustrations breed around these cases, especially when the reasons for the remaining ambiguities are outside your control. Byrna Aronson outlines a case that is fixed in her mind like a fly in amber.

A young man was found dead in his car supposedly from carbon monoxide poisoning and the official ruling was suicide. His parents couldn't believe that he had killed himself. He was about to go to college and seemed to have everything to live for.

Bryna quickly began to uncover strange discrepancies in the official case. The police were trying to hide something and did everything to keep vital evidence from her. As she dug further, however, Byrna discovered that the young man was gay, and might have been involved with a group of boys who were being paid to have sex with married men. Suddenly the whole case became much more sinister, with possible motives for both suicide and murder.

It turned out, however, that the boy's parents were aware of his homosexuality and considered it a shameful secret. They decided to stop the investigation rather than risk his sexuality becoming public knowledge.

'To this day I'm haunted by that kid's picture,' Byrna admits. 'I'm haunted by the fact that I think there was criminal activity going on, whether it was related to the death or not, and I just had to walk away from it. I don't have a right to be doing the work if they don't want me to, I don't have a right to be exposing anything that they don't want me to. The parents hired me to find out the truth, but it turns out they don't really want the truth. That's the most frustrating part of this work for me.'

Nancy Poss-Hatchl knows just what she means. 'I've had mysteries that still aren't solved. They're always present, there in the corner of my mind.' One such case involved a young girl who was found dead in mysterious circumstances. The girl, Michelle, worked part-time at a veterinary surgery, and it was here that her body was discovered. An autopsy could find no reason for her death, nor were there any clues at the scene. Three hours had mysteriously passed between the discovery of her body, when her parents were alerted, and the emergency call to the police.

Nancy was hired by the vet's insurance company and uncovered a number of strange facts about this seemingly happy and ordinary girl. It appeared that she had been in therapy, and her therapist had subsequently been charged with sexually molesting his female patients. Her relationship with the vet was also suspect. Other employees claimed he gave her expensive presents, which she was told to keep secret, and since he had access to pharmaceuticals, he may have been supplying her with drugs. Even her family set-up began to seem strange to Nancy as she dug deeper, with a distraught stepfather and a seemingly unconcerned mother keeping silence with the vet as to what had happened in the missing three hours.

The insurance company were not interested in uncovering the truth, however, merely protecting themselves from possible claims. No claims were made, which in itself Nancy found strange, so she was told to stop the investigation. 'I guess we'll never know what happened to Michelle, and that will probably still be driving me crazy when I'm knocking on heaven's door.'

Tell it to Sandra Sutherland. 'In this job, you do get an enormous amount of frustration. In 1981 I did a missing persons case which almost drove me to a nervous breakdown. A young woman called Valerie McDonald disappeared. Her parents called the cops because she had missed her father's birthday and Thanksgiving, which she never did. They had talked to her a few days before and she was fine. The cops just shrugged. She was living a kind of bohemian life in North Beach, she was very beautiful and the cops said she'd probably gone off to Reno to become a hooker and paid absolutely no attention.

'A week later, her parents hired us. An hour and a half after we had been hired, I found out that she had told friends she was afraid of the managers of the hotel where she was staying. She had expressed physical fear of these guys, and she was seen with them the evening before she disappeared. They had recently been released from San Quentin prison and had unbelievably long rap sheets for violent assaults and rape. An hour and half, and I did it the hard way by going down there and knocking on the doors of the other residents, and saying, "What about these guys?" The police could have done it on their computer in thirty seconds.

'This was eight days after she had disappeared. It turns out they held this girl prisoner for eleven days and tortured her before they killed her. If the police had got on to it immediately they might have been able to find her before she was killed. These killers had this intellectual, fascist attitude towards it. I've got copies of one of the guys' diary. There's one entry; "The ice maiden in her frozen beauty, hair flowing in the stream." They'd encased her in concrete and put her in an iron tub and dropped her in a river somewhere between here and Oregon. They've never found the girl's body. We found the receipts for the cement.

'One of them was later killed in a shoot-out with the Mounties and the other two are now in prison on other charges that arose from the investigation into what happened to Valerie. The Mounties admitted to me that they had listened in on a conversation between one of the guys who is now in prison in Canada and his girlfriend, who is one of those liberal, do-gooder young women who falls in love with violent toads. Anyway, this woman said to him, "The blonde girl's dead, isn't she?" And he said, "Yes." Those guys scared me to death and they're about to get out of prison. In the whole twenty-four years I've been a private eye, I think they're the only two that I feel really scared of. I think they might really come after me when they come out of prison, they've threatened me already. They are really evil guys these two.

'I can't say this was one of my favourite cases. I won't think about Michael Jackson fourteen years later even though I earned a lot more money. I don't even think about John De Lorean much. But I still think about Valerie McDonald.'

That'll Do Nicely...

I've worked in most parts of the world, and the cases tend to be major league. One case I did that got a lot of publicity was the American Express scandal about five years ago. Our client, Mr. Safra, is the world's richest private banker. Suddenly these articles started appearing in the world's press linking him to heroin trafficking in the Fifties and to the laundering of the $40 million missing from the Iran Contra affair. These articles were mostly in the anti-Semitic, right-wing press, the Le Pen people in France. Safra has banks in North America, South America and Europe. He's a very old-fashioned, cosmopolitan Lebanese Jew who now lives in Geneva and he felt that his family name was being dragged through the mud. Normal lawyer advice is, 'Start suing, what do you care what they say?' But he was determined to get to the bottom of this, so we were hired.

Safra himself actually had suspicions from the beginning that American Express was behind this, which made me think he was a paranoid lunatic. I'm thinking, why would American Express do something this unbelievably sleazy? They're this great corporation, I have two American Express cards myself. I didn't buy it at all, but he wanted to find out if his suspicions were correct. So we did this whole undercover operation. The first thing I had to deal with was my accent. I only have to open my mouth and people say, 'Hey, you're Australian!' and in certain areas, I know the alert goes out, 'It's Sandra Sutherland!' But on other occasions, it gives you a whole air of separation from anything people might assume you could be doing.

Now, about the only place in the world Safra doesn't have banks is Australia, so I have to come up with a good story to cover why an Australian would be looking into this. I sat in my house in Italy thinking about this for about a week and gradually I came up with this story that I would be a journalist working on the definitive book on a major Australian banking scandal from the Seventies. Back then, a bank was set up by the CIA in Australia to launder the CIA's drug money from South East Asia. There were two partners; one was an Australian crook and the other was a CIA agent. The Australian partner was ultimately found assassinated in his Mercedes with a bullet through his brain. The CIA agent disappeared never to be seen again. My cover story was that the Safra banks were showing exactly the same MO as the Australian bank had when it was laundering the drug proceeds. So maybe the CIA guy who disappeared in Australia has done a deal with Safra as a front and they are laundering the Iran-Contra money in the same way. I am a journalist out to crack this, plus reveal the identity of the original Australian crook's killer. The final chapter on this unbelievable scandal which America has never paid any attention to. That was my cover story.

So I went round to all the people that had written the articles about Safra in the various countries and said, 'Your source obviously knows all about these Safra banks and this laundering operation. Chances are he must know something about the Australian scandal, is there any chance you could put me in touch with him?' I was trying to draw this guy out. It got to the point where this guy was leaving messages at my hotel before I checked in, when nobody knew where I was going. Of course I'd been booking my hotels through American Express...I like taking risks!

We hadn't nailed him at this point, but we'd drawn him out and we knew who he was. Finally, he started trying to warn the journalists off and told them I was CIA. Here's this crazed person in such a state of paranoia that this was the only construct he could put on what I was doing. He's getting more and more perturbed because he can't get a handle on who I am, and he can't connect me to America in any way. He got hold of the translator I'd been using in France and took her out to dinner. He tried to worm out of her who I really was but all she knew was the cover story. He started slamming things down on the table and screaming at her in the fanciest Chinese restaurant in Paris, then he stormed out.

When she called me to tell me this, I frantically bought a ticket to France. We'd had a couple of ex-FBI guys doing surveillance of the American Express headquarters, and I brought the surveillance photographs with me. This guy was in the spread, and she picked him out straight away. The photograph showed him meeting a senior American Express official in the executive parking lot. So we had him totally nailed. The guy who we had shown was the source of the stories about Safra was linked right into American Express, just as Safra had originally suspected. American Express paid out eight million dollars to charities of our client's choosing, to make the whole thing go away.

That was a case where I think I slipped past people's assumptions because I was a woman. It was much easier for them to believe I was a journalist than to suspect I was an investigator.

SANDRA SUTHERLAND
San Francisco

11

Going Underground

*I've always enjoyed undercover work because it gives a flavour
of someone else's life. You get to experience another career, another
way of life without having to commit yourself to that forever.
It satisfies your curiosity about what other people do with
their days. You get the best of all worlds.*

ZENA SCOTT-ARCHER
Liverpool

In recent years, women in the USA and the UK have moved into the workplace in higher numbers than ever before, including the Second World War, when so many men were off fighting that we got our first chance to do things we'd never done before. This time, many of the jobs are poorly paid, part-time and invisible. At the same time, women have broken through into executive and management jobs in unprecedented numbers. We still occupy only a fraction of the top jobs, but there are enough of us there for it not to be a matter for comment when a woman takes on one of those roles. So for the woman private eye who's prepared to work undercover, the opportunities have increased enormously.

As with surveillance work, to be a successful undercover operative, a PI has to be able to blend in. Although the women who do this job are strong, individualistic personalities, they understand that working undercover means toning themselves down, making themselves unobtrusive and uninteresting.

The other key element is to have a good cover story. The easiest thing is to go for a background as close to your own as possible, without giving away key details that could lead to someone being able to track you down after the job is over and you have exposed them to sacking, prosecution or a civil lawsuit. The cover story needs to be thorough, and, like a method actor, you have to live it. You have to double check your own reactions against the persona you've adopted to make sure you're staying in character. But you can't just opt to be the quiet, withdrawn type to guard against making mistakes, because it's generally important to win the confidence of the people you're spending time with, to get them to open up and provide the information you need to do your job.

You have to research the role so that you look right, which is where the observational skills of the PI come into their own. If you're acting the part of a divorcee working as a temporary secretary, you don't arrive at work in a brand new BMW with diamond studs in your ears and an Armani suit on your back. Equally, if you're being presented to the board as a time and motion consultant, you leave the jeans and sweatshirt at home. In one of my Kate Brannigan books, her boyfriend comments that she doesn't have a wardrobe, she has a disguise kit. That's because she recognises the value of never standing out. Whether she needs to look like a tart or a Tory, she knows what will look right.

As a journalist, I found undercover work the most nerve-wracking area of the profession. I've infiltrated religious cults, pretended to be the owner of a clothes shop to expose sweatshop racketeering in the fashion industry, and acted the role of a businesswoman looking for a male escort for company functions. Every time, I was scared witless that I was going to slip up and reveal that I wasn't who I said I was. I guarded my tongue so carefully that at times I'm sure I must have appeared like Forrest Gump's sister as I struggled to find the answer to a question I hadn't anticipated.

The one thing you've got going for you is that most people are not suspicious by nature. We tend to accept people at face value, until they give us good reason to do otherwise. That's something that worked to Pat Storey's advantage in a major undercover operation she carried out.

The job was to look for criminal activity in a shop and she had gone in as a sales assistant. Her story was that she was divorced and living in the area temporarily and she was pleased to discover what a good actress she could be. But things nearly came unstuck when the shop was broken into. Pat was able to describe to the police two women who she had seen in the shop who she thought might be involved in the robbery. The police believed they were the girlfriends of the men they had picked up for the job and wanted Pat and another shop assistant to make a positive identification of them at court.

'I'm the one with a motor, so next morning me and this other woman get into my car. I drove off and suddenly I remembered I wasn't supposed to know the area. Thinking on my feet, I said, all dizzy blonde, "I'm driving out of here, but I don't even know where I'm going! Do you know where the court is?" I have to let her direct me, and we get there by the most circuitous route possible! Of course, I walk into court and straight into four solicitors I do work for...."Hello Pat, how are you?" I'm thinking, go away! I just blanked them, and they obviously cottoned on that I was up to something because they all smiled and walked away. The girl who was with me never even picked up on it, can you believe it?'

Being recognised becomes even more of a problem if a PI becomes well-known. Zena Scott-Archer has become quite a famous face in the Liverpool area where she works. She still does undercover work, however, and has never been caught out. The only time she has resorted to a disguise is when she was investigating a bingo hall and had to dress up as an archetypal bingo lady—head scarf, flat shoes, lisle stockings and a string bag. But dressing up wasn't enough, Zena found she had to get in character too. 'I didn't really pay much attention, until one woman sitting near me leaned over and said, "You've missed number fourteen!" I realised then that I needed to concentrate on playing, otherwise I'd be even more noticeable than if I hadn't worn a disguise. I still never won a thing, but at least I was able to complete the job without arousing suspicion!'

When Sandra Sutherland told me she has regularly worked undercover, I was surprised. Sutherland and Palladino is the kind of high-profile firm where investigators appear on television newscasts and press conferences at the shoulder of their celebrity clients. Also, in spite of having lived in America for over twenty-five years, Sandra still has a strong Australian accent. But because people are either so trusting or so arrogant that they don't believe anyone could be on their tail, Sandra gets away with it every time.

'I virtually never get spotted, which I put down to the fact that I always do my research very thoroughly before I go in on an undercover operation.' The classic example is an operation she undertook on a case in order to prove that a search warrant which had been used on her client, who was charged with possession of a warehouse full of marijuana, was invalid. The search had taken place in the California wine country so Sandra posed as an Australian journalist doing a story on the wine industry. She then came up with an ingenious excuse to ask the police questions about drugs raids.

'I went down to the local library and went through all the old local newspaper files to see if I could find a story about the wine industry and a story about the local drug enforcement unit in the same issue. After a long and dusty search, I finally found an edition that had just that, and armed with my photocopy, I went off to the drug unit's office. I said I'd been doing this story about the wine industry and I was reading through the local papers—and I'm waving the story at them! I'm enthusing at them, saying, "I couldn't believe my eyes, here in this small town there's this elite unit! In Australia we're having the same problem with this enormous marijuana industry in these small idyllic rural towns. It's appalling, maybe we can learn something from you guys."'

There is nothing like a bit of flattery to get people off their guard. The police fell for Sandra's story, hook, line and sinker. They allowed her to stay with the drugs unit for a few days, took her to a safe house and partied with her when they were meant to be on duty. She soon discovered that the officers were small-town cowboys arresting people for drugs possession then turning them loose to sell the dope for them. The case that Sandra was working on was the biggest they had had and soon they were boasting to Sandra about it, explaining how they got the search warrant from an out of town judge so that they could put anything they liked into it.

It didn't take long for Sandra to get the evidence she needed and when the case came to court even the judge was absolutely stunned that the men had done nothing to check Sandra's identity. But worse than that, while the investigation was going on, Sandra was interviewed by a magazine for a cover article. Not one of these hotshot detectives ever noticed that this friendly Australian journalist's face was plastered all over the newsstands in an article headed 'Farewell, My Lovely Gumshoe'!

Because working undercover demands total immersion in someone else's world, it inevitably provides a different perspective on your own life. Sarah Di Venere, queen of the disguise kit, discovered that on a long undercover operation she did early on in her career, and it has had a profound effect on her own attitudes. Sarah was hired to work undercover in the factory of a large manufacturing company that made components for automobiles and spacecraft.

'I was working on the production line, the lowest form of life, it seemed to me. I would leave home about four in the morning to get to work. Most people made around $5.25 an hour, they got one week's annual vacation, and it was a very difficult transition for me, because I was used to being a pampered real estate person. I was used to making phone calls when I wanted, but when you work on an assembly line, you have to ask permission to go to the bathroom, never mind to make a phone call. There was no smoking, no drinking, no chewing of gum. The work conditions were terrible, the noise of the machinery and the pollution of the chemicals. There was no air conditioning, it was hot as hell.'

Five months on the production line saw Sarah nailing a drug ring and exposing a crooked foreman selling jobs to immigrants. And she came away from it with a new-found awareness. 'You really start to think how fortunate you have it. It's like another world. Now, I've got a lot more sympathy for people who do work in those plants. It was hard for me to realise that there are people who came from other countries and had nothing who appreciate that wage, they appreciate their little house and mortgage. I was able, I think, to obtain a better understanding of values and materialism, and it changed the way I think about the society I live in.'

Not only did she have to endure the difficult work conditions but she also had to socialise with the most undesirable of the employees, in order to find out who was using narcotics. To make matters worse, the foreman fell for her and bought her a diamond ring. Sarah was extremely thankful that she had insisted on completely false personal information on the office computer, although the company had assured her that no one had access to it, because the foreman had checked all her personal details. If she hadn't been so cautious she could have had this man bursting into her real life, with all the dangers and problems that would have brought.

It demonstrates just how careful a PI has to be to protect her identity and how crucial it is that her disguises and ruses work. Often it's no exaggeration to say that it's her life on the line out there. Again, early in her career, Sarah learned valuable lessons on another undercover case.

She was investigating a boating accident in which a speed boat had hit a pontoon boat knocking a man into the water and leaving his wife clinging to the sinking boat. The man drowned and Sarah was sent to discover who was responsible.

The boat had been hit near a seedy lakeside bar, so she started hanging out there, pretending to be a recent divorcée looking for a cottage. After a week, people started to wonder why Sarah was asking so many questions and became increasingly suspicious. Sarah invited a police officer who was a friend of hers to go to the bar with her for protection but while he was away from the table a man approached her, claiming he wanted to show her something outside. Once outside, he and another man began beating her up. They were about to throw her into their car when her friend came out and chased them off. 'I learned a big lesson; never ever leave with someone without telling your partner where you're going. Nothing teaches you faster than being scared!'

In spite of the dangers and fear she was exposed to on that assignment, Sarah successfully identified the helmsman who had run down the pontoon boat and her evidence secured an indictment.

But role-playing always holds its risks. Even when you are not found out the strain of having to be someone else can take its toll, as Jean Mignolet discovered. Her most difficult undercover case involved her going to a psychiatrist regularly for eight months to investigate claims that he was sexually abusing his clients. 'It was probably the most difficult case in the world for me, because of who I am and what I do. I have good self-esteem, I'm very positive and confident. But I had to be this Jewish American Princess with a trust fund, one of those insecure girl/woman types, looking for a man to be daddy.

'I had to crawl up into the foetal position on this guy's couch and he played daddy with me. I even took acting classes during that time to help get into character. It was so different from who I was. I'd walk out of a session with this man and it would take me an hour to reprogramme myself. But we nailed him. He was always touching, always using inappropriate behaviour. I needed therapy after the therapist! It was horrible.'

Undercover work is certainly not for the timid, nor for lovers of routine. An appetite for new experience is something Zena Scott-Archer, who in the course of her undercover work has been everything from a nurse to a fashion model to a librarian, has always regarded as an essential qualification for the job. 'You need to love change and accept the unexpected,' she says categorically. 'You have to have an open mind and a thirst for knowledge. I've soaked up all sorts of things over the years. I've always enjoyed undercover work because it gives a flavour of someone else's life. You get to experience another career, another way of life without having to commit yourself to that forever. It satisfies your curiosity about what other people do with their days. You get the best of all worlds.'

Sometimes, the role itself becomes almost more engrossing than the undercover assignment, as Diana Middleton found out to her surprise when working undercover in a factory. She was pretending to be a time and motion expert and spent a lot of time talking to the workers and seeing how everything was done. She became quite an expert and at the end of the week, not only was she able to tell the boss where the goods were disappearing, but she also gave him several suggestions about more efficient ways to run the factory!

Truth, Justice and the American Way

The case I'm doing right now has been the hardest I've ever done. It's a capital case, it's real complicated and it's been the longest running. I called one of the police detectives a couple of weeks ago and said, 'I wish I could tell you this was it, but I think we're joined at the hip for the rest of our lives.'

Walter has been missing since July 1992. Literally missing. He worked at the Alameda Naval Station as a coin collector from the vending machines. There is no evidence of a murder. The little safe out of his van's missing. Money estimated at $2700 to $3000, mostly in quarters, is missing. Three men were charged with capital murder with special circumstances. Kidnapping, robbery and murder. Clifford worked at the naval station, also servicing vending machines. The second man, Lamarr, was his brother. And the third was Frank.

Walter was kind of a goofy guy, naive, thirty-five, probably an alcoholic, probably gay, probably a drug user. There's evidence to this effect. Walter lived with Lou, a guy who was quite a bit older than he was, probably late 50s. Walter used to refer to Lou as his stepfather, and he was right under his thumb. Lou's main concern when Walter disappeared was that he couldn't cash his wages check. Within a month and a half he moved into a trailer and had his phone cut off, which is a very odd thing for someone close to a missing person to do. I find they always stay where they are, keep the phone number connected, live in hope for years, because there's always that question mark, even if logic tells you that person is dead.

Clifford was in his late twenties. He had one juvenile shoplifting conviction, but hardly even a traffic ticket since. His brother, Lamarr, is an ex-felon. He kidnapped a lady for her car when he was eighteen years of age and tried to kill her because he didn't know what else to do about her. Lamarr did his time and was released on early parole in 1985 because he was a model prisoner. He had been living a clean, exemplary life ever since. He had a girlfriend, a job; he didn't drink, he didn't do dope, he went to work on time every day. Clifford and Lamarr are half Hawaiian half Caucasian. Frank is a black guy they grew up with.

Frank turned state's evidence. The prosecution story goes that Frank and Lamarr went with Clifford to work early in the morning. They hung around the rec centre while Clifford did his job then they followed Walter's van out of the facility. Frank said that when Walter stopped the van, they got out and talked then Lamarr grabbed Walter, had Frank bind his hands behind him with duct tape, taped across his mouth and threw him in the back of the van. Clifford went back to work, Lamarr and Frank took Walter's van and a car to Fairfield, a town about 45 minutes north of here.

They stopped in a little parking lot in a park, and took Walter bound and gagged out of his van and put him in the trunk of the car, left the van there, and drove back in the car to Clifford's house. They unloaded some of the cash and then they went to pick Clifford up at work. With Walter still in the trunk. They go back to Clifford's house to count the money. Two little girls are playing outside and they see guys either taking bags out of the car or putting them into the car, they're not sure which.

This is an apartment complex with stalls where the cars are parked along the drive-thru. Two maintenance men are driving through in a pick up and all of a sudden they see this trunk pop up and they see what looks like a guy in the trunk bound and gagged. Instead of doing anything about it, they drive off.

As they are driving away they see somebody come out of the apartment, slam the trunk down on this guy's head, get in the car and drive off the other way.

They get to the security gate and as they are excitedly telling the security guard what's going on, the car drives past and they say the driver is Clifford. Meanwhile, Frank claims he said he wasn't having any part of this and he ended up walking or hitchhiking all the way from San Pablo the thirty miles back to Oakland to his grandfather's.

Frank's grandfather is a well-known drug dealer in Oakland. He knows how the law works, and he sets up a meeting between Frank and the FBI, who are involved because this happened in a military installation. So Frank tells his story and the agents go out and talk to Clifford. They say that Clifford tells the same story. But the strange part about this is that they have tape recorded and video-taped every other interview in the case except this one. And they claim that in this one and only unrecorded interview, Clifford made his one and only confession. Which Clifford denies absolutely.

Lamarr hears that he's wanted now and he turns himself in. The only evidence they have is the statement from the little girls saying they saw them with the money bags, and the maintenance men who saw a body in the trunk of a car which Clifford may or may not have been driving. The Feds literally completely dismantle Clifford's car looking for a hair, a fibre, a fingerprint connecting it to Walter, and they find nothing. Not a smidgen. You just can't clean a car out that well, it's not possible.

Let me tell you the story I've put together recently. Walter and Frank ripped off the van and the cash.

Walter and Frank had some kind of a drug transaction going on and Walter was short on cash. And he and Frank decided this was an easy rip. There is also a question about whether Frank's gay, and what his exact relationship to Walter was. For whatever reason, Frank ended up killing Walter and ran to his grandfather for help. Grandpa knows that to get Frank clear, they have to have somebody else in the frame. Grandpa knows about Lamarr's felony conviction and decides the sensible approach is to put it all on Lamarr, who was my client. Lamarr is the perfect patsy because he has a similar record. So Frank goes over to Clifford's and makes sure somebody sees the body there, makes sure Clifford and Lamarr are tied in to it even though they don't know anything about it. Then he goes to the FBI.

After Frank testified, I set out to find somebody that he had told a different story to. I went to the jail where he had been held and started interviewing inmates and I found one that he had been friends with. He was facing a kidnapping charge too, and they would look up case law and compare notes. This guy's story was that Frank had admitted killing Walter and that he knew somebody at a mortuary that cremated the body. We got him to testify, but the jury didn't believe him.

I found out afterwards, when I talked to the jurors, that they had decided they wouldn't accept any testimony that wasn't corroborated. So they accepted everything that was corroborated by Frank's testimony and threw out all the exculpatory evidence I had amassed because it didn't tally with what Frank said. It never seemed to have occurred to them that Frank had had every opportunity to tailor his testimony to fit any other evidence. Plus Frank had set up some of the evidence in the first place precisely so it would corroborate his story. Juries never cease to amaze me.

It hasn't ever been the way I thought it was when I grew up—truth, justice, the American way, mom, apple pie. It's not like that. It's always been a win or lose game. I've probably become very jaundiced since I've been in this business. In my experience, once the DA files charges on a case, his office has invested in a conviction. It doesn't matter what the facts of the case are, it's about putting another notch on his gun. The prosecution's conduct was so bad in this case. The DA withheld information. Anything that didn't agree with the prosecution version of the case was withheld. We only found out about it in the middle of trial because an honest FBI agent just happened to be asked the right question on the stand. We found out there was this whole file we knew nothing about. 250 pages' worth of exculpatory information.

There were interviews with people who had witnessed what happened at the park, when the body and the cash had been transferred from the van to the car. I went back up there two years later and I found those witnesses and they still remembered vividly what they had seen. I spoke to people who said, 'The cops talked to me and I gave exact descriptions of what those men looked liked and none of them looked like your client.' People who said that the car they saw definitely was not Clifford's blue Maverick, it was a brown and orange station wagon. Someone who said, 'I saw the whole thing, I watched them for about half an hour, and I don't understand why the police didn't ask me to do a photo line-up because I told them I could positively identify the men I saw.' Things like that. Not one of those witnesses could identify Lamarr or Clifford as one of the people they'd seen.

But the judge doesn't care. He doesn't want to be seen as a judge that's soft on crime. The position is that Lamarr was convicted on all counts. Clifford has been found guilty of kidnap, but not of murder. Lamarr is looking at Death Row or life without parole. Clifford is awaiting sentence.

But Frank is free. He's out on the streets, scot-free. Frank's immunity agreement gave him complete federal and state transactional immunity. That means that no matter what evidence we find on Frank, he cannot be tried for this case unless we can prove that he lied, which we're working on. What we're focusing on now is the appeals process. I keep telling myself it's not over till it's over, but sometimes I get so angry at the way the system has completely screwed these two innocent guys.

FRANCIE KOEHLER
Oakland

12

Legal Liaisons

*Solicitors like to think they don't need us but they do.
We do all their dirty work. We do the work they either don't
want to do or would rather their clients didn't know they did.*

CHRISTINE USHER
Hampshire

In real life the police hate us.

SANDRA SUTHERLAND
San Francisco

It's no wonder that private eyes sometimes feel like nobody loves them. The two groups that perforce they have most dealings with certainly don't. To many of the lawyers who put work their way, they're a necessary evil. A bit like the bin men, their work is vital to the smooth running of the system, but nobody would want to have one around the house. To the police, they're not even that desirable. At best, they're a nuisance, at worst they're radical underminers of the system who want to show up all officers of the law as corrupt or stupid.

It's true that private eyes have something of the maverick in their make-up, however conventional they may appear on the surface. It's still so unlikely a job for a woman that they have to have a powerful streak of individuality and independence in order to get into the job in the first place, never mind to stick with it for years. But in spite of all the movies and TV programmes that feature maverick cops and lawyers, the truth is that to be successful in either of those fields, it's necessary to conform to a large extent. Inevitably, that means that cops and lawyers are going to clash with private eyes on a regular basis, conformists versus iconoclasts.

The issues of morality and ethics also play a part in these troubled relationships. It's a commonplace that many police officers are prepared to manipulate the truth to a greater or lesser degree to secure arrests and convictions. And lawyers are hired mouthpieces, paid to represent their client, however sleazy, morally bankrupt or criminal they may be. But because of their fierce commitment to their independence and the honesty of what they do, it seems unavoidable that the women eyes will find themselves in conflict with one or other of the official arms of the law.

The relationship with lawyers, however, is often crucial to the success or failure of a private investigator's business since they are the source of the bulk of their cases. In effect, PIs pick and choose among lawyers, discarding the ones they can't get along with and sticking to the ones with whom they have a working relationship. Christine Usher sums it up when she says, 'Solicitors like to think they don't need us but they do. We do all their dirty work. We do the work they either don't want to do or would rather their clients didn't know they did. I get on very well with the solicitors and insurance companies that I work with, but I've reached that point by a process of elimination.'

That experience is one that seems to be common on both sides of the Atlantic. In New York, Susan Lauman says, 'If you think PIs are sleazy, you should see some of the lawyers. One firm rule I have is that I don't take cases privately. If someone calls me up out of the blue, I ask them to come back to me through their attorney. I only work through attorneys, and even then I'm picky about which attorneys I'm prepared to work for. My other rule is that I need to know something about an attorney and the way he or she operates before I feel comfortable taking work from them. When a new lawyer comes to us, I ask around about them on the grapevine. If I don't like what I hear, suddenly I'm way too busy. The reason for that is that you simply don't know what people will do with the information you uncover for them. Lay people especially frequently abuse the information, using it in criminal or dangerous ways, and attorneys aren't exempt from that either. I don't want to feel responsible because work I've done has contributed to somebody getting hurt.'

When they are faced with practices they don't like, PIs are ruthless about walking away from paying customers. Helen Kliner's first client was an attorney who was personally recommended by a friend of hers, so she felt she could trust him. However when she got to know him better, he began boasting about the money drug gangsters gave him to defend them and even offered her an untraceable gun given to him by one of his clients. Despite the fact that he was giving her a lot of work, and money, she decided she could no longer work for him.

Nancy Barber has also sacked a client, for a very different type of unethical behaviour. 'I think when investigators interview people that they don't always explain enough about what's going on and why people are being interviewed and what's going to happen to them,' she admits. 'Once you give their names to an attorney, it's like throwing meat to sharks. That is why I am very careful about the clients that I take. I could probably make a lot more money and take a lot more work, but I'm very selective. I have to enjoy working with a person, I have to know them and trust them.'

Nancy found out that one of her clients had taken on para-legals to reinterview the people she had spoken to on an asbestos litigations inquiry, without making it clear which side of the case they were working on. To her, this was a violation of the trust her interviewees have shown in her by allowing her to invade their privacy and take up their time.

That was the last she had to do with the client, and despite the fact that it was one of her biggest sources of income, she does not regret her decision. 'I have to live with myself. I have to sleep at night. If my work is being used in a less than desirable fashion, I'd rather do without the money. I know I can only control things up to a certain point, but I'm not giving that up.'

No matter how careful investigators are in selecting the lawyers they work with, problems do arise. 'Attorneys are usually very stupid and don't know how to talk to people,' Blair says in uncompromising tones. 'I've been absolutely appalled at the way attorneys treat people we need in support of our clients' survival! You get these "holier than thou" attitudes, and also a complete failure to understand the realities of life out on the streets. And they are so arrogant, they won't listen to anything that contradicts their world view.'

In the worst case, this can even endanger a PI's life. Blair once accompanied an attorney who wanted to get some background information on his client. To her horror he brought out his video camera in the middle of an extremely dangerous neighbourhood and started filming the streets. Nothing Blair could say would convince him to stop it. Sure enough when they retraced their steps their car was stopped by a group of gang members and dope dealers who were far from happy about being filmed, thinking that they must be police. Blair had to do a lot of fast talking to get them out of the situation alive.

What annoys Blair, and many of her colleagues, most about attorneys is that they expect miracles from the private investigator and seldom show any real regard for the possible results of what they are asking. One case she is working on involves a family which is seriously damaged. The attorney wants her to find out things from the child which he has never discussed with anyone and won't listen when she asks for a child development psychologist. Blair is no trained psychiatrist and she is not willing to take the responsibility for helping the child cope with the things she draws out of him. As far as the attorney is concerned, the important thing is getting the right result, not showing compassion for the client. They might be working on the same side, but the two are approaching it from very different angles. 'I sometimes think lawyers are a separate species,' is Blair's exasperated conclusion.

Yvonne Twiby would agree. 'With some of the solicitors, you wonder whose side they're on. I did a murder inquiry about ten years ago. In the first three days, the police had made so many mistakes, and those are three days you can't get back. A reclusive forty-year-old man had a smallholding in Shrewsbury and a bunch of the local yobbos befriended him. Then he suddenly disappeared. His elderly parents were worried. He'd signed up for a college course but didn't show up, and they were convinced that something had happened to him. They went to the police, who just said, "Oh well, he's an adult, we can't do anything about it."

'But his parents were convinced that he hadn't just gone away so they kept going to the police. The coppers used to pop round now and again to the smallholding to check if he'd turned up, just to keep the old couple quiet. For two years the police were going down there regularly, they even had a police sniffer dog down. These yobbos had in fact killed him and buried his body in the orchard. Aren't our policemen observant?

'How it came to light was that a new Superintendent arrived who wanted to clear Shrewsbury of all the petty crime. So they picked up all these kids on suspicion of one thing or another and one had a credit card belonging to this missing chap so they arrested him. Eventually, one of the other yobbos told them where the body was buried so they charged the lad they'd arrested with murder. This kid is screaming innocence. He'll admit to helping to conceal a body, but there's no way he's admitting to the killing. The solicitor was new to the area and he wanted to make a name for himself and he'd been making all his own enquiries, generally winding people up and causing total chaos. The barrister got so fed up with him, he told him to instruct proper inquiry agents. So he comes to me. He's got all these theories and he's saying, all eager beaver, "How are you going to do it?"

'"I haven't got a clue," I said.

'He said, "You must know how you're going to do it! You're a professional!!"

'I said, "Until we get to Shrewsbury and I have a look round, I'm not making any decisions about how I'm doing this."

'The solicitor really got up my nose throughout the case, he was always telling me how I should do it. He couldn't keep his mouth shut about anything, so when I got to Shrewsbury I found that all these people who were going to be essential witnesses had gone to ground because they'd heard private detectives were in town. Luckily, nobody ever takes me for a detective. So I'm sitting in the pub with the client's girlfriend while the rest of the yobbos sat round planning their shop-lifting list!'

Eventually, at some risk to herself, Yvonne uncovered the identity of the real killer and the person who had supplied the shotgun. 'I went to the solicitor and said, sussed it, got it, know who did it. The next thing is he's shown copies of my reports and the statements to the police. They promptly went round and arrested all the defence witnesses. They told them that if they wanted to avoid being charged as accessories, they should support the existing police case against our client, so they all did deals. At the trial, the prosecution simply didn't call those witnesses, and we couldn't call them because they were down as prosecution witnesses. I just could not believe it. We were stuffed. We had all this evidence that we couldn't use because the solicitor was stupid enough to hand the defence over to the police on a plate. He just shrugged and said, "Oh, we'll get him off on appeal." It was just this massive ego trip for him. The poor old client got life.' She shakes her head, the bitterness of defeat still obvious after ten years. Then her mouth curls in a wry smile. 'And I waited eighteen months to get paid for it.'

If it's not the lawyers screwing the job up, it's the legal system. From the bureaucracy that surrounds the licensing process to the appeals courts where she does much of her work, Byrna Aronson has found her best efforts frustrated by the machinery of the law. The problem with the American appeal system is that it concentrates more on the process of the law than on actual justice. It's up to the PI to prove not that the defendant is actually innocent—in Byrna's experience the judges are not even interested in this—but that they did not have a fair trial. This means showing that serious mistakes were made during the trial or that evidence 'could not have been available'. Sometimes the only hope is to generate enough publicity so that the public starts to care, the press starts to take it up, and the court can be pressurised to turn around a different kind of decision. But, as Byrna puts it, 'that's no way to run a justice system'.

The OJ Simpson case put the American legal system under an unprecedented spotlight, with every step of the trial watched avidly coast to coast on live television. While I was in New York, I discovered one of the city's colleges was running a course called 'OJ 101', designed to take lay people through the process of the trial so that they would understand what was happening on their TV screens. Every American PI I spoke to was eager to know what I thought of the circus, as an outsider. Not one of them was convinced of Simpson's innocence, citing his history as a wife-beater and womaniser. But however much they condemned what was happening, they were all fascinated by the machinations of both prosecution and defence. 'I'm disgusted by the OJ Simpson case,' Sandra Sutherland confessed. 'I know all the defence lawyers. I've worked for some of them. But watching their stunts has made me disgusted with criminal defence. It's been a pantomime, a travesty, a cynical exploitation of the insatiable media. It has shown up everything that is rotten in our system, but the depressing thing about it is that I can't see anybody rushing to make changes as a result.'

Before I could feel too self-congratulatory about the British legal systems, Jennifer Paul reminded me of one of the problem areas she encounters indirectly in her work. It's an element of the Scottish criminal justice system that she, along with many others, would like to see abandoned—the 'not proven' verdict. A murder case Jennifer worked on perfectly proves her point. Her client was accused of brutalling raping and murdering a schoolteacher but the evidence was not conclusive and the verdict was 'not proven'. He is not in jail but he can't return to his old life either. Some of his neighbours think he did it and are terrified of him; others think he didn't do it and that the killer is still walking free, so they're afraid for their safety too. It's a totally unsatisfactory conclusion for everybody—the accused, his friends and relatives and the community.

Jennifer adds, I think you've also got to remember that the decision a jury reaches is not necessarily down to hard evidence. It's down to the people sitting on that jury. I've sat at the back of the court and watched them pick jurors and I've seen how solicitors use their challenges to keep certain types of people off juries. They don't want people who are well educated, or people who have a bit of nous about them. I would never ever get on a jury. Journalists don't get picked for juries. You either want the unsuspecting type who doesn't want to believe the worst of people or the ones who are themselves clearly streetwise and probably on the fringes of crime. I know everybody says, OK, it's flawed, but it's the best system we've got. Maybe, but it wouldn't hurt to take a look at it and see if there's not a way to make it work better.'

They may have their criticisms of the system and its representatives, but unlike the private eyes of fiction, whose week isn't complete unless they've done a good breaking and entering, the real women investigators have a healthy respect for the law. They see at close quarters the effects of breaking it, and that as much as their personal codes of ethics makes them careful to stay on the right side of legality. It's not always easy to do, and sometimes the lines get blurred, as René Olsson explains. 'You're supposed to be doing the right thing, good versus evil, all that stuff. Sometimes you get so close to that line that you're not supposed to cross. But when you feel like you're inches away from some key piece of information that you really need to nail a case down, you get this obsession and the line is lost and you don't know which side you're really on. Sometimes you do cross that line to get your information. Something inside you drives you on.

'I don't like crossing that line, I don't like subjecting myself to doing anything illegal. I don't want to do anything illegal and I don't want to even have to worry about it. It's too risky. You can only check your clients out so much. You can go and get tons and tons of information for your attorney and report exactly what went down, but what they use is something else. But sometimes the obsession for the answer just overrides good sense. In this game, it's often a real blur between where the good guys are and where the bad guys are.'

Often, it's small, very human things that start the downward slide. Lynn McLaren once dealt with a case in which her client was beaten up by six police officers after being stopped on a minor traffic violation. The cops who stopped him were a woman officer and a male officer. The male officer accidentally tripped and fell over, and he was so angry at looking foolish in front of the woman officer that he lost control. The beating was so brutal that the man's legs were broken in five places.

'All the time I was working that case, I knew those cops were going to be found guilty. But the jury didn't agree with me, and those cops walked away. This was before the Rodney King case in Los Angeles, and when that case came up, I said to all my friends right away, "These cops will walk. This is not a race issue, it's a power issue, and juries are not willing to take power away from the police." That realisation has altered my approach to every job I've done since. It really made me think about the assumptions I was bringing to my work.'

Private eyes who have been police officers have to make a huge mental adjustment that goes way beyond understanding that they no longer have a warrant card or a back-up team. They have to understand that they're no longer part of the system; rather, they're part of a system of checks and balances that is there to police the system they've been working within. They have to make the shift from being part of a tight-knit supportive community to being on the outside, able for the first time to see how that community is perceived by the rest of us. That can be a shock to the system, as Christine Usher discovered. 'I was quite surprised and disappointed when I realised that once people were aware that I wasn't a police officer, they would tell me things they wouldn't have told me when I was in the service. I think there is a problem with the relationship between the police and the public, and probably I'm quite pleased that I'm no longer a member of the service.

'These days, the only real contact I have with the police is when I get done for speeding again,' she adds with a rare flash of humour. 'Of course, I still know police officers, but I'd never ask them to supply me with information that isn't in the public domain. I expect my staff to stick to my code of ethics, so I can hardly turn round and ask a police officer to breach confidentiality when I know I'd sack someone who did that in my business.'

The degree of cooperation between police and investigators depends entirely on the kind of work they're doing. In the area of domestic violence, police and PIs work closely together, on either side of the Atlantic. They regularly swap information about the whereabouts of violent husbands, with the PIs referring women to their local police Domestic Violence Unit and the police referring women back to the PIs when they need someone to serve their injunctions. In recent years, the police forces in American and Britain have started to treat domestic violence seriously. They understand the importance of confidentiality and a lot of their information about battered and abused women and kids doesn't make it on to the police computer, because they understand that the men who commit these offences are often people who have access to their system, either directly or indirectly through the old boys' network. Diana Middleton has seen evidence of this for herself. She serves more policemen with domestic violence injunctions than any other profession. Having been a police officer, she understands the stresses, but doesn't accept that that is any excuse.

Although Jennifer Paul works the criminal defence beat, she has still managed to maintain a good working relationship with the police. 'It's very much a case of you scratch our back and we'll scratch your back with the police. I've discovered that it doesn't do you any good complaining about the police because they have memories like elephants.' Instead she goes out of her way to be polite and accommodating to the police officers she comes into contact with, and even passes on the odd bit of information that comes her way during her job. In her experience, if you make the effort the police will occasionally go out of their way to help you in return.

Domestic violence apart, however, Jennifer is in a very small minority of women eyes who admit to anything approaching a working relationship with the police. For men, though, it's often a different story, especially since so many of them have been coppers themselves. Although she's married to an ex-policeman, Pat Storey is under no illusions about the job. 'The police don't like us,' she said candidly. 'They really don't. For instance, we were looking for a guy recently and he's known to the police, not for anything serious, but I knew that the local police would know where he was likely to be found. I knew there was no point in me even crossing the threshold. But Tony will get to the sergeant on the strength of being ex-Job, and there's an instant rapport even though he's a PI now. The copper isn't going to tell him anything that he shouldn't tell him, but he'll point him in the right direction, which he wouldn't do for me. If I go in to the police station I get absolutely no cooperation whatsoever. I'm a female, I'm a PI—on your bike. They don't want to know.'

Often the police will be not only unhelpful to PIs, but positively disruptive. Yvonne Twiby was advised that when doing a long surveillance it was best to inform the local police force. She did this once when the local beat bobby knew the man concerned. He went straight to him and told him he was under surveillance. Now Yvonne only informs the police when she believes there may be a breach of the peace, such as when she has to retrieve a child from a parent who doesn't have custody.

In America, the situation is, if possible, worse. Asked about police cooperation, Blair guffaws heartily. 'We don't trust the police because no matter how accommodating they appear to be, you're going to be at each other's throats in court. They have their own agenda. The police usually feel we're trying to get a guilty man off when all I'm trying to do is get this gentleman a fair trial. They can get nasty sometimes. Not giving us information, being in the way. I was trying to do a series of interviews recently and everywhere I went, the police raided. I said, "What the hell is going on here?"

'"Hey," they said, "There's no call to be so hostile when we're doing you a favour. You don't need to go looking for anybody any more, they're all in the county jail." Great.'

PIs can tell similar stories of the district attorneys, the American state prosecutors. They often find information being withheld by the DA's office, legitimate requests being 'forgotten'. Whether it's a result of the pressure of work on the DA or the political need to be seen to be putting away the bad guys, it doesn't make the PI's job any easier.

Sandra Sutherland has the last word. 'In real life, the police hate PIs. They hate that we show them up, they hate that we get to the truth when they've gone for the easy option. I think the reason tame cops are always attached to the fictional private eyes is that in the prevailing American ethos, there's no room for private investigators unless you give them a connection to law and order. The reality that we're in fact crucial as a countervailing force is too complex for the American popular mind. It sounds incredibly pompous, but I said this years ago and it's still true. We are the only people in criminal defence that actually check to see that police power is being applied appropriately and not corruptly. If we didn't exist, in a theoretically democratic society we'd have to be invented. In a society as filled with inequity as this one, someone's got to do this kind of stuff.'

Everybody Loves Good Neighbors

When the recession hit in the late Eighties, we were all scraping around looking for new sources of income. I pioneered a new concept called the professional witness scheme. I work with the local council gathering evidence to assist them in eviction procedures against undesirable tenants. Once I'd got the scheme up and running, I told my colleagues in the Association of British Investigators about it, and several of them have now started running similar schemes in their own areas.

Being awarded the ABI Investigator of the Year award came out of the blue. I was really proud to start with, but it's brought me more headaches....I've had so much publicity, and that's not what you really need as a private investigator. I got the award because of the methods we developed to present evidence in the professional witness scheme. That scheme in itself had generated enough media coverage in the year before we got the award but fortunately they kept my name out of it. They identified the person conducting the investigations as a woman detective but that was all.

Then after I got the award, one of the Sunday tabloids, the real gutter press, did an expose story on me even though I refused an interview. They identified me as 'the spy next door', and blew my cover sky high. I've still got to work in my town. That's what upsets me; now the people in Sunderland know for sure it's Brenda Balmer who's the council's professional witness.

The project started in about 1990. The City Council were having problems on their housing estates and didn't know what to do so they got in touch with the

Crime Prevention Officer. The police couldn't help, but they suggested the council should get in touch with me. I had a meeting with this council officer and he showed me the Tenants' Charter. I sat and read it and said, 'Well, the only thing I can think of is to try and get evictions for harassment, damage to property, storing stolen property and drug dealing, all those sort of things.'

He said 'Do you think we can?'

'Well, there's no harm in trying,' I said. He took it through his channels and eventually came back to me with the green light. We got started in about August of 1992. That first project took two years; it's still going on and I'm still in the middle of work on that particular estate, which is partly why I'm so browned off about this publicity. It compromises operations and it could put me and my operatives at risk.

Some of the investigations were done with surveillance from vehicles, and others involved the council giving us a property and us moving in. For example, there was one we did next door but one to a property. We had three vanloads of stuff in there. We moved in as though we were new tenants. You can't just move in with a suitcase. You can't let them suspect you're not properly moving in. We never left our gear in the house, the cameras and radios and mikes, we always took it out with us every morning. Anyway, this lass we were investigating was about nineteen. She had a three-year-old child and she had a four-bedroomed council house. It was ridiculous giving a child a bloody great big house in the first place. She was using it as storage for stolen property, it was a brothel, there was drug-taking going on. It was a place of ill repute in all ways. The little thieves would come to her house at night, and by one in the morning they were going out to do jobs and then coming back to store the stuff. They'd smashed the whole interior to pieces.

It was one of the best jobs we've ever done in terms of gathering information. We spent three weeks there. We kept surveillance from about five o'clock at night till eight o'clock the next morning, looking like we were living there but 'going out to work' during the day. We could see who was going in and out her front door and we had some long-range listening devices as well. Of course, we weren't able to identify who was going in and out by name, so when we do this kind of job, we identify them by giving them nicknames. Then we put that nickname on our worksheet, names like 'Blue Cap' or 'The Limp' so that we can identify them to each other.

We had that much evidence in a fortnight it was incredible. Then the local paper heard about the scheme and wrote a half-page article—'Have You Spies Next Door?' It even named the estate we were working on. All the tenants had to do was figure out who were the new faces. We'd given them no reason to think we were anything other than new neighbours, but I knew we were living on borrowed time.

That night, while I was asleep, the little buggers shinned up the drainpipes and nicked my directional mikes from off the upstairs window sills. I knew then that we were definitely sussed. We were out of there so fast you wouldn't believe it. We just grabbed our equipment and went. Luckily, it was too early for most of them to be up and about. We had to send the council round later to pick up the rest of our gear.

The positive side of it was that we had enough evidence for the council to evict this woman, and it was the first case of its kind in the country. We've done other successful ones since, though we've had one or two other near things. One time, some kids tried to set fire to our van, and another time a gang of teenage thugs tried to frighten us off with baseball bats and rocks through the window.

When that journalist wrote his daft story, he obviously wasn't thinking about the consequences. I suppose it never occurred to him that he could have got somebody hurt.

BRENDA BALMER
Sunderland

13

Techno, Techno, Techno

*Never throw anything out that you don't want someone else
to read. I've learned one thing, you never say anything
crucial over the telephone; there's a scanner right there.*

SARAH DI VENERE
Chicago

*Some of the young male investigators can be a bit brash.
They've got all the equipment and the mobile phones, but
people don't talk to them they way they talk to an older woman.*

SALLY ISTED
Southsea, Hampshire

There's no question that the development of electronic technology has changed the way investigators do their jobs. From miniaturised cameras to computer databases, it has provided them with a new generation of tools that have left them with mixed feelings. Some have embraced them joyously with both hands; others have their reservations. But all acknowledge that the technology is here to stay and can't be ignored.

The clients too are aware of the changes, and their expectations of what an investigator can do for them have been correspondingly inflated. The trouble is that the gadgetry we fiction writers cheerfully throw around in our books and scripts is often too expensive and also too illicit for all except the biggest or the most unscrupulous to use. But because they've read about it or seen it on TV, the clients expect everything to be at the fingertips of every operative, and they expect results yesterday.

Interestingly, the women all maintain that it is the men who are more interested in acquiring the latest piece of technical gadgetry. The boys want toys to play with, while the women are more wary. It's not that they don't feel competent to use the state of the art electronics; it's that they believe human interaction is still the most effective and accurate way of assembling much of the information they need to do the job properly. They tend to be far more selective in their use of tricks and electronic wizardry. Brenda Balmer is happy to use high amplification directional mikes when that's the only way she's going to succeed in a professional witness surveillance; but it's always a last resort when other techniques have failed or are inappropriate. When it comes to sticking tracer bugs on cars or hacking computer databases, most women eyes prefer to leave it to others.

Like Sarah Di Venere. 'I have a friend who is a PI in Chicago, and this guy is a real character. He's always calling up the newspapers and scamming them with stories of what he's done. He's been indicted for tapping and he's been in jail and I don't understand how he got his licence back. He's hated by other investigators but I tolerate him because he's good for information.

'He was on TV once telling the reporter, "I have this equipment that I can point at a car down the street and it allows me to hear everything that's being said in there." Next thing is, I have clients calling me, asking if I've got one of these gadgets that lets you listen to people's conversations in their car. Now, equipment that good costs thousands of dollars and nobody except the CIA has got it! Investigators do not run around with that type of' money. So I call this guy and tell him how pissed I am at him for mouthing off about this gear, and he just laughs and says, "So what if I don't have the stuff? It makes great copy, Sarah. My phone has been red hot today."

Typical male hot shot! Women just do not pull that kind of stunt. Even if I had that equipment, the last people I'd tell would be the TV station.'

Sarah isn't against using gadgets, however. She wouldn't be without her scanner, that clever electronic eavesdropping gadget that allows its owner to pick up other people's mobile phone calls. She also has a tapeless recorder built into a pen which can record short snippets of information on a digital chip. She doesn't use it to record people unawares, but to keep a note of vital details such as number plates when she's at the wheel and can't use a pen and paper.

One of the most commonly used pieces of equipment is the video camera. It's perfect for recording evidence from surveillances, particularly in insurance cases where proof is needed that the claimant is really fit for work. But like many of their colleagues, Sally Isted and Pat Wingate generally think that flashy equipment is no substitute for good investigation. 'Some of the young male investigators can be a bit brash. They've got all the equipment and the mobile phones, but people don't talk to them the way they talk to an older woman.' Nevertheless, they have used video cameras in their insurance fraud work. On one occasion, they were investigating a mobile hairdresser. They rented a bedsit and booked her to do Pat's hair. Sally videoed everything on the pretext that she was a friend who had come from Bournemouth to go to a school reunion with Pat, and was practising with the video camera her brother had lent her for the occasion.

The video evidence proved that the hairdresser could still work, and showed exactly how agile she was. Sally had even persuaded her to video them, which proved that she could comfortably handle something heavy and awkward.

A video camera takes on the role of an undercover spy when a company is too small to be infiltrated by an undercover agent without setting off alarm bells. These days video cameras can be amazingly small and discreet and can be hidden anywhere. Janet Wilson sometimes installs hidden video cameras in her pub surveillance work, but believes it is vital for an agent to visit the premises too. 'A camera can't tell you that you can cut the atmosphere with a knife. It can do a lot of the basics, and provide evidence, but it can't interpret what it sees.'

This is a belief that is repeated again and again by the women eyes; however sophisticated technology is, it can only provide raw information, not process what it sees. The skill comes in that interpretation and in knowing how and when to exploit the technology at the PI's disposal. The more technologically advanced the equipment is, the more the PIs have to learn in order to use it properly.

One example is the polygraph, or lie detector, a machine that measures a number of physical reactions such as breathing, blood pressure and pulse while the subject is questioned to show when he or she is lying. For Susan Lauman, it's been a fascinating new departure to learn how to exploit the test to the full.

'At first, I was very sceptical about using the polygraph. In the past, I'd been involved in a couple of cases where people failed the polygraph test, although they insisted they were innocent, and I believed them. I thought, "Hey, this thing really isn't reliable." Then later, both of them broke down and confessed. So the polygraph was right even when I was convinced it was wrong. Since then, I've come to realise that in the hands of a good operator, nobody can beat the polygraph. They might manage to keep a pretty tight grip on themselves, but you run that test a couple of times and you can spot where the lies live.'

One of the major growth areas in big commercial centres like New York is white collar crime. The shift into computerisation has handed some fraudsters the perfect opportunity to help themselves to huge wads of other people's cash. Those in the know reckon the banks only admit to about ten per cent of what they actually lose through electronic fraud. If they told the truth, everybody would be closing their accounts and reverting to socks stuffed with gold coins tucked under the mattress. Such computer crime can be incredibly difficult to uncover because the perpetrators are intelligent, highly skilled and cover their tracks with care. In such cases a polygraph can play a vital role, as Susan Lauman discovered.

'We used the polygraph to break down a suspect in a big computer fraud case. A spectacular sum of money—in the region of $12 million—had been removed from New York banks and transferred by a very complex and obscure route to the Cayman Islands. From quite early on in the case, we could see how the fraud had been carried out, but it took us a long time to get from there to the people who had actually done it. There were two of them, and building proof against them was very, very difficult because what they'd done was very clever and they'd covered their tracks extremely carefully.

'We got one of them to agree to take a polygraph test, because he was an electronics whizz kid and he thought he could beat it. He'd beaten the bank's computer system, and he thought he could do the same with the polygraph. He was wrong. We could see straight away the guy was lying to us, and we could see exactly which questions were provoking false responses. Now, this knowledge was a very persuasive tool to use to put pressure on him to confess, which he finally did. This was a guy with no money at all. The whole thing had been like a game to him. He was a computer freak, and he did it simply because he thought it could be done. It was a challenge, him against the machines. It was totally satisfying to catch him out like that.'

When it comes to computer technology, many women eyes are ambivalent about its benefits. Increasingly, public information is being stored on computer, which means that private eyes are forced to access their sources electronically whether they like it or not. There are undoubted benefits. New technology and access to computer databases means that an investigator is no longer tied to the hours that public records facilities are open; they can search the databases at other times, they can work in the middle of the night if they need to. It saves having to run around to three or four different places to look at different records; that in turn saves the client money, and for people who have a commitment to getting the best value for the client's dollar, that has to be a significant cost-saver.

What worries many of the women I interviewed is the accuracy of many of the on-line databases. Byrna Aronson, happy to be called a Luddite, explains. 'Computers generate so much misinformation. We've had exposés in this country about how between fifteen and twenty per cent of computerised credit records have mistakes in them. Well, that's a lot in my business. For me to come up with one fifth of my information incorrect would not be helpful to me or my client.'

Sandra Sutherland found computer inaccuracies sent her running around in circles on one case. She was trying to find her client's long-lost sister but could find absolutely no records under the family name, Beaulieu. In desperation she asked to see the old ledgers from which the database she was using was drawn. She noticed that in the spidery handwriting on the ledgers 'u's and 'n's looked very similar. She returned to the computer and typed in the name Beanlien and up popped the information. A simple typing error had almost left her stranded.

It's not just that databases can be inaccurate, or even, as is often the case, out of date. There's a whole mine of human information that an experienced PI can find on written documents that disappear on the computer. Evidence of forgery for instance, such as different inks or handwriting, alterations or deletions. As Sandra Sutherland points out, a hacker doesn't leave any traces but paper documents cannot be altered without evidence. Often the PI won't know what they are looking for until they are holding a piece of paper in their hand and something jumps out at them. Perhaps the writing is quavery or illiterate, which might give vital clues to the character or state of mind and health of the writer.

Technology puts barriers between the investigator and the information. Even relatively old technology like the telephone. That's why Sandra Sutherland's agency never does interviews on the telephone unless there's a very good reason why they have to. For one thing, it's a lot easier to say no on the phone than when facing someone who has come to your doorstep. Showing an interviewee a face can allay their fears and build up trust. The PI can also get a lot more information when they can see their subject. Is she smelling of gin? Is she in an old chenille robe at ten o'clock in the morning? Does he have survivalist magazines on his coffee table? Are they telling the truth or does their body language show that they are lying? Face to face conversations tend to go on longer, they are more spontaneous, more discursive. It could be in the general chit chat that precedes or follows an interview that the PI picks up what they really need to know.

'People can always get more than computers,' says Jane Quinney. 'A computer can't knock on the door. A computer can't tell you what the house is like, or what the area's like.' Jane's agency has often been called in when computer traces have failed, usually because the information on the databases is out of date. But the rise of agencies that only do computer tracing has brought problems for investigators who believe that the best way to obtain results is to get out on the street and use their wits. Many of these computer tracing agencies are willing to work on a no result no fee basis. That's fine if you are doing multiple traces which are nothing more than typing a name into a computer, but it's not acceptable to agents who have spent time out on the streets following up all the possible sources of information. They believe that it's only fair that they get paid for their time, whether or not they actually come up with a result.

Some women eyes also believe that the advent of database technology has made people either lazy about or ignorant of the other resources that are available. According to Blair, 'The problem is computers can turn people off the simple things. Even attorneys have the wrong idea about what technology is there for. I had an attorney call me from Los Angeles to ask me for a zip code and I said, "Here's the deal. I'll share the secrets of the trade. I'll tell you what I would do. I'd call the Post Office. Better still. I'd take five minutes and walk over to the Post Office and look in their zip code book." Like, idiot, I don't have to do this, send one of your paralegals to the Post Office or the library. It's going to be a lot cheaper than me getting it for you from the computer. So many people forget the simple things. They forget how to use resources that are free and available to everybody. The reference desk at the library is one of my all time favourite sources because if you handle it properly, the person who picks up the phone is going to go the distance for you. These are people who like their work!'

There are women eyes who have enthusiastically embraced the wonders of modern technology. Nancy Poss-Hatchl delights in the way it speeds up the job and gives her clients better value for money, though she confesses that if it wasn't for the help of her husband Sidney, a retired aerospace engineer, she'd have trouble working out the finer details of the computers. Her company is on line to several databases which provide information on everything from criminal records to property transactions. As I watched, she typed in a subject's name to the property database. Within seconds, we were looking at a comprehensive list of the houses the subject owned, when he bought and sold them, how big they were, how much he'd bought and sold them for and what mortgages were outstanding on them.

Mistaking my look of horror for amazement, she said gleefully, 'It's terrific, isn't it? It's so fast. I get enquiries from all over the world, and I can deal with them almost instantaneously. People love it when they get a fax back within a couple of hours of sending their inquiry.'

Nancy worries about the fact that access to information is gradually being whittled away in California. It's no longer possible to obtain forwarding addresses or details of names and addresses from car licence plates. But as someone who looks for the positive in life, she accepts each shutdown as a challenge. When one door closes, she immediately takes a crowbar to a window. For example, nearly everybody gets a traffic ticket some time and traffic tickets are in the public domain. She can run a licence plate through the traffic ticket records and pull out a name and address that way.

Jean Mignolet has become an enthusiast of computer technology because so much of her work now involves background checks. Because Miami is a place where nobody comes from and everybody moves to, background checks are de rigueur for everything from marriage to employment. In the state of Florida, there is a huge amount of information in the public domain, so Jean can sit at her computer terminal and run down background on people very easily.

Jean has created a personal database of everyone she meets, containing all she knows about them, their work and their interests. With 2,000 contacts logged onto her computer she can be almost certain that whenever she wants something, one of them is bound to know how she can get it. But such technology cuts both ways; hackers can get into information stored on a computer and in a job where client confidentiality is so vital, this is a serious risk for a PI.

Even the most ardent technophiles agree that it's important to combine traditional and modern resources. When Nancy Barber is researching the history of her asbestos claims, she starts off with the old-style methods. This may mean going through old phone books, city directories and company records. 'Everybody who thinks being a private investigator is so glamorous should see me sitting in blue jeans and teeshirts on the floor of a public library going through dusty city directories,' she laughs.

Only when she has got as much information as possible this way does she turn to her computer. 'I never even turn on the computer, I never punch in a name till I've done the basic research. My complaint about some investigators that do the same kind of work I do is that they'll spend a fortune on database searches before they've even figured out anything about the person's life.'

Pat Storey, on the other hand, starts with the computer. 'The first thing I would do when I get a trace enquiry is database searches. If I've got a name and address, I put that straight into the database to check out if they're still living there, and who else is listed at 'that address, if your target turns out to have moved, that often gives you another name to use to help trace where they are now. Secondly I would do a credit search on them; what credit do they have? What cards do they have? Do they have hire purchase agreements? Are they keeping up with the payments? Now, if they've moved, they will almost certainly have told the credit card companies, and that new address will be in there. Now you have a door to go and knock on.'

Once she has the computer evidence Pat will go out on the street, talking to neighbours, checking out the subject's house and car, to find out the story behind the statistics. 'A lot of so-called tracing specialists will say, "Thank you for your instructions, we've traced him to 123 Acacia Avenue." That's no bloody good at all. Is it a better house than he had before, or much worse, does he rent now where he had a mortgage before? Is he working when he's said he's not, is he living with someone? The client gets a proper status report from us, because we understand the value of the human element.'

It's easy to become infatuated with the glamour of technology. I know; I once spent hours setting up a computer template to print out the address labels for my Christmas cards. It took longer than it would have done to write out the whole lot by hand. But probably because computers and technology have the reputation of being a boy's world, the women eyes are more wary of becoming dependent on something outside themselves than most of their male counterparts. As a result, they seem to have managed to be selective, only embracing those elements of technology that really help them do their job more effectively. Most importantly, they never forget that when it comes to solving puzzles created by people, nothing can beat the human touch.

Where There's a Will . . .

One case I remember talking over with Sue Grafton involved an inheritance. I was contacted by a bank in New Jersey who were looking for a woman who was due to inherit $60,000. They needed to find her so they could close the estate. All they knew was that she was believed to be in Seattle.

It turned out one of the weirdest cases I've ever worked on. This poor woman had left her family practically twenty years ago. The family were very well educated, very wealthy. The daughter rebelled against her family and just went totally off the rails; she became a drug addict and got in with a bad crowd. She went her separate way and they hadn't heard from her since.

One of the reasons it was so difficult to find this woman was that she did not exist in the traditional sense. No trace of a social security number. Nothing. She wasn't working, she didn't appear ever to have worked. She didn't have a driver's licence. She didn't have a car. Didn't vote. None of the things that normally would enable you to trace her.

Eventually, someone in the family came up with this approximate address so I checked with the Post Office in Seattle and we got lucky, and managed to find the apartment building. I thought that was it, settled. No such luck.

This woman was just impossible to get to. She never seemed to come out of the building, and it had security access only. Mail was returned to sender unopened. She just didn't want to deal with anything or anyone that had anything to do with her family. In the end, the bank sent me the cheque, and I went up to Seattle to sort it out. They also sent me this woman's high school picture, obviously about thirty years out of date, but she was a beautiful young woman. She had a real happy smile and was a very sweet looking lady.

The woman I saw was not smiling. Even when she tried to smile, all you could see was sadness. She wore some kind of scarf thing on her head, so I couldn't even see the colour of her hair. She would never look me in the eye and her body language was very meek, very insecure. She had ended up living with her husband in this dank, disgusting, horrible little one-roomed unit. You couldn't really call it an apartment, it was so small and dingy. It was March when I went to see her and the Christmas tree was still in the corner. There was only one lamp in this entire room and it had a forty-watt bulb in it. All the windows were boarded up. There was one little card table with two chairs that didn't match, plastic plates; a very, very horrible looking existence.

I tried to engage her in conversation and her husband cut her off every possible moment that he could. She was like a delicate flower and he would just cut her down and act like she wasn't even in the room any longer. Her husband was suspicious of the money. I'd gone there with the investigator I'd been dealing with in Seattle, a guy named Ron. Picture this. Four individuals in this tiny little room where there's only two chairs and a bean bag where if you sit in it you end up like a turtle on your back. Now, I'm the one with the briefcase, I'm the one with the cheque, I'm the one with the case history, I need to talk to the woman but the husband thinks that Ron, being the man, is the one who knows what's going on. I'm talking to the woman, the husband cuts her off and then tries to pick up the conversation with Ron. Ron keeps saying, 'I don't know anything about this case,' and looks at me and I start all over again. Every time I spoke to the woman, the husband cut her off and took up the conversation with Ron.

Finally after about an hour of this ridiculous scene, I gave her my card and told her to call me at the hotel. I said if she didn't want the money, she could give it to charity, for God's sake! $60,000, there's a lot of things you can do with that kind of money and if she was really stuck, she could always have signed it over to me! The thing was, it was shit or get off the pot time. The bank needed to close out the estate, and they needed her either to take the money or sign a waiver saying she wasn't prepared to accept it. But she wouldn't do either; she just wanted no connection with her family.

As a last resort, I talked to the landlord, and she was pretty cool. She said they always paid their rent on time, in cash. They'd been living there for years on end. I suspected that they were actually dealing drugs because the landlord said that they never were up during the day, they were always up at night and she hardly ever saw the woman. Everything was always cash, they didn't have a checking account, nothing. It must have been in the mattress! I ended up having to come back to Santa Barbara with this $60,000 cheque. Can you believe that, in this day and age?

BJ SEEBOL
Santa Barbara

14

Women Against Violence Against Women

The depressing thing about domestic violence is the number of cases that come around again.

JOAN BEACH
Washington DC

I feel it's important to help women not to be victims.
I've done a lot of pro bono work with abused women and
children, and part of that is helping those people
understand that they are not to blame.

SARAH DI VENERE
Chicago

Although young males in their twenties are the social group most likely to suffer violent death at the hands of another, it is clear that when it comes to suffering regular, systematic, demoralising violence, women are the principal victims. It's not street violence that degrades them and turns their existences into living hells. It's domestic violence. It happens in their homes, the places where they should feel secure. It happens at the hands of the very people who they are told will love and protect them—husbands, lovers, sometimes even children. And it happens in such a way that, as often as not, they feel that it is their responsibility and that they must bear the burden of guilt for what has been inflicted upon them.

For those of us who have never been battered, it's easy to believe that it could never happen to us, that we would walk away forever from someone who inflicted that kind of damage on us. No matter how sympathetic we know we ought to be, there is some corner of our minds that feels a grain of contempt for women who stay and allow themselves and their children to be abused. It's not that simple, though. Often women who are battered in adulthood have been abused as children; they equate battering with love because they don't have any other experience to compare it with. They also love their abusers. They know deep down that their lover wouldn't be battering them if only he could get a job, or gain recognition for his talents, or stop drinking, or pay his debts, or quit doing drugs, or she could stop the baby crying, or, or, or....The list is endless, but for the victim of the battering, there's always an excuse, always a catalyst over the distant horizon that will stop it happening.

It's not just something that happens among the poor and the badly educated. Spousal battery, as they call it in America, can happen anywhere. Hollywood stars like OJ Simpson do it. Doctors do it. Lawyers do it. Lots of policemen do it. Pam Quinney, who works in genteel, Georgian Cheltenham, sees it all the time.

'Mostly they're victims of the recession. Their businesses have gone into debt and they're looking at bankruptcy. That's sometimes when the marital problems start. It's a big strain. The husband might have lost a good job. He's out of work, there's no money coming in and it puts a lot of pressure on the marriage and sometimes it just explodes into violence.'

Sometimes women scrape together the courage to make a bid for escape. They grab the kids, pack a few things and head for the women's refuge. Or they resolve to be really brave and stay in the house, determined to keep him out, temporarily at least. That's where their lives collide with women PIs. They're the ones who serve the injunctions that are supposed to keep their abusers away from them.

Mostly, the injunctions come via solicitors. Sometimes, they come directly from the women themselves, who have managed to negotiate the shoals of the legal system single-handed and find themselves the possessors of an injunction with no idea how to serve it. Often, they turn to the police Domestic Violence Unit for help and advice, and the DVUs pass them on to the private eyes.

Then the women eyes have to serve papers on men who are already demonstrably violent. The theory is that men are less likely to hit women who are not their wives than they are another man. It doesn't always work out that way, though, since some of them are outraged to be served with an injunction by a mere woman.

The experience of dealing with domestic violence from this angle shapes the women eyes' work. Some of the women who do criminal defence work simply refuse to accept clients who are charged with violence against women. Others will accept such cases, but only on the basis that they would rather it was them re-interviewing the victims of crime than a man.

What they all acknowledge is the profoundly depressing nature of the work. It's hard to gain satisfaction from putting a barrier between women and their abusers when, as often as not, the woman takes her partner back and walks willingly back into a situation that she kids herself will be different. Months, weeks or even days later, papers land on the PI's desk with the same names, the same addresses and the same pain.

'There was one particular chap in Chester, he was a real sod,' Jackie Griffiths recalls, an edge of anger in her voice. 'He looked like Tom Selleck but twenty years younger. He had this little wife, four foot six, six stone, and he was beating hell out of her, smashing up the home. I went serving papers on him half a dozen times because his wife kept taking him back and taking him back, and he'd thrash her again, so I'd be serving him again. That happens a lot; sometimes I get despondent about it, but more often it makes me angry.'

The final straw came for Jackie when the man turned on her, as she served him yet another set of papers in a pub. 'He turned and he grabbed my wrist. The barmaid was shouting at him to let me go. I told him very quietly to let me go. He said, "It's always women, always erring women, isn't it?" We're standing there in this Mexican stand-off, and he's got my wrist in this really tight grip. I'm fairly tall but he was above me, and I'm saying, "Let me go. I'm a match for you any day." And my knees were going like castanets, and I'm thinking, God, I hope he believes it because I don't! He finally let me go and I walked out but he came out of the pub after me. I jumped in the car and went off like a bat out of hell.

'Of course, his wife took him back again and a few weeks later, the solicitor phoned up and said he had more papers to be served on this chap. I said, "Sorry. If she wants them serving, she can serve him herself. It's my body going on the line. Every time I go up against him I'm running a bigger and bigger risk of getting thumped, and for what? I am not risking myself for her to be stupid and keep taking him back. I'm not serving him again!" It wasn't fear so much as anger at the futility of it.'

It's the only time Jackie has been attacked while on the job but she admits that she always feels nervous when serving papers on men for violence against women, particularly when she has read the affidavit describing what they have done. However much it helps to be prepared, she sometimes feels that ignorance is better than knowledge in these cases.

Unfortunately, evidence on paper isn't always necessary since it's there to be seen with her own eyes. She recalls another case when she couldn't find the man she was to serve and in desperation went to ask his wife where he might be. Jackie found her covered in bruises and was immediately outraged that any man could treat a woman so badly. Her outrage turned to frustration when she heard the man's voice from inside the house and realised that he had been taken back once again.

Although she tries to understand the fear such women suffer from, Jackie admits that she finds herself exasperated and depressed by them too. At times it has made her consider giving up the job and finding an occupation without the emotional strain.

What stops PIs like Jackie from giving up is the belief that they can do some good, and help improve the lives of some of the women they encounter, even when they seem to be permanently damaged. Jennifer Paul worked on a harrowing case involving incest where it seemed that three women's lives had been utterly ruined. The three sisters had been abused for many years by their uncle and grandfather and all had carried the scars through into their adult life. One had become a lesbian, but it seemed to Jennifer it was not because of a genuine love of women but more a result of her hatred of men caused by the abuse. The second had physical problems with her womb, the third was mentally unbalanced. After many years, the women found the strength to have their uncle and grandfather charged. Jennifer admits that she questioned the value of this course of action.

'Sometimes I think to myself they shouldn't have to go through it all again in the witness box, but on the other hand, maybe it gives them a feeling of catharsis, or a sense of power, that they've finally taken action against the men who made their lives hell.'

Sarah Di Venere would agree with this. She believes that it is vitally important not just to get women out of situations where they are in physical danger but to help women not to be victims and to understand that they are not to blame. In the pro bono work that she does for abused women and children, she has seen how many forms abuse can take, both mental and physical.

At times mental victimisation can be as brutal and damaging as physical violence. Sarah once had a woman (who was on the verge of a nervous breakdown) referred to her by a psychiatrist. Her husband had been telling everyone that she was mentally unstable and even a drug addict, and constantly telling her that there was something wrong with her, until she had finally begun to believe it. Sarah discovered that the husband was having an affair and was placing mental stress on his wife to pave the way for getting out of the marriage on the excuse of her mental instability. Solving the case, and giving back the woman's sense of self-worth and self-confidence was immensely satisfying to Sarah.

Sarah has also developed techniques for helping women who are being oppressed by stalkers, something which in her experience is much more common than people realise. A woman who is plagued by a stalker cannot get help from the police unless an actual crime has been commited. Following her around or constant telephoning isn't a crime, however threatening it may be. Luckily Sarah has found that following a stalker is easy for a woman because these men discount women totally. If it crosses their mind that somebody might just be taking action against them, they'll imagine in their arrogance that it must be a male detective or police officer. Sarah is able to stalk the stalker and video them harassing the victim. This gives her something solid to take the police; even if they can't actually charge him with anything they can at least talk to him and let him know they are watching him.

'We have to tell women, "Don't just sit back and let people walk all over you," and then we have to empower them to act for themselves,' Sarah explains. "I always tell women, never go out without one of those disposable cameras. If you see somebody following you, take a picture of them and get their licence plate. When they realise they've been spotted, they know they're not going to be able to get away with it and they'll disappear like all bullies do when they see somebody is prepared to stand up to them.'

Sometimes the bullying batterers are so arrogant that they actually think they can use a woman investigator to further their pursuit of their victim. Christine Usher recalls a man who tried that. 'He wanted to find his wife. As I probed deeper, it became clear she had taken out an injunction against him. We'd done a little bit of work for him by this stage and I thought, suppose he gets this address, he's going to go round there and get aggressive towards his wife, so I made him sign a waiver. I said if I continued with the job, I would also inform the local police that he knew where she was. He wasn't happy about that and we didn't finish the job. Whenever I feel a little uneasy about clients, I always say to them, "Look, I'm not going to assist in any offence that you might want to commit, and if I feel at any time that you are going to commit an offence, it is my duty as a professional and as a citizen to report it." That's what I tell them and at least they know where they stand.'

Perhaps surprisingly, it's not only men who are guilty of violence against women. In spite of the mythology that lesbian relationships are somehow more tender and caring than heterosexual ones, women also batter their lovers. Byrna Aronson has been closely involved in a case of this type in the course of her pro bono work for battered women.

'The Governor of Illinois had reviewed a number of cases involving women who had been sent to jail for killing partners who had battered them. He decided that several of these cases were genuine self-defence. So he gave these women amnesty and they were released.

'The Governor of Massachusetts decided that was a wonderful PR stunt. So he set up a commission where any woman who was in Framingham (the Massachusetts state penitentiary for women) who thought she might qualify could send in an application for commutation. Now, when you are charged with murder in Massachusetts, you are not allowed to bring in evidence about the person that is killed; their history of battering, their terrorising of you, their abuse. That's not allowed as evidence in self-defence. You can only bring in what was going on at the time of the crime. These women who have been battered for years have a lot of evidence that was never allowed to be heard in court. So their attorneys were trawling through their pasts, looking for any witnesses to these prolonged histories of abuse.

'One of the eight women who have applied for commutation is a black woman jailed for killing her lesbian lover, and she has a lesbian attorney representing her. Believe me, this is a case nobody wanted. But her lawyer approached me, and I said I'd take a shot at it. I hated the idea of what this woman had been through, regardless of who had done it to her.

'I read the case and visited my client who didn't want to talk to me about shit, didn't want to answer my questions. She was typical of a lot of battered women, feeling guilt, feeling hopeless, sometimes feeling like she deserves to be in jail, other times feeling she should not be incarcerated for defending herself. This woman was also terrified of the family of the victim. With good reason, as I later found out. But having agreed to take the case on, I was prepared to run it into the ground.

'There was one person who had witnessed some horrendous injuries that the dead woman had inflicted on my client. The problem was that she is the ex-girlfriend of my client's brother, and she had filed charges against him for molesting her children. So there is no love lost here.

'I figured, this woman is not going to want to talk to me, but I couldn't pass up the possibility. I had such trouble finding her. Nobody knew where she'd moved to. I tracked back to the neighbourhood she used to live in. I talked to people she knew and I heard she might work for a bank. Somewhere. Eventually I narrowed the area down and started going into all the banks around there. At last, I walked in the door of one of these banks, and there she was, sitting behind her nameplate.

'I convinced her to come meet with me. I knew she was crucial because, as opposed to most of the other people in this case, she's a very credible witness. She's employed, she has been for years, she's a bank officer, she's living essentially a middle-class existence. She has no axe to grind because she is not exactly a big fan of my client's family. And she has witnessed enough to convince anybody that it was self defence. She would be the perfect witness and I knew she would not want to talk to me.

'She had coffee with me but she was not prepared to be involved. Not for justice, not for pity, not for anything. All I could get from her was a promise she'd go home and think about it and meet me again. Next time we met, I produced the tape recorder and my list of questions, and she answered every one. Then she told me she absolutely would not testify. If I subpoena her, she won't show up. If she's forced to show up, she won't answer any questions. If she's forced to answer questions, she'll be a hostile witness, destroying the credibility of other witnesses we have to the abuse. I was going crazy inside, because she was a goldmine of information. So I worked on her with everything I knew. Eventually, she agreed that if I typed up an affidavit, she'd think about signing it.

'Anyway, the lawyer and I prepared the affidavit and I met her again. Will she sign it or won't she? I am trying to impress on her that her evidence is crucial to my client's future. That my client wasn't responsible for her brother's terrible actions. That I'm not asking her to lie. That this woman is in jail for the rest of her life if the truth cannot be told. That two wrongs don't make a right. She decides she wants to take the affidavit home and think about it. I'm waiting for her call, and the tension is killing me.

'She asks for another meeting and straight off, she signs the affidavit and I notarise it. I can't believe the turnaround. And she says, "Do you want to know why I'm doing this? Because my daughter told me to. My little girl said whatever your client's brother did to her, that was no reason for me not to do the right thing. And that she needed me to do the right thing." This was all very poignant, but I'm so delighted, I'm thinking, "Honey, I don't care if you just stood on your head and spit wooden nickels!" I knew she had just made my case.

'My political experience told me that my client never had a snowball's chance in hell of being released. I knew they were going to have to turn some of the women down out of political expediency and that she would be one of them. But that was no reason for me not to do everything that was humanly possible to overturn her conviction.

'The commission said hers was a case of mutual battering, a concept, by the way, that has no legal standing. The victim was twice the size of my client, she had come in drunk and had started abusing my client, who happened to be cutting up meat at the time so she had a knife in her hand. But the commission said that was nothing to do with battered woman syndrome. It's much harder for people to see battery between two women in terms of a lesbian relationship.

'Out of the eight, I think three got their sentences commuted and a couple got early parole. My client's still sitting there.'

René & Anna's Excellent Adventure

The company I work for buys up and turns around large debts. We're talking seven figures and above. We're not in the repo trade. We're not in the car loan business. It's piddly dollars. But we'd bought the loan on this huge building in Alaska and ended up having to foreclose. We didn't want to own that building when winter time came because the heating bills were going to eat us alive. A company wanted to take it off our hands and part of the deal was we took over 160 car loans. We found a buyer for the 125 car loans that were still being paid on, and the guy that I work for told me to go find the other thirty-five cars that were in default.

These cars were all in the Los Angeles area, so my sister Anna and I headed down there for a month. Our job was to track the cars down and then call the guys with the repo truck to come pick them up. We were working really bad areas, heavy gang turf. I must have been out of my mind! I had been doing this cushy financial work, and then suddenly, the Seattle Sisters hit LA...! We went to these big repo guys, and said we were looking for these cars and we wanted them to be on call for us, and they said, 'Really? Two little girls from Seattle? Hey, we've nothing against you guys but this is LA, this isn't Seattle and these cars have been gone for a long time and the reason is because people can't find them down here. If you get one car consider yourself lucky. If you get five cars then you're superior to anybody down here.' Well, we got all thirty-five!

We had done three weeks of advance telephone work, pretexts, licence checks on everything to at least get leads before we even got down there, so once we arrived we just started setting up routes round all these places we had to go check. That first day, we asked the repo guy for directions to the first address on our list and he sort of stepped back in horror and said, 'You don't want to go there, that's Watts!' Now, I've never taken kindly to being told what I can and can't do, so we went off anyway. We didn't realise exactly where we were going; it was the first and last time we did that. We left the repo place, drove right into the middle of Watts in the middle of the day and then found the truck! It was right where we thought it would be!

So within half an hour of leaving the repo guys, we called them to say we'd found the truck, they should come pick it up. They never came. They said, 'OK, we'll go get it at night, we can't go in there in the daytime, get out of there, it's a bad area.' We'd gathered that by then. We were driving right through the middle of drug deals and Anna said, 'If anybody hits us, René, just keep driving!'

We were there a whole month and every day I called them and said, 'You guys pick up that truck yet?'

'Oh, we didn't get to it. Oh, we went and it wasn't there.' Bull! They were afraid to get it. Now Anna and I made these promises to each other that we weren't going to take risks, but there's degrees of risk and everything's relative and after a while you get so obsessed with getting what you need that it gets real personal and you lose sight of what's sensible. And I knew I was not going to leave LA without that truck.

The night before we were due to leave, I called Larry the repo guy and said, 'We have to go get that truck. I'll give you a $200 tip on top of the repo fee. Only, don't tell my sister!' So that night when Anna was asleep, I snuck out and met Larry just after one.

It was way too early to be in Watts. The street life was still buzzing. It only quiets down in there between three and six in the morning, but we were just so gung ho about finally getting this truck that we didn't care! When we got to the house, there was a heavy chain across the driveway, but luckily it was unlocked and Larry just pulled the chain free. Otherwise we'd have been in the realms of illegality, and I don't do things that could get me arrested. We couldn't believe our luck, because it was real quiet on the street. Larry's going, 'This is incredible, we're going to hook it and we're gonna be gone!'

All of a sudden we hear this screaming, and this woman comes running from across the street. She runs right behind the tow truck, races up to this house and starts pounding on the windows. 'Get out here, get out here, look what they're doing!' Larry is half way hooked up, and suddenly we're looking down a shotgun barrel. Larry is about 260 pounds, six foot four and he is dwarfed next to these people that come out of the house. And they were wearing skirts! They were huge! And they're shouting, 'What are you doing?'

And Larry's gabbling, 'I'm taking this car, it hasn't been paid for, there's my paperwork, I have to pick it up.'

And I'm standing there, on the mobile phone, going, 'Yes, Officer, we are at the address we gave you and we're picking up this truck and we want you to hang tight until we get out. No, I don't anticipate any problems, we should be out of here in about five minutes, just stay on the line.' Of course, there is no officer on the line, since the police had already refused us back-up. I was just making up this conversation, and I started thinking, God if my sister wakes up and sees I'm gone and calls the phone number...if the phone rings right in the middle of this spiel, we're dead! But our luck held. They just stood there and we picked up the truck and we drove off and Larry just started screaming. We were happy to walk away.

I didn't confess to Anna till about three weeks later, because I'm supposed to be the big sister, the good example. When I admitted what I'd done, she pointed out very forcefully that I had been real stupid. And she was right. I didn't have a gun with me in Watts.

The LA trip was wild. That's one of the wildest things we've done. You feel like a criminal, you're sneaking around garages at four in the morning. The repo guys were amazing. I'd be saying, 'Larry, how the hell are we going to get it out, there's four cars parked in front of it.' Well, Larry goes in and he moves all those cars around, pulls cars out and puts them all back. Can you imagine? You come out next morning and your car is gone, but all the cars that were blocking it in are exactly where they were? I tell you, these repo guys are braver than I am.

RENÉ OLSSON

15

Point of Impact

Somebody once asked me how I get my job done without telling lies…

LYNN McLAREN
Santa Barbara, California

If people do find out what I do, they make the usual boring comments about trench coats and hanging around on street corners.

MAUREEN JACQUES-TURNER
Hull

Being a private eye is one of those jobs where other people think they know how you spend your days. They have a mental picture of car chases, picking locks, tense confrontations with criminals, the toting of guns and the spying on adulterers; a potent mix of exoticism, glamour and sleaze. The one thing they get right is that it's a job that's mainly done by men.

It's also a job that people feel qualified to make judgements about. They just know that it's faintly disreputable, that its practitioners are inevitably unscrupulous, probably amoral and almost certainly sexually promiscuous. There are certain jobs that are subject to condemnatory judgements like this, and they're usually occupations that have some moral dimension to them. More often than not, the critics are people who have never had to make a moral decision in their entire careers. 'When people find out I'm an investigator, they think that I spend my days following someone else's husband, and that does irritate me,' Christine Usher admits. 'That's maybe one per cent of my business. They have no idea of how hard we work and what we actually do.

'When one lady, who I'm actually quite friendly with now, heard what I did, she said, "Don't you have a conscience about invading someone's privacy?" Well, no, I don't have a conscience about it. I'm just doing a job that I've been instructed to do, rather like the solicitor who has been instructed to act for one client against another person. I don't decide the rights and wrongs of the issues, I simply supply the information I've been contracted to provide. I know the job will be done ethically, because I have strict moral and professional codes that I stick to.'

Often, people are taken aback to find a woman doing the job. As Jennifer Paul observes wryly, the ones who are the most critical of the kind of thing they imagine she does for a living are the very ones she wouldn't be surprised to find herself pursuing. Zena Scott-Archer remembers the hypocrisy that she discovered among her own social circle about her job. Now widowed, Zena was married to a pharmacist. Her husband was extremely supportive of her career but the reaction from his colleagues was very different.

'When I told my husband's colleagues and their spouses that I was a private investigator, they really didn't think it was a very "nice" job for a respectable chemist's wife. I'd start to tell them some amusing anecdote and they would clear their throats and change the subject. But all of them, one by one, came to my door when their son got married to a trollop and they wanted to know how to get him out of it, or they had bought a house and been gyped on the contract. As soon as they were in trouble they would come and say, "I wonder if you'd be able to help me?" All they could ever imagine was that my work was somehow sleazy. They had no concept of the reality, or the satisfactions.'

It's a widely held opinion among those who consider themselves 'respectable'; they either tut-tut in disapproval or demand to hear all the PI's most sordid stories. On one occasion Zena gave a talk at a ladies' guild and was worried that her stories might be a bit old. 'I said, "Some of the stories are a bit...I'm searching for the word...Some of the stories are a little bit hoary."

'"Never mind," the chairwoman said, "we're very broadminded here!"'

Byrna Aronson has found a more positive reaction from the women she encounters, who are often pleased to see a woman doing such an unusual job, while the men are more often suspicious and disbelieving, even if they try not to show it. 'Sometimes people don't show reactions but you know from their body language they're having one. I know that I do not fit people's image of a private investigator, but that only shows the limits of their imaginations.'

Yvonne Twiby agrees. 'British people have to put you into a category. People make assumptions about what I am; I don't have to do pretexts, I just rely on them thinking I'm a hairdresser or a businesswoman. It's quite strange really. People don't quite know what to say when they find out what I do. They seem to think you can't be a private investigator unless you're six feet tall and wide as a doorway. I'm tiny, and I can see them thinking, she's the detective? I always smile sweetly and tell them to watch out because I'm the heavy gang.'

Reactions like this make it understandable that many women eyes are disinclined to admit what they do for a living to all but their closest friends. She may play down her role as an investigator, but Maureen Jacques-Turner shares that reluctance with her fellow operatives. 'When people ask what I do, I get real cagey. Even at my badminton club, they don't know what I do. There's one woman there who's really nice, but we have dealt with her husband and I don't want her to connect me with that at all! He's a constant debtor, we have him at least twice a year.' But as well as preserving one's social life, it's also a way of avoiding the assumptions people immediately jump to. 'If people do find out what I do, they make the usual boring comments about trench coats and hanging around on street corners. Either that or they get all excited and demand that I tell them all about my cases. It's quite insulting, in a way. If I was a lawyer or a doctor, they wouldn't react like that.'

Knowing about the job may change the way people look at her, but Maureen and other women eyes have also found that it changes the way that they look at others. The private eye has to be wary and streetwise at work, always assessing people and never taking them at face value. Inevitably this filters through to their private life too. Byrna Aronson admits that she will always check out a doctor's qualifications before making an appointment and Maureen often drives different ways home to make sure she is not followed.

This wariness is only one example of the way that their work has an impact on the lives of the women eyes. This is not a nine to five job that they can shrug off at the end of the working day. It affects their lives in all sorts of unexpected ways, as Blair explains.

'There are moments when I'm just crazy and at those moments I call up the office and say I won't be in today. I'm just going to sit here and work this out of my system. Those are the days when everything becomes too much. The court system, the prison system, the social system, the cultural system.

'This is a job that can take you over. It's difficult being on the road, away from your support systems and your home. In a way what makes me good at my job is also a curse; I have an imagination. I can walk into almost any set of circumstances and find a way into this person. I never try to be better than that person. If you listen to them carefully enough you will find a thread of conversation that will connect you as human beings and it will be honest because if you lie to somebody you're dead meat. There's also that aspect of insinuating yourself into a person's life, and when the case is over, that person is not in your life any more and I haven't figured out a way to resolve that yet. I find that difficult. You get so close to someone, it can be very intense, sometimes you end up being the person that knows things about them that nobody else in their life knows, truly hideous things, and you have to deal with it when they realise that you've gotten those things out of them, and sometimes they feel rage or they want to be your friend. To get you have to give and that can sometimes be dangerous for me.'

When the stresses of the job spill over into their lives, the PIs have to find solutions as creative as those they come up with at work just to stay sane. For Nancy Barber, that meant buying a second home a couple of hours' drive north of San Francisco where she now spends half her time. Others put aside time for hobbies and relaxing pastimes—dancing, writing, playing with children—or simply pamper themselves with luxuries, from trips to the ballet to expensive underwear.

There are things that are open to most people in the course of their work that are definite no go areas for private eyes. A high percentage of people meet their sexual partners in the workplace. That's not an option for the women eyes. Divorcée Joan Beach admits, 'Falling for the clients is a temptation, of course it is. I recently did a job for a man that I felt really attracted to, but there was no way I could allow myself to become involved with him. I have erected a kind of mental barrier between myself and the work, as a simple form of self-preservation against the emotional havoc my work with children would otherwise cause me. Any kind of emotional entanglement with this man would have destroyed that, not to mention my objectivity.'

It is not a discipline that the male PIs impose on themselves in Joan's experience, however. Many of them will sleep with a client given half the chance.

Being a private eye does make a positive impact on women's lives, however. Several spoke of the self-confidence it had given them. Jackie Griffiths, for example. 'You have to develop a certain toughness in this job to survive. When something bad does happen, you learn to pick yourself up and get back on your feet and do the job, otherwise you'd fall to pieces.' The resilience helped Jackie cope with the aftereffects of a bad car crash which left her feeling that she would never have the nerve to drive again. She believes that without the confidence the job gave her she would never have gone back on the road.

Freedom is another thing the women eyes get from their job. Many are their own bosses and can pick and choose the hours they work and the jobs they do to suit their lifestyle and inclinations. It's a gift that those with children are particularly grateful for.

There are other benefits too, perhaps less immediately obvious. Several of the women eyes I spoke to had at one time or another found themselves investigating hairdressers or beauty parlours and got a free haircut or makeover on the job. Others have had free dry-cleaning, wallpaper and clothes in the course of the inquiries they've done.

The gains are not all financial. It seems a vital trait of the woman eye is a love of knowledge and a desire to learn. The jobs they do introduce them into different worlds and teaches them numerous skills, from soldering to film-making. Sally Isted reaped an unexpected benefit from a domestic inquiry. Her client was convinced her husband was having an affair and wanted him followed. He was a member of a video club and so she joined. The woman's fears were proved unfounded, but though she got nothing from the job, it gave Sally the chance to learn to improve her skills with the camcorder.

Of course there are also social and emotional gains from the job. As well as the delight in jobs well done, in solutions reached and lives altered for the better, many women eyes find strong friendships through their work. It's seldom the clients and the targets of investigations who penetrate the private world of women eyes, but they often form bonds with colleagues and contacts. As crime writers do, they meet as often as they can, when the pressures of the job and home allow, through their organisations, using the excuse of professional development seminars to keep the tax man off their backs while they catch up with old friends and make new ones. And these professional friendships run deep. Maureen and Richard Jacques-Turner had no qualms about their teenage daughter going off on an extended trip round America because they knew she was going to be passed from private eye to private eye like a valuable parcel. It's not surprising that these strong bonds of friendship spring up so readily; nobody except another woman eye knows the pressure and the strains of the job.

By far the greatest point of impact for the women private eyes is their domestic life. As Pat Storey has pointed out, one of the key differences between men and women PIs is that the women have homes to run, whereas most of the men have wives who take on the burden of the domestic work. Of the women I spoke to, half are married. Another couple are living with someone. The rest are either single, divorced or widowed, in roughly equal proportions. About two thirds of them have children. There's no question that domestic responsibilities place a greater burden on the women than their male counterparts. For example, Jennifer Paul's only regret about the job is that it means she can't always be with her children between the hours of five and nine in the evening, because that's often the best time to catch witnesses at home. Men seldom feel guilt because their work prevents them from having quality time with their children; women always do.

It's one area where there is a wide divergence between the real and the fictional women PIs. Convention dictates that the detective is a loner, freed to crusade by the absence of ties, an outsider who can see more clearly because of their emotional distance from the rest of humanity. It's one convention that has spilled over from the traditional male PI novel almost intact. These heroines seldom manage to sustain intimate relationships, whether with members of the opposite sex or even with female friends. I can only think of a couple of fictional women private eyes who are mothers, and one of those, Marele Day's Claudia Valentine, lost custody of her child in a messy divorce. When my PI, Kate Brannigan, was confronted with having to take care of her lover's son from his previous marriage, she found herself at a loss for the first time in her career. The fictional PIs have always seemed to me to tend towards being emotional cripples, and it's one element of the genre I've always found least credible, which is why Kate Brannigan does have a steady relationship with a man and a nexus of close female friends. She sees things clearly not because of her distance from the rest of us, but because she's close enough to understand what motivates people. I was relieved to find that as far as that aspect of my work was concerned, I'd managed to reflect reality.

Often, the pressures of family life mean that the women have less opportunity to meet their colleagues than they would like. Meetings of PI associations tend to be scheduled for times when work is slackest. But women who have partners and children want and need to spend their Sundays with their families, so something has to go by the board. While the men are relaxing over a drink, swapping stories and tips, the women are home doing the ironing or taking the kids out for the afternoon.

Sometimes, the only way to balance motherhood and being a PI is to take the kids along too. Nancy Poss-Hatchl was once baby-sitting her grandchildren when an urgent job came in and she had to hotfoot it down to an industrial site where a vast factory was being demolished. Her grandchildren were completely fascinated by the sight of the huge wrecking ball swinging from the crane and crashing through the upper storeys of the factory. 'Other grandchildren ask grandma to take them to the zoo. Mine ask to go watch demolitions,' she observes wryly.

When Pat Storey started her business, she worked solo initially. 'I just used to chuck the kids in the back of the car with a burger and a cola and work like that. They've been great camouflage on some scams. We had a classic case involving a quarry where lorries were going in and loading up, but there was no paperwork and they were taking these loads off illicitly and selling them on the black market. The quarry was losing vast amounts of money. We hired a caravan and drove it to a lay-by near the entrance of the quarry. We took the wheel off, and Tony, my husband, got the kids and the dog and walked them up and down and had a picnic and changed the wheel, and no one took a blind bit of notice of us because we didn't look suspicious. I was inside the van behind closed curtains, logging all the vehicles going in and out. Registration numbers, times in and out, the lot. Then we got all the bills of lading from the company and went through them so we could target who had been in and come out with a full load but hadn't actually signed for it. We got the lot of them!'

Helen Kliner also finds the family useful camouflage, and doesn't mind taking advantage of her children's sharp eyes. If she takes them out on a job she tells them that they're going on a spying mission and she want them to look for a certain licence plate or a certain car. She even pays them if they manage to spot anything.

When Susan Neary was a child, that was exactly what happened to her when her parents were working their cases. Now she's mother to a three-year-old and stepmother to Brian's three daughters from a previous marriage. Her own childhood experiences have clearly taught her how to juggle the demands of running a home and family with the pressures of a job that never has regular hours.

'When we were kids, on Saturdays Dad would say. "Let's go to Brighton for the day," but we always knew that Dad would be working on the way and that would pay for the day out. We used to all pile into a Mini, three kids and a Labrador dog and Dad and Mum and off we went. Dad would make one or two calls on the way, serving process or making background enquiries, and I can remember thinking, "I just want to get to Brighton, I'm not interested in what he's got to do." Looking back, I'm now doing those things to my own children! It's quite funny because I can remember thinking, "I'm never going to do this to my kids!"'

It's less easy to deal with the kids as they get older and start to realise the implications of mummy's job. Then, like their fathers and grandparents, they often start to feel apprehensive. Sandra Sutherland admits that her children used to worry about the dangers of her job. As they have matured they have learnt more about what their mother is capable of as an individual and worry much less. Being the children of a PI does have advantages too though. What could be more glamorous in the playground than the idea of a private eye just back from another dangerous mission?

Whilst they clearly do worry about the dangers their partners face on the street, most of the men who live with the women eyes seem supportive. They help with the childcare, they even help with the jobs from time to time. Sometimes, ironically enough, the women treat their husbands as men have traditionally treated their wives, keeping them in the dark so they won't go worrying their pretty little heads about things. 'What he doesn't know about can't worry him,' as Sarah Di Venere puts it.

For Susan Neary, however, being able to discuss the job with her husband Brian, who works with her, is vitally important. 'Whatever you're doing, you need to be able discuss it with somebody who knows the ins and outs or is at least prepared to listen and try to understand. When you get wound up, you get high, it's like a drug. If you're enjoying your work and it's going well, it gets the adrenaline pumping. You can't just walk into the house and switch off. We tend to go off into the kitchen and cook a meal together and discuss the day's work.

It's a great wind-down. Also, neither of us is ever giving the other one a hard time because work's getting in the way of family life—we're each as bad as the other in that respect!'

Sadly not all the women eyes find such an understanding partner. It isn't only the fear of danger that their husbands don't like. Some can't cope with their wife's independence and success. When Joan Beach married her second husband he was excited by her seemingly glamorous career, but he soon felt threatened by her capability and success, and was even angry when important clients telephoned her. It was as if her success undermined his masculinity. Unsurprisingly the marriage did not last.

René Olsson has also found that men can feel very intimidated by her achievements and obvious financial independence. As a young single woman she finds the job interferes with her social life and particularly her love life. When she first meets people she can't tell them what she does in case she finds herself having to follow them the next day. When she does develop a relationship her partners find it hard to accept the unpredictability of her lifestyle. You have to be pretty keen to keep dating someone who never knows when or whether she'll be home.

When it comes to the love-life, however, the job has its pluses as well as its minuses. There's nothing like having the skills of a private eye at your disposal when you think your man's cheating on you. Jean Mignolet had no qualms about using her expertise close to home. 'I discovered after six years of seeing this guy that he was cheating on me so I set him up. I got other operatives to do surveillance on him back in LA where he lives, then I used the evidence to humiliate him completely. He should have known better than to fuck with me. I'm a professional. I do this sort of routine stuff standing on my head.'

Being deceived was not just a personal insult but also a professional one for Jean. 'No way was I going to stand back and let him humiliate me professionally as well as personally. It had nothing to do with me being an emotional female, it had everything to do with me being the best private investigator I know. It was about self-esteem. I will never be a victim.'

The wiser men who date PIs know not to take such risks. 'The best thing is the stuff they tell you on the first or second date because they're afraid that you're going to find it out!' laughs René Olsson. 'All their dark little secrets come spilling out, and you get more out of them than some people discover in a whole marriage!'

René's choice of career has caused some family tensions too. Her mother wasn't pleased about her taking the job but was even more unhappy when her sister Anna followed her into the business. Now her youngest sister, who is only fourteen, has expressed a desire to be a PI. René sympathises with her mother's unhappiness, since her sister's decision to join her put her on the other side of the fence. Here was her kid sister, who she felt protective of, taking on a job which she knew could be extremely dangerous. It is something René found hard to come to terms with until she saw how competent Anna was. Although she enjoys working alongside her sister she admits it still worries her. 'I couldn't live with myself if anything happened to my baby sister—I'd always feel it was my fault for getting her into this business.'

In spite of the personal and domestic problems that go with the job, though, few women eyes can even imagine finding any other job that would give them the same buzz. According to René, once you've become a PI, giving up can be positively fatal.

'I really thrive on working hard and doing a good job on cases where I really make a difference. I think about all the detectives that I've known, and when they retire, they all die so fast. Six months, maybe a year. They retire and they're gone. It's frightening. I tell all my friends in the International Council of Investigators, don't retire!'

The Slave Trade

There was a very wealthy, powerful man and he had much, much money. He also had a villa in Mexico. He would hire servants in Mexico and say, 'Let me take you to the United States, where you will have a better life.' He flew them up in his private jet, avoiding the immigration authorities, but when they got there, the man's wife would lock the women up in a room, only allowing them out to work. She would also beat them. The whole house was locked up, and it was surrounded by this man's huge estate. It was totally private. These women never got paid, and there was something like six or seven of them there at any one time.

A couple of times, one or other of them contrived to get to a telephone. But they didn't speak any English, they didn't understand the phone system and the operators only speak English, so they had failed to communicate with the outside world. Finally, one got out. Somehow, she managed to make it to the nearest house, which was miles away across the desert. They thought she was nuts and called the police. The police were going to lock her up. But because this is California, they have some officers that do speak Spanish. Somehow, this distraught woman managed to convince them that she wasn't crazy, she was telling the truth. The police raided the place. They found a bunch of women so upset and nervous they were literally shaking. The women didn't even know where they were, they just knew they were somewhere in America. Eventually, the man and his wife were convicted of slavery.

The man then had a heart attack and his doctor said that it would kill him to go to prison, so he never served time. In spite of his alleged poor health, he's still alive some years later. But the wife did go to prison.

One of the worst aspects of the case was that he could easily have afforded to pay all those women good wages. He was a major league businessman, head of an empire with coast-to-coast outlets.

Afterwards, all the slaves filed lawsuits. I was hired by this man's insurance company who were facing huge damages because it had never occurred to them to put in their policy, 'We don't insure against lawsuits involving slaves'. I mean, what company would think to put a clause in indemnifying themselves against lawsuits resulting from slavery in the 1990s in America? The way we got my clients off the hook was by saying the man and his wife had committed a criminal act, which invalidated the policy. But that was a really wild case. Slavery in the USA!

NANCY POSS-HATCHL
Santa Ana

16

Truth is Stranger than Fiction

We always make it quite clear to anybody who comes to work for us that we don't act the way they do on television.

DIANA MIDDLETON
Hornchurch, Essex

Way back at the start of my investigation into the lives of the women eyes, I rang the Metro Newsdesk of the *Chicago Tribune* and explained why I was visiting the city. They passed me on to their veteran crime reporter. I asked if he knew any real-life women private eyes operating in Chicago. The man on the end of the phone chuckled and said, 'You should be talking to a lady called Sara Paretsky. She's the expert around here.' The first myth, that of the hard-bitten reporter who is the private eye's right hand and second pair of eyes, died right there.

I didn't tell the man I'd already taken his advice. Like most of us, Sara Paretsky didn't know any real women PIs when she started writing her internationally successful series of VI Warshawski novels. It didn't take long for them to find her. 'I've met several now,' she revealed. 'They tend to approach me when I'm doing book signings. It's gratifying to be told by the real professionals that I'm not getting it too outrageously wrong.'

These days, Chicago is as famous for its architecture as its most famous gangster, Al Capone. But the tour Sara gave me of VI Warshawski's Chicago took in more than the smart downtown buildings of The Loop, where her fictional PI has her offices. 'Chicago is still like a patchwork quilt of ethnic neighbourhoods,' Sara explained as we headed for the South Side, where VI grew up. 'We've got the fourth largest Hispanic population in the USA, including a Hispanic Chief of Police. We've got the largest Polish-speaking community in the world outside Poland—quarter of a million of them. After the Depression, when the rail link was put in to Mississippi, poor blacks migrated to the city for work in the steel mills and other heavy industry. Now there's only one steel mill left, and the jobs have gone. And that's hit the black community worst of all.'

By now, we were cruising a network of streets where two white women in a smart car was enough to turn heads. 'It wouldn't be wise to be around here after dark,' Sara said, a note of sadness colouring her voice. Potholed streets, decayed steel mills, houses where the only recent paint job was the graffiti. It was almost a relief to move on to the poisoned marshes around Dead Stick Pond, scene of one of VI's most threatening brushes with death. The stink still clung to my nostrils hours later. It's not hard to see how Sara finds Chicago such fertile soil for a series of novels that pit the individual against the corruption of the establishment. Sarah Di Venere and Helen Kliner certainly find no shortage of work.

'I think there's a large correlation between the characters that you write about and what really happens on the street,' Sarah says. 'I've read a lot of private eye novels. The crimes the fictional women investigate are a lot more dramatic than most of the ones we cover in real life, but the novels are often quite accurate about the way we live and the way we approach our work. Not knowing what kind of case you're going to have from week to week; finding yourself in strange areas and having to be careful of how you go; working all hours of the day and night. You may go home thinking you're finished for the day, then something strikes you so you will get back in your car at ten p.m. or early in the morning and on Sundays because you figure the person who's been avoiding you will be home.'

Sarah even recognises the little details of the fictional PIs' lives—living off junk food, having a special bar or coffee shop to hang out in. It seems the crime writers have got some things right.

The women eyes fall into two broad categories—those that read and enjoy mystery fiction, and those who never touch it. The ones who never read it usually say that they read to escape, not to be reminded of work. And besides, their own cases are more interesting than anything we writers can imagine! For those who read extensively in the field, Sue Grafton, the biggest seller among women PI novelists, is by far the most popular writer. Her character Kinsey Millhone strikes most chords with the women who do the job for real, scoring high on how she goes about the job and on her attitude to the people she comes into contact with.

Santa Barbara, where Sue lives and works, is one of the more prosperous towns on the California coast. Since one of the great truths is that where there's cash, there's crime, Santa Barbara has proved fertile ground both for fictional and factual crime. The town was first given its pseudonym of Santa Teresa by Ross Macdonald, and the baton has been picked up with equal panache by Sue. The local bookshop's massive mural of writers with California connections features her prominently in the foreground. But that's not one of the things she pointed out as she gave me the Kinsey Millhone tour.

Like most writers with a strong sense of place, she has a clear picture in her head of where Kinsey lives—in a quiet street a couple of blocks from the ocean- and where she works—near the police department, just down the street from a courthouse that looks more like a Spanish mission. When she started writing the series with A Is For Alibi, she didn't know any real women private eyes. Now, Lynn McLaren and BJ Seebol, the two women private eyes who work the real Kinsey Millhone beat, have become friends as well as sources.

Lynn says, 'I read the fictional PI novels as a form of relaxation. I enjoy Sue's books best because I recognise so much in them. She might call it Santa Teresa, but I know where she's writing about and she gets it right. Santa Barbara is a great town to live in. If it wasn't for the gangs and the graffiti, it would be perfect. But the gangs are starting to build in this town, and I don't think they're just here on a visit. Because Sue lives here, she recognises the changes as they happen, and she incorporates them in her books. I swear I even recognise particular police officers!' Like Lynn, BJ is a fan of her fictional counterpart and found it extremely flattering when people assumed that Kinsey was based on her because they both drove Volkswagen Beetles, although she's quick to put paid to this idea.

Byrna Aronson is a great devourer of crime fiction. 'I like reading mystery books because I find them entertaining, but at the same time they make me think. The ones that I like best are the ones where I also learn something about other people's worlds. They're good at filling in the gaps in my knowledge, giving me solid background in areas I didn't know anything about before. My favourite mystery writer is Sara Paretsky. My favourite PI character is VI Warshawski. I think Sara has done a remarkable job of creating not just a PI but a rounded character. I don't think that any PI could stay alive doing the things that VI does, you certainly couldn't make a living. Your hospital bills would be enormous, if not your cemetery bills. But as a read, I think they're wonderful. They challenge people.'

Byrna admits to have been influenced by reading Nancy Drew as a child, while René Olsson's mother believes that she only became a PI because she read too many crime novels at an early age. These days René believes that they are compulsory reading for women eyes, 'Because the fictional women detectives in them are always driven by a sense of justice, and they care about the people they deal with.'

That's not to say that the women eyes don't have criticisms of their fictional counterparts. They get irritated by the way some of the heroines deal with violence, leaping instantly back into action after injuries that would fell the toughest football player. They wish the fictional eyes had private lives that more accurately reflected the reality of having partners, households and children. They deplore their consistently terrible taste in men. Jean Mignolet complains that they never have a big enough caseload at any given time; 'I have thirty cases sitting on my desk today, and that's not unusual. I couldn't eat if I did as few cases as the detectives in books,' she comments wryly. Maureen Jacques-Turner comments bitterly that private eyes in books always manage to find parking spaces.

Susan Lauman reckons that because of the fiction, everybody now thinks they know how she spends her days. 'Mostly, they're wrong. It's a lot less exciting than the books, but try getting people to believe that now. They also now have these unrealistic expectations of how quickly I can get results. The one thing that I wish you fiction writers would show is that cases are never solved in two days. There's a lot of long, boring tedious stuff you have to do to get a case to work out, and a lot of the time you need a large slice of luck to get things to drop into your lap. Sometimes, the luck takes a long time coming.'

I found in my investigations that truth is indeed stranger than fiction. The women I met were more diverse in their personalities and their work than I could ever have envisaged. If they have one thing in common, it's that they all give really good directions. I never got lost once.

I didn't find Kate Brannigan or Kinsey Millhone. What I did find was a group of women far more varied than their fictional counterparts. In fiction, the women private eyes tend to range in age from late twenties to around forty. And at forty, like VI Washawski in *Tunnel Vision*, they start wondering whether they're getting too old for this game; should they pack it in and settle for a quiet life alligator wrestling? The real women have a far higher age profile, from grandmothers in their sixties to single women in their early thirties. Their average age was forty-five, demonstrating that the truth is certainly tougher than fiction.

They don't look like investigators of fiction either. They look utterly normal. You wouldn't look twice at any of them in the supermarket queue. Most fictional women eyes don't even know what a supermarket is for.

Their background motivations are different too. Most of the fictional women PIs came into the game because they had some sort of involvement with the legal or law enforcement system. They've grown disenchanted with its ability to right wrongs and come up with the correct answers; these are women with some kind of mission, whether their authors state it overtly or not. But that's not what brought the real women eyes into their career. Those who have been cops didn't leave the police because they were disenchanted with the morality or effectiveness of the force. They had more personal reasons. Most of the others fell into it by chance, never having a burning desire to be a detective. So although they may have developed certain passions for justice along the way, most of them didn't start the job with any kind of burning desire to right wrongs and change society by being a private eye.

Their politics cover a similar range, however, both in terms of feminism and conventional politics. In life, the women range from radical lesbian feminist to those who deny they are any kind of feminist, while acting like any other product of the seventies' Women's Liberation Movement. Their politics range from a left-wing mistrust of government to the belief that Margaret Thatcher was a damn good role model. So in fiction, though there the tendency is towards the left and middle ground. It's hard to think of a fictional PI who would think of Thatcher as anything other than a terrible step backwards for the cause of women.

But the key to the difference between the fictional detectives and their real counterparts is in their relationships to other people. Sometimes, reading crime fiction, I'm tempted to give the heroine a shake and say, 'Get a life!' So many of them struggle to maintain any kind of friendship, never mind a bond with a lover. I can't think of one who's married. It's one of the things I wanted to make different about Kate Brannigan, who has a nexus of close women friends with whom she does normal things like shop and gossip, and a man with whom she has a permanent, close relationship which mirrors reality in its emotional swings.

The real women PIs seem not to have a problem in this area; most of them have children, half of them are married, some even have grandchildren. They have achieved the delicate balance between dangerous, demanding career and domestic comfort. They do the things other wives and mothers do; Jackie Griffiths made her daughters' wedding dresses, Sarah Di Venere bakes the chocolate chip cookies she uses to bribe doormen, Pat Storey feels the need to cook the dinner even though she and her husband arrive home at the same time from the same job. These women may be mavericks professionally, but personally they are generally far more conformist than the imaginary eyes.

What they have in common with their fictional counterparts is their tenacity and commitment to their clients. When a case grips them, the bill is the last thing on their mind. Sure, they want to be paid. Who doesn't? But in any case that engages their hearts as well as their minds, where the quest becomes almost an end in itself, these women will go the extra mile for their clients without pausing for a second to consider how much of their time and effort is going to be paid for. And no matter how professional and hard-headed they profess to be, it's clear that cases like that are not uncommon.

I expected to be daunted by them, to feel inadequate and intimidated by their hard-nosed professionalism. I thought I'd feel inferior to the women who did in reality what I only fantasised about. I certainly didn't think I'd feel comfortable enough to like them. But none of them was interested in that sort of one-upmanship. I'd forgotten how powerful an equaliser curiosity is. These women are successful at what they do because they have a natural, healthy curiosity about everyone and everything they encounter. They were as interested in my world as I was in theirs; they had almost as many questions for me as I had for them. But I never felt interrogated; instead, it felt like the early stages of getting to know someone you think might end up as a friend.

The work they do is extraordinary, and behind the facades that are often remarkably ordinary, the women eyes are extraordinary too. Smart, strong and sure of themselves, they walk the mean streets to their own beat. On my quest, I met women whose lives and stories are as powerful, as scary, as interesting and as exciting as anything I could imagine. I've only been able to tell a fraction of those adventures. The remainder will fuel my fiction for some time to come.

An Interview with Val McDermid

Val McDermid was raised in Kirkcaldy, a small town in an industrial area on the East coast of Scotland. With the class system still very much an integral part of British society, the author is proud of her working-class background. Val's mother was a bookkeeper and shop assistant, and her father worked in the ship yards before going on to work for the town council.

Due to the few recreational outlets in Kirkcaldy the extra curricular activities organised by the school were highly popular. "It was very much a local tradition to make sure your kids had a better life by seeing to it that they got a proper education," McDermid says. "I was lucky because the school I went to was not merely focused on academic excellence, they were also very much interested in developing a child's personality."

What did Val do in her free time? "Besides smoking behind the bike shed?" she says with a chuckle. "Well, I played hockey, I was in the debating team, I was in the choir and the orchestra....I couldn't be bothered with drama since I was this little fat kid who was never going to get the leading role." She couldn't see the point of attending rehearsals just to stand at the back during a scene not doing anything.

When the time came for Val McDermid to decide what she wanted to do after she had left school she announced that she would like to study English. The establishment view was that promising pupils went to the universities of Edinburgh or St. Andrews; others had to 'make do' with those of Stirling or Dundee. It's was typical for Val that she decided to go to St. Hilda's in Oxford instead. The school board were not at all happy about her choice. They wondered why she was so intent on going to a university in England since graduates always returned to Kirkcaldy again anyway.

"I'd had a sense in my teenage years of being different," McDermid says. "A knowing that I was different but not having a name to put to that difference. I presumed it was because I was 'creative' since I knew that I wanted to be a writer. I knew instinctively that I had to break out of that set pattern that Kirkcaldy expected, otherwise I would go crazy."

Fortunately she was supported in her decision by her English teacher who helped prepare her for the university entrance exam. "I was sixteen-and-a-half when I went down for my interview—which is very young for an English university entrance—and I remember the college principal telling me that they had never taken anyone from a Scottish state school before. 'Well,' I said, 'then it's about time you started!'" Val says laughing. Nor had the college accepted anyone as young as her before. How would she feel if they offered her a deferred entry instead? Not starting that year but the year after? Putting on the thick Scottish accent she had as a girl McDermid echoes her reply, "I'm not hanging about wasting a year! I'll go somewhere else instead!" Embarrassed at the memory of her self-assured adolescence the author shakes her head and says, "When I think about it now I go hot and cold." Mary Bennett, the principal at St. Hilda's, told Val some years later that the interview board felt that they couldn't let anyone with her degree of confidence slip through the net.

Val McDermid has very fond memories of her time at St. Hilda's. "I went to Oxford with the attitude that these people had the keys to the kingdom, and I was damned if I was leaving until they had handed them over." Apart from the common ups and downs that students encounter, Val had a fabulous time and enjoyed the opportunity of intensive study. She actually did do some work then? "Oh yes!," she says smiling, "Maybe not as much as my tutors would have liked, because I was very involved in student politics and I was also the president of the Junior Common Room."

During her college days Val made a profound and important discovery that would have a lasting impact on her life: "I learned that there was a name for the difference I had felt, and that it was that I was a lesbian," she says. When Val came out about her sexuality, she generally received much support from her immediate circle of friends and acquaintances, and she feels this was largely due to the burgeoning feminist movement of the 1970s. Not surprisingly women's causes have remained important to her ever since.

It was also at St. Hilda's that one of Val's tutors introduced her to the works of Dashiell Hammett. Not that she hadn't read any crime novels before, but it was an introduction to an area of the genre she had not yet encountered. "There wasn't enough money to buy books when I was growing up," Val recalls. "They were far too much of a luxury, so I always ended up at the library. I read all sorts, books by Enid Blyton, Nancy Drew, the Bobbsey Twins—God help me, historical books, poetry. It was all very eclectic."

Since both her parents had jobs, she used to spend holidays and most weekends with her grandparents. When she had worked her way through her stack of library books she was left with the reading matter her grandparents owned: a copy of the bible, and Agatha Christie's *Murder at the Vicarage*, the latter having been left behind by a previous house-guest. "The times I used to read and reread *Murder at the Vicarage!*" Val says smiling. She went on to enjoy many other Agatha Christie's and also discovered additional crime writers of the Golden Age, writers such as Ngiao Marsh and Dorothy Sayers. Later McDermid graduated to more contemporary authors like Ruth Rendell and PD James. However, after the traditional British crime novels the hard-boiled Americans were a breath of fresh air, and they would prove to be of great influence on her own writing.

After graduating Val McDermid was offered a placement with one of the regional newspapers of the Mirror Group. Two years later she was taken on by *The People*, in those days one of the major British tabloids. Wasn't that a waste of her education? "No, that is a popular misconception," she says with a patient smile. "Actually tabloid journalism is much harder than writing for *The Times* or the *Telegraph*. When you are working on a story that generally does not run longer than ten paragraphs you learn a tremendous economy of language. You also become much more resourceful in tracking down your own stories and sources. Many of the broad-sheet journalists take what's fed to them."

Because of the increasing concentration on sex and gossip McDermid has no great sorrow for the diminishing respect that tabloid journalism in Britain has been receiving over the last ten years. She worked for *The People* when it was considered the best investigative newspaper in Britain. "We broke a lot of big, important stories. Stories varying from animal welfare to the fire risks in old people's homes. The law was actually changed as a result of the reports about retirement homes," Val adds proudly.

Despite the idealistic conviction that her work could inform as well as entertain, McDermid grew weary of having to fight to report sensationalistic news stories with some degree of restraint. The result was that she increasingly started concentrating on her fictional work. When Val finally decided to put a stop to her career as a journalist, three of her crime novels had already been published.

As mentioned earlier, Val McDermid had decided on a writing career at a young age. It was during her placement with the regional newspaper that she started work on her first manuscript. The arrogance that she would write the great British novel aged twenty still makes McDermid cringe, but at the time it seemed entirely feasible. "I wrote this novel of tortured human relationships, of angst and pain and grief and tragedy," she recalls. "It was completely over the top, and it was rejected by every publisher I had sent it to. Then I showed it to a friend of mine who was an actress, and she said it might make good play." Laughing, McDermid remembers her reaction, "I thought 'Yeah, I can do that! Cross out all the descriptive bits and add some dialogue to cover the transitions.'" After making the alterations Val showed it to the person in charge of the local theatre company, and to her amazement he agreed to put it on. When the play, *Like A Happy Ending*, was also produced on BBC radio Val had visions of being the new Harold Pinter. A problem arose when she was unable to work out what she had done right and subsequently she became increasingly frustrated when she was unable to replicate her earlier success. Ensuing attempts were all met by rejection, and with a grin Val recalls the ultimate humiliation: being fired by her agent. "When the person who stands to make 10% of everything you write thinks you're never going to make another penny, then you know you should really give up."

Yet she still felt she had a story to tell and that it was only a matter of finding the right vehicle. The breakthrough came when someone gave her a copy of one of Sara Paretsky's books featuring female private investigator V.I. Warshawski. The genre offered the helpful framework of body, sleuth, suspects, and an ending with a denouement. This, coupled with the age old advice 'write what you know about', suddenly made it crystal clear to her that she should use her investigative journalistic background and write a crime novel. Val's detective, Lindsay Gordon, would be a lesbian reporter. It was only later, when McDermid had gained more experience in writing fiction, that she felt confident enough to create her own British private investigator.

Despite the fact that five Lindsay Gordon novels have been published, it was Val McDermid's intention to write only three. *Report for Murder* was set at a girl's boarding school; *Common Murder* was inspired by the women's peace-camp at Greenham Common, the American airbase in Britain that stored nuclear weapons; and both books were written to allow the shocking close of *Final Edition* to have its full impact. (*Final Edition* was re-titled *Open and Shut* and *Deadline for Murder* in the US.)

"Usually an author sketches out a history for their protagonist but I was very inexperienced and it took me two books," Val says laughing. "The third book was the one I wanted to write and I couldn't figure how to get there without writing the first two first." Expecting the third instalment to be the end of Lindsay, the author then had an idea for the book that was to become *Union Jack* [*Conferences Are Murder* in the US], a crime novel about trade unions, and it seemed logical to bring back the politically aware Gordon. The most recent instalment in the series, *Booked for Murder*, appeared in 1996 and took a satirical look at the world of publishing.

Did Val have difficulties finding a publisher? "Well, to some extent I imposed my own limitations," she says. "I finished the first draft of *Report for Murder* in 1985 and I was fairly confident that there wasn't much point in my sending a lesbian crime novel to a mainstream publisher—I don't think they would have taken it. However, if I wrote a new lesbian series now Harper Collins [UK publisher of her (heterosexual) Kate Brannigan novels] wouldn't think twice about publishing them."

Yet even The Women's Press, the British publisher of the Gordon books, occasionally had some objections to certain issues raised by the author. Lindsay is not particularly politically correct, and the publishing house was not happy with the lesbian killer in one of Val's books. "It was ridiculous," she says. "I got a lot of stick for creating a lesbian murderer. It was as if I was somehow letting down the sisterhood by indicating that lesbians could be wicked. One of the problems in the feminist lesbian movement is that we have shoved under the carpet some of the issues that are very important. For example, there is lesbian domestic violence but for a long time it wasn't allowed to be acknowledged outside the closed community. I find that very sad because it really diminishes the pain of those women and that is deeply damaging to people's lives."

Another matter that upsets Val are publishing houses who refuse to accept manuscripts by authors who do not share the sexual or ethnic background of their protagonists. "Writing is an act of imagination and creativity. I'm not black, does that mean I can't put any black people in my books? I'm a lesbian, perhaps I shouldn't put any straight people in my books because I don't know how they feel....Better not have any men in my books either because I'm not a man!" Fortunately Val did not pay any attention to such silly notions.

After her first three Lindsay Gordon books, Val McDermid wanted to write novels that would allow her the financial freedom to become a full-time author. Knowing that a lesbian protagonist would not be a commercially viable option for a big publishing company in the early 80s, McDermid also felt that she needed to develop new characters if she was to grow as a writer. That is how private investigator Kate Brannigan came into being. In creating her PI Val acknowledges the trailblazing influence of Sara Paretsky, Sue Grafton, and Marcia Muller who together are considered to be the founding mothers of the contemporary female hard-boiled private eye genre. It was these women who, for Val and many of her sisters in crime, indicated that is was possible to write crime fiction that reflected women's lives in present day settings, be they urban or otherwise.

Inevitably, Val moved her female PI in different directions because her novels are largely set in Britain where society functions very differently from the United States. "Apart from the obvious differences," she says, "like not living in a gun culture, and private eyes not having to be licensed, British social structures and politics operate in ways that make some avenues of investigation easier and some more difficult."

Having been spurred into action by Sara Paretsky, McDermid feels that the tone of her books have more in common with those of Sue Grafton. Says Val, "I enjoyed the lighter feel of the Kinsey Millhone novels, and I suppose they made me realise I could allow my humour fuller rein than I might otherwise have done."

This did not mean that McDermid would create a detective in the classic mould, one of those types who remained untouched by violence. Val herself had been the victim of a beating and knows how damaging the after-effects can be. "Some writers are prone to putting their characters in a situation of violence, yet the next day they leap out of bed and quite cheerfully get on with things as though it never happened," she says.

The assault on Val occurred during her time as a journalist, the incident even making the front page of the newspaper she worked for. 'OUR VAL BEATEN UP BY BIG DADDY', read the headline, Big Daddy being a popular English wrestler. McDermid was badly shaken after the beating she received from the huge wrestler. The question that had led to her attack related to a domestic matter, and Val recalls, "He'd clearly been contacted a fair few times over this story that day and it was kind of sensitive. I rang the bell and when he opened the door I said who I was and he started hitting me! I was trying to get away from this guy and he was punching and shouting at me. My photographer just legged it, he didn't even try to get a picture!". She briefly laughs at the memory, but then becomes serious. "Women who get battered usually have far worse injuries. I didn't have any broken bones, didn't have much in the way of bruises....It was very painful for a few days, I was very stiff and it hurt every time I moved, but more importantly it undermined the view I had of myself. I had this self-image of a woman who was powerful and who did her job well, but for six months after that every time I knocked on a door I could feel sweat on the back of my neck as if it was all going to happen again. Most writers write about violence in such a way that it is absolutely clear that nobody has ever lifted a hand to them in anger."

Val McDermid's British private investigator is the Manchester based Kate Brannigan. The young heroine is a partner in an agency that specialises in computer fraud and security systems. In all of the Brannigan novels the main story-line is accompanied by one or two sub-plots, not always necessarily connected to the central story. In *Dead Beat*, the first in the Brannigan series, Kate's relationship with pop-journalist Richard saw her tangled up in the search for the missing muse of a rock-star. *Dead Beat* also introduced readers to the secondary characters who re-appear throughout the books: Kate's business partner Bill; their secretary Shelley; and her friends Alexis, a journalist, and Chris, an architect, two women in a stable lesbian relationship.

Less stable is the relationship of Kate and Richard. It survives because of the conservatory connecting their adjoining homes. Whilst the glass structure allows Kate to maintain her fiercely fought independence, it also enables them to drop in on each other without too much formality. In *Kick Back* all was still well between them, but when Richard was innocently jailed for possession of drugs in *Crack Down*, Kate's efforts to clear his name disturbed the balance of their relationship and put it under a huge strain. This became most evident in *Clean Break* when Kate, chasing a band of art-thieves through Europe, had a huge row with Richard. In the opening sentence of *Blue Genes*, which focused on new developments in in-vitro-fertilisation techniques, readers were met with a nasty shock in the opening pages when confronted with the announcement of Richard's death. In the most recent Brannigan title, *Star Struck*, Kate's love life has settled into a comfortable and happy stage, allowing her to concentrate on body-guarding the star of a gritty British soap drama.

"My personal feeling about Richard," says Val, "is that he is a strong man in the sense that he is able to put his ego to one side and let Kate get on with her life. He doesn't feel the need to control, he doesn't feel the need to tell her what to do, and mostly he doesn't feel the need to interfere. There have been occasions where he does do so with fairly disastrous consequences, but those are instances where he does so out of concern. He is usually very laid back." What frequently amuses Val is that a lot of men think Richard is a wimp, but virtually every woman she knows asks her whether he based on someone real and how they can meet him."

Commenting on her PI's relationships Val says, "I was quite keen that Kate would be somebody who had a life. I didn't want her to be this emotional cripple, a maverick with no friends and no lover. That is what I learned from Marcia Muller's Sharon McCone series: the importance of working with other people as part of a team." The other relationships that are important to Kate are those with her female friends. McDermid included this aspect because she thought it was important to reflect that women have started to network with each other in the way that men had been doing for generations. "I wanted to show the kind of relationships that women have together, the closeness, and the completely non-judgemental nature as well," she says. "Women will weigh in to help without being asked. They do it without expecting anything in return. It's just 'You're my friend, you need this'."

Val McDermid thinks it is inevitable that the protagonist in a first novel is either going to be the writer's alter-ego or their imaginary best friend. Val says that Lindsay is her alter-go, and that Kate fits the 'best friend' category. When asked whether her two heroines will ever meet McDermid is shocked by the idea. "God, no! They'd hate each other," she says. "The clash of egos would be a nightmare, they'd be arguing all the time. Lindsay would just dive straight into things and Kate would be saying, 'You stupid bitch, what did you do that for?'" Laughing Val adds, "It would just be too stressful to write."

What both fictional women do have in common with each other as well as their creator is their sense of humour. "They find the same things funny," the author says. "They crack the same kind of jokes because I can't invent a sense of humour. I wouldn't know if it was funny."

1995 was a big year for Val McDermid. Not only did she win the Gold Dagger from the British Crime Writers' Association for her first psychological thriller *The Mermaids Singing*, it also was the year that *A Suitable Job for a Woman: Inside the World of Women Private Eyes* was published. How did this non-fiction book come about? "An editor suggested it to me," Val says, "and it sounded like a project that would be a lot of fun as well as incredibly interesting. I just couldn't resist—after all, how often does a publisher say, 'Here's some money, go and wander around America and Britain talking to interesting women.' And that isn't even taking into account how useful the trip would be as a source of information and anecdotes for my future books!"

When asked if she would care to mention any stories that didn't make it into the book, the author grins and admits, "Well, there were one or two, but I was sworn to secrecy on those..."

With *The Mermaids Singing* Val McDermid took on a completely different literary genre. The psychological thriller dealt with the gruesome manner in which a serial killer tortured men to death, and responsible for cracking the case were policewoman Carol Jordan, and criminal profiler Tony Hill.

Why the sudden change in direction? "I have asked myself the same question," Val says, "and the short answer is that it came from my dark side. The idea for the plot came to me in a flash. I was driving down the motorway listening to the radio, and something the broadcaster said must have triggered some strange synaptic junction in my brain. It was as though some dark angel was hovering overhead and said 'here have this', because the plot suddenly fell into my lap."

Val had to pull onto the hard-shoulder of the motorway and write down the idea for fear that she might forget some of the details. "I'm not used to having ideas like that," she says. "Most of my plots take a long time to develop. I start off with something that I am vaguely interested in, and I find that over a couple of years I acquire lots of bits and pieces of information about it. Then gradually something emerges as a story."

In its early stages Val McDermid had difficulty researching *The Mermaids Singing* because most book-shops and libraries didn't have books on medieval tools of torture. "Can you imagine the looks I got when I said: 'What have you got on medieval torture? Preferably illustrated.'" Val says laughing. On holiday in Italy the author had a lucky break. In Florence she saw banners advertising a new museum on criminology. "The small print said it was a museum of criminology and torture," Val explains, cheerfully going on, "So I thought 'Hmm, this might be interesting.' I didn't buy the illustrated catalogue, but I went around making lots of notes and taking loads of photographs." The thing McDermid found most memorable and extraordinary was the craftsmanship that went into these 'engines of torture' as she calls them. "They weren't just thrown together with a few nails....The pears that I describe in the book were made of silver with beautiful decorative engravings on them. If you saw one of them you would say, 'What a beautiful object.' Then, when you heard what it was for, you'd feel faint and sick."

Two years after *The Mermaids Singing* came the sequel *The Wire in the Blood*, which was published in the United States by Poisoned Pen Press in 1998. The limited American edition featured the added bonus of an intro-duction written by Michael Connelly, and the copies were signed by both authors. It again featured Carol

Jordan and Tony Hill who this time set out to prove that a television celebrity was also a serial-killer. Val explains the book's premise, "Most of what we know about psychopathic offenders comes from interviews conducted by the FBI. They virtually all come out as having IQ's well above the average. Now these are the ones we know about because they have been caught.... Presumably this means that the brighter ones are still out there." *The Wire in the Blood* tells how Tony and Carol set about convincing people that someone with a high profile and tremendous public popularity was a murderer. "How would you convince people that Roseanne Barr was a serial-killer...." Val says, immediately cracking up at the idea. Still laughing she tries again, "Okay, try to convince people that Bill Cosby was a serial-killer."

A third instalment is being researched at the time of this interview, and in a few days the author is travelling to Belgium, Holland and Germany to do some background research on commercial waterways. All McDermid will say at this stage is that Carol Jordan will be based in Germany, and that she is attached to Europol, investigating the smuggling of drugs and illegal immigrants into Europe. Tony has gone back to academic life, but he is persuaded to return to semi-official active service when Carol hears about a serial killer who is killing psychiatrists in Europe. Val adds that, "The story has its roots in Nazi war crimes, but also confronts contemporary European problems of refugees and the economics of international crime."

Before the third Hill and Jordan instalment comes Val McDermid's non-series novel A *Place of Execution*. It found it's origin during an event Val shared with Douglas Wynn, a true crime writer. He talked about a case history of a murder trial where the body of the victim had never been found. That was the seed of inspiration that set the wheels turning in Val's head, though A *Place of Execution* is far removed from the events of the real case. Parts of the novel, that spans three decades from the 1960s onward, are set in the limestone landscape of the Derbyshire Peak District where the author used to live. "It's a cross between a period police procedural and a psychological thriller," she says, adding, "It's not the start of another series, but a genuine stand-alone novel. It's me spreading my wings and trying to do something a bit different. There will be another Brannigan, but not for a year or two."

Currently Val is engaged in a joint project with New Orleans crime writer JM Redmann. The end result will feature Redmann's series PI Micky Knight as well as McDermid's Lindsay Gordon, and will see the two sleuths getting together to solve a murder in the Big Easy. "We're writing alternate chapters," explains Val. "It started as a light-hearted bit of fun, but we're ten chapters into it and it's starting to look suspiciously like a novel," she says grinning.

Coinciding with the Knight/Gordon project is *Killing the Shadows*, another stand-alone novel. "It's a serial-killer-thriller with a central character, academic psychologist Professor Fiona Cameron, who is very unlike Tony Hill—she's a number cruncher," the author says, "not a touchy-feely psychologist." As she explains the plot further Val's face again lights up with grin. "Someone is killing crime writers—and since Fiona lives with thriller writer Kit Martin, she has a vested interest in finding out what is going on."

Writing these more commercially orientated novels Val McDermid sometimes finds herself accused of selling out. "Yes, I've heard that," she says, "and it is rubbish! I would argue that by writing the Kate Brannigan books I have given lesbian crime fiction a much wider audience. We all know the way crime readers read: they find a new writer and will go out and buy everything that person has ever written, even the obscure out-of-print first novel that got remaindered. After the Kate Brannigans many straight readers turned to Lindsay Gordon and found out that reading lesbian fiction needn't be alienating. Then they went on to buy other feminist lesbian thrillers they hadn't considered reading before," Val concludes.

Fans of Val McDermid know they can swing either way and still get a good read.

© Copyright Adrian Muller, 1999.

Fiction

Report for Murder (Gordon). London, The Women's Press; New York, St. Martin's Press, 1987, and Duluth, Spinsters Ink 1997.

Common Murder (Gordon). London, The Women's Press, 1989; Duluth, Minnesota, Spinsters Ink, 1995.

Final Edition (Gordon). London, The Women's Press, 1991; in the US as *Open and Shut*. New York, St. Martin's Press, 1991; as *Deadline for Murder*. Duluth, Spinsters Ink, 1998.

Dead Beat (Brannigan). London, Gollancz, 1992; New York, St. Martin's Press, 1993.

Kick Back (Brannigan). London, Gollancz, and New York, St. Martin's Press, 1993.

Union Jack (Gordon). London, The Women's Press, 1993; in the US as *Conferences Are Murder*, Duluth, Spinsters Ink 1999.

Crack Down (Brannigan). London, HarperCollins, 1994; New York, Scribner 1995, and Harper, 1996.

Clean Break (Brannigan). London, HarperCollins, 1995; New York, Scribner 1996, and Harper, 1997.

The Mermaids Singing (Hill & Jordan). London, Harper-Collins, 1995; New York, Harper, 1996.

Blue Genes (Brannigan). London, HarperCollins, 1996; New York, Scribner, 1997.

Booked for Murder (Gordon). London, Women's Press, 1996.

The Wire in the Blood (Hill & Jordan). London, Harper-Collins, 1997; Arizona, Poisoned Pen Press, 1998.

Star Struck (Brannigan). London, HarperCollins, 1998.

A Place of Execution. London, HarperCollins, 1999.

Non-Fiction

A Suitable Job for a Woman: Inside the World of Women Private Eyes. London, HarperCollins, 1995; Arizona, Poisoned Pen Press, 1999.